AMSTERDAM

THE ROUGH GUIDE

WK 36

£1·25

D0452793

ROUGH GUIDE CREDITS

Series Editor: Mark Ellingham
Editorial: Martin Dunford, John Fisher, Jack Holland, Jonathan Buckley
Production: Susanne Hillen, Kate Berens, Andy Hilliard
Typesetting: Greg Ward and Gail Jammy
Design: Andrew Oliver

Continued thanks for help, information, and encouragement on this new edition to: Odette Taminiau (VVV Amsterdam), Marcel Balthus (NBT London), Henny van den Berg (GVB Amsterdam), Gary Smith for his piece on nightlife, Stephen Burn for Gay Amsterdam listings, Rob Jones for copy-editing, Jackie Jones, Donald Hutera, Ken Wilkie, Laura Jongeneel, John Fisher, Sue Weightman, Andy Holzman, Bridget Bouch, and Mark Krone.

And **thanks** too to all those who have written in with contributions and advice on Amsterdam: Caralyn Longhurst and Ian Peterson, K. S. Masters, Paul Tensby, R. Hayes, G. S. Woods, Michael Bird, Mark Taylor, Chris Taylor, Tony Hallas, Sarah Williams, R. Barinowsky, Brian Lomas, Ruth Pollak, Judy Morris, Barrie Wood, A. Graafland, Celia Hurst, Faith James, Shane Beadle, John Fitzgerald, Penny Spencer, Helen Copperman, Lisa Barnett, F. E. Bradley, Victoria Lavender, Philip Anscombe, F. Ross, G. Tierney, J. Wakefield, Peter Flaherty, Roger Gaitley, Pete Coombs, S. J. King, G. Earley, G. E. Herbert, Julia Wright and Mr. and Mrs. J. Pugh. Please keep writing!

Published by Harrap Columbus, Chelsea House, 26 Market Square, Bromley, Kent BR1 1NA.

Typeset in Linotron Univers and Century Old Style.
Printed by Cox & Wyman, Reading, Berks.

Illustrations in Part One and Part Three by Ed Briant; Basics illustration by Helen Manning
Contexts illustration by David Loftus

224p.
Includes index.

British Library Cataloguing Publication Data
Dunford, Martin
  Amsterdam: the rough guide. – 2nd ed. – (The Rough Guides)
  1. Netherlands. Amsterdam. Description and travel
  I. Title II. Holland, Jack III. Series
  914. 92'3

ISBN 0–7471–0203–1

AMSTERDAM

THE ROUGH GUIDE

WRITTEN AND RESEARCHED BY
MARTIN DUNFORD AND JACK HOLLAND

With additional contributions by

Sara and Jon Henley, Mark Fuller, Peter Glencross,
Sue Weightman and Bernadette de Wit

HARRAP-COLUMBUS ■ LONDON

CONTENTS

PART ONE BASICS   1

PART TWO THE GUIDE   23

More for Adults: Skating (108), Jogging (109), Canoeing and Horseriding (109), Tennis, Squash and Table Tennis (109), Swimming (110), Saunas and Gyms (110), Bowling, Carambole, Chess, and Draughts (110), Football (111), Hockey and Basketball (111), Gambling (111), Pole Sitting (111).

■ 5 DRINKING AND EATING 112

Food: An Overview (112), Food and Drink Glossary (114), Drink: An Overview (116), Bars (117), Coffee Shops and Tea Rooms (126), Women-Only Bars and Coffee Shops (128), Gay Men's Bars and Coffee Shops (129), Restaurants (130).

■ 6 NIGHTLIFE 139

Concert Halls and Multi-Media Centres (140), Live Music (141), Pop and Rock (142), Jazz and Latin (143), Folk and Ethnic (145), Contemporary and Classical (145), Discos and Clubs (146), Film (149), Theatre (150), Dance (151).

■ 7 OUT FROM THE CITY 153

Haarlem (155), Leiden (160), Gouda (164), Delft (165), Muiden and Naarden (167), Utrecht (168), Alkmaar (171), Marken, Volendam and Edam (172).

PART THREE   CONTEXTS   175

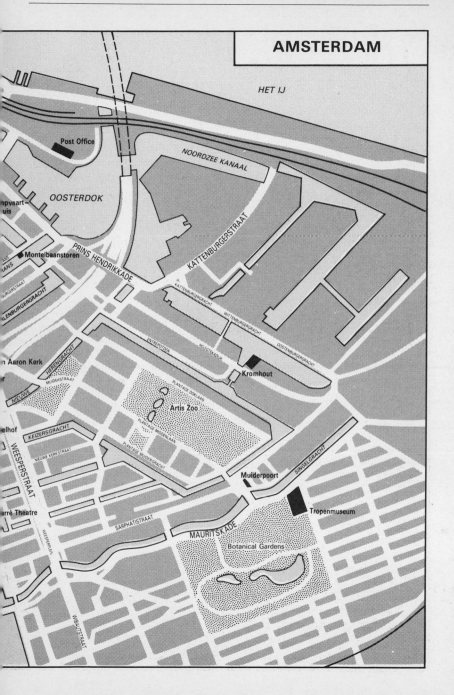

AMSTERDAM

HET IJ

Post Office

NOORDZEE KANAAL

OOSTERDOK

epvaart-
uis

■ Montelbaanstoren

PRINS HENDRIKKADE

KATTENBURGERSTRAAT

RGERSTRAAT

LENBURGERGRACHT

KATTENBURGERGRACHT

WITTENBURGERGRACHT

OOSTENBURGERGRACHT

ENTREPOTDOK

HOOGTEKADIJK

Aaron Kerk

HERENGRACHT

Kromhout

MUIDERSTRAAT

NIEUWE

PLANTAGE DOKLAAN

Artis Zoo

elhof

KEIZERSGRACHT

PLANTAGE MIDDENLAAN

NIEUWE KERKSTRAAT

PLANTAGE MUIDERGRACHT

WEESPERSTRAAT

Muiderpoort

SINGELGRACHT

Tropenmuseum

arré Theatre

SARPHATISTRAAT

MAURITSKADE

WEESPERZIJDE

Botanical Gardens

WIBAUTSTRAAT

INTRODUCTION

Amsterdam is a compact, instantly likeable capital: appealing to look at, pleasant to walk around, and with an enticing mix of the provincial and the cosmopolitan. The city has a welcoming attitude towards visitors, and a uniquely youthful orientation, shaped by the liberal counter-culture of the last two decades. It's hard not to feel drawn in by the buzz of open-air summer events, by the intimacy of the clubs and bars, or by the Dutch facility with languages – English, for example, is spoken almost everywhere.

The city's layout is determined by a cobweb of canals radiating out from a medieval core, which, along with planned seventeenth-century extensions further out, provide elegant backdrops for living or wandering. The conventional sights are for the most part low-key – the **Anne Frank House** being a notable exception – but Amsterdam has developed a world-class group of museums and galleries. The **Van Gogh Museum** is, for many, reason enough in itself to visit the city; add to it the **Rijksmuseum**, with its collections of medieval and seventeenth-century Dutch paintings, the contemporary and experimental **Stedelijk**, plus hundreds of smaller galleries, and the international quality of the art is evident.

But it's Amsterdam's **population and politics** that constitute its most enduring characteristics. Notorious during the 1960s and 1970s as the heart of radical, "liberated" Europe, the city mellowed only marginally during the Eighties, and despite the inevitable late-Eighties yuppification retains a resilient laid-back feel. The authorities are trying to play down the counter-culture label and boost Amsterdam's economy by cultivating a businesslike image for the city and a more conventional reputation for the arts. Sporadic battles erupt over urban development plans, as Amsterdam's inhabitants, perennially short on low-cost housing, object to the construction of yet another high-rise hotel or prestige opera house. But it's a tension that keeps the city on its toes. Overall, the keynote is tolerance, or *gezelligheid* as Amsterdammers say. Though untranslatable, the term conjures up a sense of laid-back intimacy; put simply, Amsterdam is a city that's as congenial a place to hang out in as you'll find.

Amsterdam has responded to its youth culture with a social and sensible attitude to soft drugs. Entertainment has a similarly innovative edge, exemplified by **multi-media complexes** like the *Melkweg*, whose offerings are at the forefront of contemporary film, dance, drama and music. There are some great **coffee shops**, serving cannabis products and soft drinks instead of alcohol, and the more conventional **bars** range from the traditional, bare-floored *brown cafés* to new-wave designer haunts. The city's **club** scene is by contrast relatively subdued, with its venues modest by London standards, and the emphasis more on dancing than posing. **Gays**, though, will discover that Amsterdam has Europe's most active and convivial nightlife network.

Costs – And When to Go

With the current strength of the guilder, Amsterdam is by no means a cheap city. But careful **spending** – eating in student restaurants, camping, or sleeping in hostels, etc. – enables you to do it on the tightest of budgets (reckon on £12–14 a day as an absolute minimum). If you actually want to enjoy yourself, and sleep in an ordinary hotel, £30 a day would be a realistic figure. Individual accommodation costs vary from roughly £5–7 a night for the cheapest dormitory bed, to around £10–12 per person sharing a double room in a bottom-line hotel. Main courses in most restaurants will cost you somewhere between £5 and £7, while drinking a small glass of beer in a bar will set you back approximately 80 pence. Obviously, costs for both food and drink drop considerably if you visit a supermarket.

Just about any time of year is a good **time to go**, though it's advisable to avoid the mid-winter months (Jan & Feb), when the wind blowing off the canals can be bitterly cold. High summer can be unpleasant as well, since the city gets crowded and sticky then and hotel rooms are at a premium. Spring is perhaps the best time to visit: the weather is comfortable for sightseeing and the canals are at their most alluring.

Finally, don't fall into the trap of thinking that there's nothing to The Netherlands **beyond Amsterdam**. If you're here in spring the bulbfields are in bloom, and towns like Haarlem, Leiden and Utrecht are worth a visit at any time of the year. All are reached quickly and painlessly by train; for full details see the *Out from the City* chapter.

AVERAGE DAYTIME TEMPERATURES				
	MIN		**MAX**	
	°C	°F	°C	°F
January	−0.2	32	4.3	40
February	−0.5	31	4.9	41
March	1.5	35	8.1	47
April	3.8	39	11.6	53
May	7.5	46	16.0	61
June	10.5	51	19.1	66
July	12.5	55	20.5	69
August	12.5	55	20.5	69
September	10.5	51	18.3	65
October	7.3	45	14.0	57
November	3.8	39	8.8	48
December	1.1	34	5.7	42

$$°F = (°C \times 9/5) + 32$$

PART ONE

THE
BASICS

GETTING THERE

BY TRAIN

British Rail operates combined **boat-train** services from London to Amsterdam's Centraal Station. Two daily departures run from Liverpool Street via Harwich and the Hook of Holland; four from London Victoria via Dover and Ostend (Belgium). Total journey times are similar on both routes (10–12hr), as are fares, which start at about £64 for an ordinary return (five day excursion tickets are available for £50). Basically, the choice really depends on how long you want to spend on the water. If you opt to travel at night, cabin supplements start at around £10 per person. For British Rail European enquiries, phone ☎01/834 2345.

Those **under 26** can go much cheaper: a *BIJ* (youth) ticket goes for about £43 return through *Eurotrain*, 52 Grosvenor Gardens, London SW1; (☎01/823 7131), plus branches nationwide, or most other student/youth travel agents. Another cash-saving possibility for those under 26 (and resident in Europe for six months) is the **InterRail pass**, currently costing £145 from any major UK railway station or student/youth travel offices, which is valid for one month's travel on all European (and Moroccan) railways, and gives half-price discounts on British trains and some cross-channel ferries. This could cut costs significantly if you're intending Amsterdam to form just a stopover on your European travels. A variation on the standard card is the **InterRail Flexicard** (£135), which provides the same benefits as the *InterRail* pass but is valid for any ten days within a month.

BY COACH

This is a good option if you're over 26, since fares are roughly the same as for under-26 rail travel. Your choices are between **coach and hovercraft** (daily services via Dover–Calais) and the slower **coach and ferry** (normally overnight via Dover–Zeebrugge). Journey times by hovercraft are about ten hours, by ferry about thirteen hours.

Costs are much the same across the board: *Eurolines*, operated by *National Express* and bookable through their agents country-wide, offer daily departures from London by hovercraft for £41 return (students £38), or two nightly departures by ferry at the same prices; *Trailblazers* also have an allocation of seats on this service, plus they can book accommodation in advance – something worth taking advantage of in high season (see below). Otherwise, *Hoverspeed City Sprint* offer two morning departures daily, bookable through most travel agents or British Rail travel centres.

COACH COMPANIES
Hoverspeed City Sprint (☎01/554 7061).
National Express/Eurolines (☎01/730 0202), plus agents nationwide.
Trailblazers (☎01/727 1898).

BY PLANE

Flight deals to Amsterdam **from London** are many and change frequently, but are obviously the best option if saving time is a priority – London to Schipol takes as little as 45 minutes. Most airlines offer some sort of discount fare in the neighbourhood of £70 return, perhaps less if you're a student. An unrestricted ticket will cost well over £100. To find the current bargains, study the ads in the Sunday travel sections of quality newspapers (*The Observer* especially) or, if you live in London, scour the back pages of the listings magazines *Time Out* or the freebie *LAW*.

Charter fares are hard to find, but most airlines offer special cut-rate fares at, currently, around £70 return, sometimes less if you're a student – the conditions on which vary, but usually involve spending a Saturday night away

AIRLINES AND AGENTS

Air UK (☎0345/666777).

British Airways, 421 Oxford St., London W1 (☎01/897 4000).

British Caledonian, Victoria Air Terminal, Victoria Station, London SW1 (☎01/668 4222).

British Midland, (☎01/581 0864).

KLM, Time and Life Building, New Bond St., London W1 (☎01/568 9144).

London City Airways, (☎01/511 4200).

London European Airways,(☎01/328 4000).

Netherlines, Luton International Airport Terminal Building, Room 15, Luton LU2 9LY. (☎0582/459906).

STA Travel 86 Old Brompton Rd., London SW7 and 117 Euston Rd., London N1 (☎01/ 937 9921).

Transavia, (☎0293/38181).

Campus Travel, 52 Grosvenor Gardens, London SW1 (☎01/730 3402).

Travel Cuts, 295 Regent St., London W1 (☎01/255 1944)

---

or booking a maximum of two days in advance. Regular fares start at well over £100 return, and a number of airlines fly the route, so departures are plentiful. Bookings can be made through the airline direct, but if you want to be sure you're getting the best deal, book through an agent.

As far as **flying from other parts of Britain** goes, if you're under 26 and/or a student you can fly from British regional airports (including Belfast) for under £100 return through *USIT* (see above). If not, you may find it makes more sense to travel via London, or to take a package, since ordinary fares from regional airports can be prohibitively expensive.

BY CAR/HITCHING

The **two most direct crossings** to Amsterdam are via Harwich to the Hook of Holland, and from Sheerness to Vlissingen. Driving time from the Hook to Amsterdam is about one hour; from Vlissingen roughly two-and-a-half hours.

HARWICH–HOOK OF HOLLAND. *Sealink*. Two crossings daily, a night run taking eight hours, and a daytime one of seven hours. Single fares in high season are £24 per person, plus from £29 for a vehicle by day, £49 at night.

SHEERNESS–VLISSINGEN. *Olau Lines*. Two sailings daily, a seven-hour daytime ferry and an eight-and-a-half-hour night boat. Single fares in high season are £22.50 per person, plus from £35 for a vehicle by day, £50 at night.

If you want to spend **less time crossing** the water, consider instead **sailing to Belgium**, either from Dover to Zeebrugge or Ostend or, if you live in the Midlands or north of England, from

Felixstowe to Zeebrugge – from where it's a steady three-hour drive up to Amsterdam.

DOVER–ZEEBRUGGE/OSTEND. *P&O*. Six crossings daily. Crossing time four to four-and-a-half hours. Single fares in high season, £13 per person, plus from £24–63 per vehicle – unusually, it's cheaper at night.

FELIXSTOWE–ZEEBRUGGE. *P&O*. Two sailings daily, one in the morning, one at night. Crossing-time five and-a-quarter hours (day), around six hours (night). Single fares in high season £15 per person, plus from £25–65 per vehicle – the night sailing is the more expensive.

If you live in the **north of England** it's worth taking advantage of the Hull-Rotterdam service, which leaves you just an hour or so's drive from Amsterdam.

HULL–ROTTERDAM (EUROPORT). *North Sea Ferries*. One departure daily, every evening at 6pm. Crossing time 14 hours. Single fares in high season are £43 per person, plus £8 for a cabin, £54 for a small car.

FERRY COMPANIES

North Sea Ferries, King George Dock, Hedon Road, Hull HU9 5QA (☎0482/77177).

Olau Lines, Sheerness, Kent MW12 1SN (☎0795/666666).

Sealink, PO Box 29, London SW1V 1JX (☎0233/47047).

P&O, Russell Street, Dover, Kent CT16 1QB (☎0304/203388). 127 Regent Street, London W1R 8LB (☎01/734 4431).

Remember that, in all cases, there are special, extra-cheap **excursion fares** available if you're only going for a short time. Also that for those **under 26**, or a **student**, *Eurotrain* do cut-rate car-ferry tickets. If you have kids, *Sealink* have the best deals: on day crossings children up to age 13 may travel free, and at night go for fifty percent discount; other companies tend to give a fifty percent discount across the board.

Any **travel agent** can provide further information on prices and timings, and book tickets in advance – more or less essential in high season. Or you can contact the ferry companies direct.

HITCHING

It's relatively easy to get lifts once in Holland or Belgium, so **hitching** can be a good way of cutting costs. Bear in mind though, that since drivers have been made to account for unauthorised passengers, it's no longer possible to travel over for free in a truck-driver's cab. To make sure of a lift on arrival, talk to as many people as you can on the ferry and do your best to cajole them into picking you up on the other side of customs.

Hitching out of Amsterdam to the Randstad towns and the Hook of Holland on the A4 auto-route, take tram #6 or #16 to its terminus at the Olympic Stadium and walk down the sliproad for the southern ring road. You can't hitch on the road itself – and the police will make sure you don't – but stand just before and you should pick up a lift at least as far as The Hague, from where it's a short and fairly cheap bus or train ride to the Hook. Similarly with points south to Vlissingen and Belgium, though this time you need to catch tram #4 to the RAI exhibition centre, or tram #25 to Nieuwe Utrectseweg (Martin Luther King Park), and pick up the **A2** heading south.

PACKAGES

Don't be put off by the idea of going on a **package**: most consist of no more than travel and accommodation and can work out an easy way of cutting costs and hassle – especially if you live some distance from London, since many operators offer a good-value range of regional flight departures. Depending on the type of hotel you opt for (anything from budget to five-star are available with most companies), prices from London start at £70 per person for return coach and hovercraft travel and two nights' accommodation in a one-star hotel with breakfast, or a little over £100 if you fly. A travel agent can advise further on the best deals available, or you can contact one of the **operators** listed below:

Amsterdam Travel Service, 54 Ebury Street, London SW1 WOLU (☎01/730 3422).

Thomson, First Floor, Greater London House, Hampstead Road, London NW1 7SD (☎01/387 6510). Often the cheapest.

Time Off, 2a Chester Close, London SW1X 7BQ (☎01/235 8070).

Travelscene, 94 Baker Street, London W1M 2HD (☎01/935 1025); 22a Cheapside, Bradford BD1 4JA. 0274/392911.

Travel Young, 38 Store Street, London WC1E 7BZ (☎01/580 6762). Specialists in youth and student travel, and offering deals with multi-bedded hostel accommodation as well as good value arrangements on regular double rooms.

FROM EIRE

There are no direct ferry links from Ireland to the Dutch or Belgian coasts, but if you are a student or under 26, flights to Amsterdam direct from Dublin, Cork or Shannon can be had from IRL£140 return through **USIT** (Aston Quay, O'Connell Bridge, Dublin 2; ☎778117; and other branches countrywide). **USIT** also offer flights from Belfast for around UK£100 return. If you fall into neither of these categories, expect to pay at least IRL£150 return.

FROM AUSTRALIA & NEW ZEALAND

Cheapest option is to fly to London, to which there are plenty of good deals to be had, and pick up a connection from there. Reckon on paying around AUS$1450 return from Sydney, NZ$1450 from Auckland. **STA**, and in New Zealand, **STS**, are the best people to contact; branches in Sydney, Melbourne, Canberra, Auckland and other cities – see the phone book for details.

RED TAPE AND VISAS

Citizens of Britain, Eire, Australia, Canada or the USA need only a valid passport to stay three months in The Netherlands. The temporary British Visitor's Passport, obtainable from post offices, is also valid for the same period. On arrival, have enough money to convince officials you can stay alive. Poorer-looking visitors are often checked, and if you can't flash a few travellers' cheques or notes you may not be allowed in.

For longer stays, you officially need an **extension visa**. These are obtainable in advance from the Dutch embassy in your own country or via the *Bureau Vreemdelingenpolitie* (Aliens' Police) at Waterlooplein (open to walk-in visitors Mon–Fri 9am–12.30pm – get there early as the queues build up fast; or ring between 2pm and 4pm to make an appointment; ☎55 99 111). In reality restrictions are fairly loose for European Community passports – they're not always date-stamped when entering the country – though if you are definitely planning to stay and work it's probably best to get a stamp anyway (See "Long Term Stays", below). Non-EC nationals, however, should always have their documents in order.

Residence permits are preferably obtained from outside the country and are issued for a maximum term of one year upon proof of income from sources other than employment in The Netherlands, and sometimes not even then. **Work permits** are even harder to get; your prospective employer must apply in The Netherlands while you simultaneously apply at home; both parties must await its issuance (by no means automatic) before proceeding.

CUSTOMS

For residents of EC countries the **duty-free allowance** is 300 cigarettes if bought tax-paid in the EC, 200 if bought duty-free or outside the EC. These allowances are doubled for those living outside the EC. Wherever you've arrived from you're allowed one litre of duty-free spirits (don't bother utilising your five litre wine allowance – it's cheaper to buy it in Amsterdam). Allowances are the same when returning to Britain and in all cases apply only to those over the age of 17.

British **customs officials** tend to assume that anyone youthful-looking and coming directly *from* The Netherlands is a potential dope fiend or pornographer – strip searches and general unpleasantness seem to be frequent, particularly at airports. If it happens to you, unfailing politeness is the best tactic: those attempting to bring back drugs, pornography or flick knives can expect a hard time and most likely arrest.

NETHERLANDS EMBASSIES AND CONSULATES

Great Britain 38 Hyde Park Gate, London SW7 (☎01/585 5080).
Eire 160 Merrion Road, Dublin 4 (☎1/693 444).
Australia 130 Empire Circus, Yarralumla, Canberra ACT 2600 (☎62/733 111).
Canada 3rd Floor, 275 Slater Street, Ottowa ONT K1P 5H9 (☎613/237 5030).
New Zealand Investment House, 10th Floor, Balance and Featherstone Street, Wellington (☎4/738 652).

USA 4200 Linnean Avenue NW, Washington 20008 3896 (☎202/244 5300); 1 Rockefeller Plaza, 11th Floor, New York NY 10020 2094 (☎212/246 1429).
Denmark Toldbodgade 95, 1253 Copenhagen K (☎1/156 293).
Norway Oscargate 29, 0352 Oslo 3 (☎2/602193).
Sweden Gotgatan 16A, 11646 Stockholm (☎8/247180).

HEALTH AND INSURANCE

As fellow members of the European Community, both Britain and Eire have reciprocal health agreements with The Netherlands.

These provide for free medical advice and treatment on presentation of certificate E111. In theory you're supposed to apply for this by completing the form in leaflet SA30 (available from any DHSS office) and sending it back at least a month before you leave: in practice it's possible to take it to any DHSS contributions counter and have the counter clerk complete the form on the spot. Without an E111 you won't be turned away from a doctor or hospital, but may have to contribute towards treatment.

For non-EC citizens travel insurance is essential, and it's a wise additional cover for everyone, since policies cover your cash and possessions as well as the cost of medicines, medical and dental treatment. Among British insurance companies, *Endsleigh* are about the cheapest. Premiums cost about £11 a fortnight, available from youth/student travel offices, or direct from 97–107 Southampton Row, London WC1 (☎01/580 4311). You'll need to keep all medical bills to reclaim costs and must get a written statement from the police should you have something stolen.

Minor ailments can be remedied at **Chemists** (*Drogisterij*), which supply toiletries, non-prescription drugs, tampons, condoms and the like. A **pharmacy** or *Apotheek* (open Mon–Fri 9.30am–5.30 or 6pm) is where you go to get a prescription filled. No pharmacy is open 24 hours, but the **Central Medical Service** (*Centraal Dokters Dienst*) (☎66 42 111 or ☎79 18 21) will give the addresses of the nearest shop open outside normal business hours. To get a prescription or **consult a doctor**, again phone the Central Medical Services – something the *VVV* (Tourist Office, p.7) will do for you if you need help.

Minor accidents can be treated at the outpatients department of most **hospitals**; the most central one is the *Onze Lieve Vrouwe Gasthuis* (1e Oosterparkstraat 179, tram #3; ☎599 9111), or the *VVV* can advise on outpatient clinics. In **emergencies** dial 55 55 555 to summon an ambulance.

For urgent **dental treatment**, ring the *ADC Dentist Practice* at Wilhelmina Gasthuisplein 167 (☎16 12 34); open Mon–Fri 8am–midnight, Sat 8am–9pm, Sun 1–5pm. They will sort out an appointment for you, though without insurance the cost can be high. For advice and information on **sexually-transmitted diseases**, there's a 24-hour information line on ☎23 22 52; there's also a weekend clinic at 1e Helmerstraat 17 (☎85 33 31). For details of how to get contraceptive or "morning-after" pills, see p.14.

INFORMATION AND MAPS

Before you leave it's worth contacting the Netherlands Board of Tourism, who put out a variety of glossy, informative (and free) booklets.

Most of these cover Holland in its entirety, but some are specifically devoted to Amsterdam, with useful, if sketchy, introductory maps of the city and brief details of hotels, principal tourist attractions, annual events, etc. The Board also issues the *Holland Leisure Card*, which, for about £7.50, entitles you to (among other things) hefty discounts on domestic Dutch flights, car rental, excursions and various entrance charges in The Netherlands – a bargain if you're thinking of staying for some time.

Once **in Amsterdam**, the place to head for is the *VVV*, the nationwide tourist organisation, either at its main branch outside Centraal Station (June–Aug daily 9am–11pm, Sept–Oct daily 9am–9pm, mid-Oct–May Mon–Fri 9am–6pm;

NETHERLANDS BOARD OF TOURISM OFFICES

Australia Suite 302, 5 Elizabeth Street, Sydney, NSW 2000 (☎2/ 276921).

Britain and **Eire** 25–28 Buckingham Gate, London SW1E 6LD (☎01/630 0451).

Canada 25 Adelaide St. East, Suite 710, Toronto, Ont. M5C 1Y2 (☎416/363 1577).

Sweden Styrmansgatan 8, 114 54 Stockholm (☎8 782 9925).

USA 355 Lexington Avenue., 21st Floor, New York, NY 10017 (☎212/370 7367); 225 N. Michigan Avenue, Suite 326, Chicago, IL 60601 (☎312/819 0300): 605 Market Street, Room 401, San Francisco, CA 94105 (☎415/ 543 6772).

West Germany Laurenplatz 1–3, 500-Koln-1 (☎221/236262).

☎26 64 44, office hours only), or at Leidsestraat 106 (summer Mon–Sat 9am–11pm, Sun 9am–9pm, Sept–Oct daily 9am–9pm, winter Mon–Fri 10.30am–5pm, Sat 10.30am–9pm, closed Sun). Either office can sell you a map, book accommodation for a f3.50 fee (plus a f4 "deposit" which you reclaim from the hotel), and provide informed answers to most other enquiries.

Our **maps** are adequate for most purposes, but if you need something on a larger scale, or with a street index, look for the "This is Amsterdam" map by *Falk* (f2.95), available from the VVV and many bookshops. The traditional foldout *Falkplan* (f7) is more detailed still, though Falk's ring-bound city atlas (f10) is more convenient.

For information on what's on, the VVV issues a free weekly listings guide, *What's On In Amsterdam*, which you can either pick up directly from their offices or at selected hotels, hostels and restaurants. This gives reasonably complete, if uncritical, listings for museums, the arts, shopping and restaurants. Otherwise there's rather a dearth of critical, English-language listings sources.

Of the many Dutch-language monthly freebies to be found in bars and restaurants, the best is **Agenda**, whose listings have a more youthful slant and whose addresses, phone numbers and numerous advertisements for various services could prove invaluable.

MONEY AND BANKS

The Dutch currency is the guilder, indicated by "f" or occasionally "Hfl". Each guilder is divided into 100 cents, the 25c piece commonly called a *kwartje*. You'll also find 5c, 10c, 25c, f1, f2.50 and f5 coins, along with f5, f10, f25, f50, and f100 notes, and, rarely, f250 and f500 notes.

Guilders are available in advance from any high street bank: current exchange rates are around f3.50 to the £Sterling, f2 to the US$ and there are no restrictions on bringing currency into the country. The best way of carrying the bulk of your money is in **travellers' cheques**, available from most high street banks (whether or not you have an account) for a usual fee of one percent of the amount ordered. An alternative is the **Eurocheque** book and card, issued on request by most British banks to account holders, which can be used to get cash in the majority of Dutch (and European) banks and bureaux de change. This works out slightly more expensive than travellers' cheques, but can be more convenient. Bear in mind that you always need your passport as well as the Eurocheque card to obtain cash at Dutch banks.

CHANGING MONEY

Amsterdam **banks** usually offer the best deal for changing money. Hours are Monday to Friday, 9am to 4pm, with a few banks open on Thursday 7–9pm or Saturday morning; all are closed on public holidays (see p.11). At other times you'll need to go to one of the many **bureaux de change** scattered around town. The most useful of these, in roughly descending order, are *Change Express* (open daily until midnight); *GWK* (main branch open Mon–Sat 7am–10.45pm, Sun 8am–10.45pm); and *Thomas Cook* (open Mon–Sat 8.30am–7pm, Sun 9am–5pm). You can also change money at major department stores like *Vroom & Dreesman* and *De Bijenkorf*. All these four options charge commission on transactions, but rates tend to be better than the *VVV* counters or other bureaux de change. Hotels, hostels and campsites usually give rip-off rates.

PLASTIC MONEY

Visa, Access (Eurocard) Diners Club, and *American Express* cards can be used in most Dutch banks and bureaux de change – if you're prepared to withdraw a minimum of f300. *American Express* card holders can also take out cash or replace lost travellers' cheques by using the machine and office at Damrak 66. Credit cards are less popular than expected, although most mainstream shops, hotels, restaurants will take at least one brand. Check before you commit yourself to spending. Eurocheques are the most commonly used form of payment after cash.

USEFUL ADDRESSES
Change Express
Leidsestraat 106 (☎22 14 25)
Damrak 17 (☎26 95 84)
Damrak 86 (☎24 66 81)
Kalverstraat 150 (☎27 80 87)
GWK
Centraal Station
Other rail terminals (shorter hours)
Thomas Cook
Dam 23 (☎25 0922)
Leideseplein 31a (☎26 70 00)
American Express
Damrak 66 (☎26 20 42)
Lost credit cards
Visa (☎52 05 911)
Access (Eurocard) (☎10/457 0760 & 10/457 0759)
American Express (☎42 44 88)
Diners Club (☎557 3757)

POST OFFICES AND TELEPHONES

Amsterdam's main post office is at Nieuwe Zijds Voorburgwal 182, immediately behind the Royal Palace, and is open Monday to Friday from 8.30am to 6pm, (staying open until 8.30pm Thurs) and Saturday from 9am to noon (☎55 58 911).

Queues for stamps can be long (make sure you're in the right one, labelled *postzegelen*) and it's often easier, especially for postcards, to buy stamps from tobacconists. For the record, **postal charges** right now are: within Europe 55c for a postcard, and 75c for a letter; outside Europe 75c for a postcard and the same for letters up to 20g. The main post office doesn't handle parcels; these should be sent from the **sorting office** at Oosterdokskade, near the Centraal Station, which keeps the same hours. **Post boxes** are everywhere, but use the correct slot – *Overige* for destinations other than Amsterdam. To have friends send you something **poste restante**, tell them to address it "Poste Restante, Central Post Office, Amsterdam" and it will arrive at the main office. To collect a letter you'll need your passport. There are **other central post offices**

INTERNATIONAL DIALLING CODES

Great Britain ☎09 44   **Eire** ☎09 353   **New Zealand** ☎09 64
Northern Ireland ☎09 44   **Australia** ☎09 61   **USA** and **Canada** ☎09 1

USEFUL NUMBERS

Operator calls 06 01 04
National directory enquiries ☎008, 8am–10pm; outside these times dial 06 899 11 33 (though this is expensive).
International directory enquiries ☎06 04 18
Fire ☎21 21 21
Police ☎22 22 22
Ambulance ☎55 55 555

Collect calls Either ☎06 04 10, or for calls to the UK ☎06 022 99 44; to the US and Canada ☎06 022 91 11; to Australia ☎06 022 00 61. These numbers connect directly to the national operators and generally provide a quicker service.
To call the USA direct, dial 06 022 9111, which connects you straight to the AT&T operator in the States.

See also the Directory section for help and info lines.

at Keizersgracht 757, Kerkstraat 169 in *Vroom & Dreesman* at Kalverstraat 201 and at Stadhouderskade 41. For further locations, and information on the postal service, call ☎0017.

The green-trim **telephone boxes** are similar to the modern British kiosks and most others in Europe, with a digital display of the amount of credit remaining after depositing your money. The slots take 25c, f1 and f2.50 coins; only wholly unused coins are returned. More and more call-boxes taking only **phonecards** are appearing, and buying a card is a good way to avoid queueing. They're available from post offices and Centraal Station – f5 for the equivalent of 20 local calls. Though you may have less idea of how much you're spending while the call is in progress, it's easier to make international calls from the **Telehouse**, Raadhuisstraat 46–50

(24hrs); a discount rate on international calls is in effect between 8pm and 8am. Most hotels will allow you to make international calls, but check prices first as the charge is considerably higher than from a booth or the Telehouse. Taking advantage of recent privatisation, there are also two commercial **phone centres**, offering the same facilities as the Telehouse, though slightly more expensively: *Tele Talk Center*, Leidsestraat 101, and *Telefoon Center*, directly opposite but with an entrance in Lange Leidsedwarsstraat. For further assistance, the **Amsterdam Yellow Pages** (*Gouden Gids*)can be found in most bars and cafés and has useful information.

When dialling Amsterdam from elsewhere in The Netherlands, prefix the telephone number by the city's area code, **020**; where applicable, codes for other cities are stated in the text.

POLICE, TROUBLE – AND A NOTE ON DRUGS

You're unlikely to come into much contact with Amsterdam's police force (*Politie*), a long-haired, laid-back bunch in dodgem-sized patrol cars. Few operate on the beat, and in any case Amsterdam is one of the safest cities in Europe – bar-room brawls are highly unusual, muggings uncommon, and street crime much less conspicuous than in many other capitals.

Nonetheless, it's always worth taking precautions against **petty crime**: secure your things in a locker when staying in a dorm; never leave any valuables in a tent; and if you've brought a car, remove everything that you might miss, especially the radio, and park in a well-lit, public place if you can't find a car park. As far as **personal safety** goes, it's possible to walk anywhere in the city centre at any time of the day

Central police stations include:
Headquarters: Elandsgracht 117 (☎559 91 11)
Lijnbaansgracht (☎559 23 10)
Warmoesstraat 44-46 (☎559 22 10)
The police **emergency number** in
Amsterdam is (☎22 22 22).

or night – though women might get tired of being hassled if they walk through the red-light areas alone; see p.14 for more on women and sexual harassment.

If you're unlucky enough to have something stolen, you'll need to report it to a police station and get them to write a statement for your insurance company (see *Health and Insurance* p.7). *See also* **Bicycling** *and* **Driving** *(p.27).*

DRUGS

Some residents claim that the liberal municipal attitude to the sale of **drugs** has attracted all sorts of undesirables to the city. This is partly true, but the "cleaning-up" of the Zeedijk, once Amsterdam's heroin-dealing quarter, seems to

have made open trafficking less frequent and the city a safer place.

Amsterdam has sanctioned the sale of **cannabis** at the *Melkweg* and *Paradiso* nightspots, and at many coffee shops, since the 1960s – buy it elsewhere, especially on the streets, and it's highly likely you'll be ripped-off. Though busts are rare, legally you're allowed to possess only 28 grams for personal use – which given the strength and quality of the dope here is more than enough. It's also acceptable to smoke in some bars, but since many are strongly against it, don't make any automatic assumptions. If in doubt, ask the barperson.

Purchasing, transporting or consuming cannabis products anywhere outside of the city is inadvisable, and attempting to take them out of the country foolhardy in the extreme. Bear in mind, also, that while there's a lively and growing trade in **cocaine** and **heroin**, possession of either could mean a stay in one of The Netherlands' lively and growing gaols. For drug-related **problems**, the *Drug Advice Centre*, Keizersgracht 812 (Mon–Fri 1–3pm ☎23 78 65), offers help and advice.

BUSINESS HOURS AND PUBLIC HOLIDAYS

The Dutch weekend fades painlessly into the working week with many shops staying closed on Monday morning, even in central Amsterdam.

Opening hours can be erratic, with some smaller shops opening only when the owner is in the mood. But they tend to be from 9am to 5.30 or 6pm, with many shops open until later in the evening, especially on Thursday and Friday in summer; some close on Wednesday afternoon.

Things shut down a little earlier on Saturday, and only die-hard money makers open up shop on a Sunday.

For a list of **late-night** shops and restaurants, see pp.100 and 138.

Though closed on Christmas, New Year's and Boxing Days, and on Mondays, all state-run museums adopt Sunday hours on the following **public holidays**, when most shops and banks are closed.

PUBLIC HOLIDAYS	
New Year's Day	Whit Sunday and Monday
Good Friday (many shops open)	May 5 (Liberation Day, 1990 only)
Easter Sunday and Monday	Dec 5 (early closing for St
April 30 (Queen's Birthday, many shops open)	Nicholas' birthday).
	Christmas Day
August 15 (Ascension Day)	December 26

FESTIVALS AND EVENTS

Most of Amsterdam's festivals aren't so much street happenings as music and arts events, along with a sprinkling of religious celebrations.

Most, as you'd expect, take place in the summer; the following occur annually. Check with the VVV for further details, and remember that many other interesting happenings, such as the Easter performance of Bach's *St. Matthew Passion* in Naarden or the *North Sea Jazz Festival* in The Hague, are only a short train ride away.

February 25: *Commemoration of the February Strike* around the *Docker Statue* on J. D. Meijerplein (see p.61).
February is also *Carnival* month in the south of Holland, centring on Maastricht, if you fancy a two-day excursion.

March Sunday closest to 15: *Stille Omgang* procession through the streets to the Sint Nicolaaskerk.
Blues Festival at the Meervaart Theatre.
Antique and Art Fair in the Nieuwe Kerk.
Arts and Crafts Market every Sunday on Thorbeckeplein until October.

April 30: *Koninginnedag* (Queen's birthday), celebrated by a fair on Dam Square, street markets, and fireworks in the evening. A street event par excellence, worth planning a visit around.
Paasopenstelling: the Royal Palace open day, falls in April.
Stadsilluminatie: not really the festival, but in April the canal bridges are lit up at night until October – a lovely sight.

May Second Sunday: *Amsterdam Marathon*.
Nieuwmarkt Antique Market each Sunday until September.
World Press Photo exhibition in the Nieuwe Kerk.

June 1–30: *Holland Festival*. The largest music, dance, and drama festival in the Low Countries, see p.140 for details.
Vondelpark Open Air Theatre. Free theatre, dance, and music throughout the summer (see p.140).
Last week: the *Festival van Verleiding* to celebrate *Gay Pride week*. Various exhibitions and theatrical productions.

July 1–21: *Summer Festival*. Informal international festival of modern theatre, music, dance, and mime.
Camel Jazz Festival. Renowned jazz musicians in the Concertgebouw.
Late June/early July:
Koepelkwartier Street Festival on Spuistraat between the Sonesta Hotel and the Spui.

August *Amsterdam 700*. Weekend-long football tournament with Ajax Amsterdam, Feyenoord Rotterdam and top European clubs.
Last week: *Spiegeltentfestival*. A large tent on Museumplein is the lively setting for new wave/jazz bands, poetry readings, avant-garde theatre, etc.
Uitmarkt: a weekend where every cultural organisation in the city advertises itself, with music, theatres, dancing, etc; either on Museumplein or by the Amstel.
Late August/early September: *Prinsengrachtconcert*, an evening of classical music on Prinsengracht outside the Pulitzer Hotel.

September First week: *Bloemencorso*, the Aalsmeer–Amsterdam flower pageant in the city centre. Vijzelstraat is the best place to see things, but it's not really worth a special trip.
Third week: *Jordaan Festival*. Street festival in a friendly neighbourhood. There's a commercial fair on Palmgracht, talent contests on Elandsgracht and a few street parties.
Hiswa te Water: state-of-the-art boat show at the Oosterdok. Illuminated canoe-row at night.

November Saturday in mid-November: *Parade of Sint Nicolaas*, with the traditional arrival of *Sinterklaas* near the Sint Nicolaaskerk.

December Though it tends to be a private affair, December 6, or *Pakjesavond*, rather than Christmas Day, is when Dutch kids receive their Christmas presents. If you're here on that day and have Dutch friends, it's worth knowing that it's traditional to give a present together with a rude poem you have written caricaturing the recipient.

New Year: *New Year's Eve* is a big thing in Amsterdam, with fireworks everywhere, especially outside Chinese restaurants. Some bars and discos are open all night.

GAY AMSTERDAM

In keeping with the Dutch reputation for tolerance, no other city in Europe accepts gay men as readily as Amsterdam. Here, more than anywhere, it's possible to be openly gay and accepted by the straight community. Gays are prominent in business and the arts, the age of consent is sixteen, and, with the Dutch willingness to speak English, French, and just about any other language, Amsterdam has become a magnet for the international gay scene – a city with a dense sprinkling of bars, saunas, discos and advice centres.

It says much for the strength of the community that the arrival of **AIDS** was not accompanied by the homophobia seen elsewhere. Rather than close down clubs and saunas, the city council has funded education programmes, encouraged the use of condoms, and generally conducted an open policy on the disease. If anything AIDS has created an even greater solidarity among Amsterdam's gays, a feeling tangibly manifested in the *Homomonument*, unveiled in 1987 as a memorial to gays and lesbians murdered in the Nazi concentration camps (see p.55).

The city has four recognised **gay areas**: the most famous and most lively centres around **Leidsestraat, Kerkstraat, and Reguliers-dwarsstraat**, a neighbourhood as popular with locals as it is with tourists; along the **Amstel and Amstelstraat**; the cruisy and mainly leather-geared **Warmoesstraat**; and the generally harder-line places near the **Station and Nieuwe Zijds Voorburgwal**. You'll find descriptions of all **bars and nightclubs** in Chapters 5 and 6, and recommended **gay hotels** on p.33, but for full details of both (and more on the resource listings which follow), pick up a copy of the *Top Guide to Amsterdam* (f12.50). This comprehensive gay guide (in English), mainly directed at gay men, is available from any of the shops listed below and most other gay bookshops around the world, or by post (£5, US$10, including postage) from Postbus 22643, NL-1100 DC Amsterdam (☎90 56 91). For up-to-the-minute listings get hold of the monthly *Gay Amsterdam* (f6.95), which has a selection of news and reviews in English.

CONTACTS AND INFORMATION

AIDS Hotline (☎24 42 44/ 24 42 45) Mon–Fri 3–8pm.

COC Rozenstraat 8 (☎26 86 00). Help, advice, noncommercial social activities, coffee shop, and notice board. Open noon–midnight. *COC* also broadcasts gay and lesbian information (occasionally in English) at 102.4 FM.

Documentatiecentrum Homostudies, Weteringschans 102 (☎23 53 85). A gay studies information centre. Fri 2–5pm.

Gay Switchboard (☎23 65 65). A 24-hr English-speaking service and the first source to contact for information on community groups, health services and the gay and lesbian scenes in general.

Gay Radio. If your Dutch is up to it, a gay and lesbian radio station broadcasting on FM 104.9 or 106.8.

Gay Jewish Group (*Sjalhomo*), Postbus 2536, 1000 CM Amsterdam (☎ 73 06 29). Monthly discussion groups for gay and lesbian Jews.

Op Je Flikker Gehad !? Postbus 55556, 1007 NB Amsterdam (☎24 63 21). Support and help group for victims of assault, rape and blackmail.

HEALTH

Jhr Mr. J. A. Schorerstichting, Nieuwendijk 17 (☎24 63 18). Gay and lesbian counselling centre offering professional and politically conscious help and advice on identity, sexuality, and lifestyle. Mon 6–7pm, Thurs 9–10am.

NVSH, Blauwburgwal 7–9 (☎22 66 90). The Amsterdam branch of the *Netherlands Society for Sexual Reform*, with booklets on safe sex and supplies of *Gay Safe*, a condom specially designed for anal sex. Open Mon–Fri 11am–6pm, Sat 11am–4pm.

BOOKSHOPS

Intermale, Spuistraat 249–51 (☎25 00 09). Amsterdam's largest serious gay bookshop, with a good stock of English-language books and magazines as well as a small gallery and coffee shop.

Man-to-Man, Spuistraat 21 (☎25 87 97). Information centre, bookshop (mainly porno) and cinema. Daily until midnight.

Vrolijk, Voetboogstraat 7 (☎23 51 42). Gay and lesbian bookshop with an international range of magazines and good secondhand section.

SERVICES

Thermos Night Sauna, Kerkstraat 58-60 (☎23 49 36). Saunas, steamroom, whirlpool, cabins. 11pm–8am, admission f22.50.

Toff's Tours, Ruysdaelkade 167 (☎73 85 29). Informal tours of the gay scene in Amsterdam – or anywhere else that takes your fancy. Useful for first-time visitors with plenty of cash.

WOMEN'S AMSTERDAM

Just over a century ago the only women out at night in Amsterdam were prostitutes, and a respectable woman's place was firmly in the home. Today the city has an impressive feminist infrastructure: support groups, health centres, businesses run by and for women, and there's a good range of bars and discos, a few exclusively for women.

Unless you're here for an extended stay, however, much of this can remain invisible. Both the Dutch lesbian scene and Amsterdam feminist circles are generally indifferent to travellers; most of the contacts you'll make will be with other visitors to the city. Outside the capital you'll frequently be reminded just how parochial The Netherlands is – attitudes and behaviour accept-

able in Amsterdam will be frowned on elsewhere, especially in the Catholic south.

Amsterdam, though, maintains equality of the sexes in high profile; the atmosphere is refreshing. The city streets are relatively safe for women travellers, although the brashness of its main **Red Light district** around O. Z. Achterburgwal can be initially intimidating. Walking with a friend is a good idea here, if only to ward off unwelcome leers. When it comes to exploring for yourself, remember to project a confident attitude – if you feel that the night is yours as well as his, problems shouldn't arise. However, the smaller backstreet red-light areas, such as those around the northern end of Spuistraat, are best avoided.

What follows are mainly information/health/ services listings; for **women's bars**, see p.128.

HEALTH, SUPPORT, AND CRISIS CENTRES

AIDS Helpline, (☎06 32 12 120) Mon–Fri 2–10pm.

Aletta Jacobshuis, Overtoom 323 (☎16 62 22). Named after the country's first female doctor, the Jacobshuis offers sympathetic information and help on sexual problems and birth control. It's possible to get prescriptions for birth-control pills here, as well as morning-after pills and condoms.

Blijf van m'n Lijf (☎94 27 58); **Vrouwen Opvanghuis voor Vrouwen** (☎26 80 80). Battered women's shelters.

De Maan, Koninginneweg 11 (☎76 16 73). Women's therapy centre with competent, concerned staff.

Meidentelefoon (☎23 14 01). Hotline for all matters of interest to women. Mon & Fri 6–9pm.

MR '70, Bachplein 12 (☎73 83 84). Independent abortion clinic.

De Rode Draad, Postbus 12042, 1100 AA Amsterdam (☎24 33 66). Prostitutes' support group.

Vrouwen bellen Vrouwen (☎25 01 50). Women's support and information hotline. Tues, Thurs, Fri 9am–noon, plus Tues & Thurs evening.

Vrouwengezondheidscentrum, Obiplein 4 (☎93 43 56). Women's health project, offering self-help groups for eating disorders, pregnancy, and menopausal problems, along with a referral service to help find non-sexist, non-homophobic doctors, therapists and clinics. Tues 9am–noon, Thurs 7–10pm, Fri 1–4pm.

Tegen Haar Wil (☎25 34 73). 24-hour hotline for victims of rape and sexual harassment.

Vrouwen Tegen Verkrachting, Herengracht 65 (☎24 76 44). Rape helpline Mon 7.30–9.30am, Thurs & Fri 2–4pm.

Drugs Vrouwen Crisis Centrum, Stadhouderskade 125 (☎75 07 41). Drug crisis centre for women.

For **babysitting services** see p.104; for recommended **nurseries and day care centres**, phone ☎085/33 66 41.

CENTRES AND GROUPS

Avalon, Roerstraat 79 (☎64 65 30). Feminist spirituality centre offering a wide range of workshops and weekend courses.

Gay Jewish Group (Sjalhomo), Postbus 2536, 1000 CM Amsterdam (☎73 06 29). Monthly discussion groups for lesbian and gay Jews. If no answer phone the Lesbian and Gay Switchboard.

De Hippe Heks, Confuciusplein 10 (☎11 22 68). Women's meeting-place.

Kenau, Overtoom 270 (☎16 29 13). Self-defence centre with summer weekend courses on Oriental defence techniques for women.

Vrouwenhuis, Nieuwe Herengracht 95 (☎25 20 66). Open most days at varying times. Organising centre for women's activities/cultural events. Worth dropping by to check out what's happening.

BOOKSHOPS AND GALLERIES

Amazone, Singel 72 (☎27 90 00). Women's art gallery and exhibition centre for cultural and social topics affecting women. Tues–Fri 10am–4pm, Sat 1–4pm.

Lorelei, Prinsengracht 495 (☎23 43 08). Secondhand booksellers with a lesbian-feminist stock and clientele. Wed–Sat noon–6pm.

Villa Baranka, Prins Hendrikkade 140 (☎27 64 80). Cross-cultural art studio with performance art, literature and poetry readings by and for women. See p.146 and *Uitkrant* for more details.

Vrouwenindruk, Westermarkt 5 (☎24 50 03). Feminist secondhand bookshop.

Xantippe, Prinsengracht 290 (☎23 58 54). Amsterdam's foremost women's bookshop with a wide selection of feminist titles in English.

ARCHIVE

International Information Centre and Archives for the Women's Movement (IAV), Keizersgracht 10 (☎24 21 43/24 42 68) Mon–Fri 10am–4pm. Up-to-date clippings service from all important international feminist magazines, and a major archive for the women's movement containing an elaborate historical collection from international sources. Also referral service for women's studies, and home of the foundation for women artists (☎26 65 89).

FEMINIST BUSINESSES

Knalpot, 1e Passeerdersdwarsstraat 2 (☎24 70 40). Garage where women teach you how to fix your car. Mon–Tues only.

Vrouwenfietsenmakkerij, 2e Ceramstraat 23 (☎66 53 218). Bicyle repair shop run by women.

Zijwind, Ferdinand Bolstraat 168 (☎73 70 26) and Gorontalostraat 30-32 (☎65 32 18). Bicycle repair shops run by women; also rent bikes (see p.27).

LESBIAN AMSTERDAM

The city's native **lesbian scene** is smaller and more subdued than the gay one. Many of Amsterdam's politically active lesbians move within tight circles, and it takes time to find out what's happening. Good places to begin are the *Saarein*, the oldest and best established of Amsterdam's *vrouwencafé*, or any of the women's bars listed on p.128.

HELP AND INFO

COC, Rozenstraat 14 (☎26 86 007). Help, advice, noncommercial social activities, coffee shop and noticeboard for men and women. Open noon to midnight. *COC* also broadcasts lesbian information (occasionally in English) on 102.4 FM.

Gay Switchboard (☎23 65 65). 24-hour English-speaking information service on health, community services and the gay and lesbian scene.

Lesbian Radio. For the frequencies of Amsterdam's gay and lesbian radio station, see "Gay Amsterdam", above.

Lesbian archives, (☎25 37 47). Mainly Dutch reference centre for contemporary lesbian culture and history. Tues & Fri 2–4.30pm.

Jhr Mr. J. A. Schorerstichting, Nieuwendijk 17 (☎24 63 18). Lesbian (and gay) counselling centre offering professional and politically conscious help and advice on identity, sexuality and lifestyle. Mon 6–7pm, Thurs 9–10am.

Vrolijk, Voetboogstraat 7 (☎23 51 42). Bookshop with an international range of lesbian magazines and secondhand books.

LONG-TERM STAYS: WORK AND A ROOF

WORK

In order to **work** legally anywhere in Holland, it's necessary to get a **work permit** from the police: all EC nationals are entitled to stay for three months, but it's only possible to stop on after this if you're in work. To obtain the necessary paperwork you'll need to tangle with Dutch bureaucracy, which can be labyrinthine. If you are planning on staying, try to get your passport stamped on entry – just ask firmly at passport control. This is because the only proof of long-standing residence the police will accept is a stamped passport. Some other words of advice: when you come bring all possible documentation – birth, marriage certificates, letters of employment, contracts, etc – with you, and put on businesslike clothes when attending any official interviews.

Actually **finding a job** isn't easy, though lately the (previously terrible) employment situation seems to have stabilised. **Temp agencies** (*uitzendburos*) provide the main source of casual, quasi-legal work, particularly during the summer. If you're prepared to tramp around to such offices twice a day and willing to take any job, you'll normally find something, especially if you're under 23 (employers have to pay substantially more to older individuals). The sort of jobs you'll find in this way vary enormously, but in the summer there's some demand in the hotel and catering industry – though you may have better results applying directly to tourist establishments. Also, it's often possible for people with typing/secretarial skills to pick up temp jobs as English-speaking typists, particularly in the holiday season.

Scanning the newspapers isn't much use save for irregular adverts from *uitzendburos* and cleaning agencies. The *arbeidsburo* (labour exchange) has been known to find work for non-Dutch speakers, mainly skilled manual workers, but this seems to have dried up considerably. Summer jobs in the **glasshouses** can occasionally be found – the best way of doing so is to head down to Aalsmeer and the bulb areas around Haarlem.

RENTED ACCOMMODATION

Reasonably priced rented accommodation in Amsterdam is in short supply, and flat hunting requires a determined effort. Much of the housing is controlled by the council, and the only people eligible for a **council flat** (more numerous since the city's big urban renewal – read demolition – programme got under way) are those holding the *urgentie bewijs* – an urgent-need certificate that you can get if you've been living here for two years but still don't have a suitable home. Anyone planning to stay a while should register at the *Bevolkings Register* (address below) on arrival, since the *urgentie bewijs* is a useful piece of paper to have – though you should only go once you've registered with the police (and keep them informed of any change of address); otherwise things can get messy.

Most newcomers, however, are forced to seek accommodation in the **private sector**, which can prove expensive. There's little chance of finding anything for much less than f600 a month – though some of the old warehouse buildings around the central harbour area have been converted into small studios and rooming houses, which are comparatively cheap, if a little tacky. (Ask in *'t Anker* bar, behind the station, for more information). Otherwise, the **newspapers** *De Telegraaf* and *De Volkskrant* are a must, with large "To Let" (*Te Huur*) sections, particularly on Friday and Saturday – though it's well worth buying them every morning (at the crack of dawn for any sort of chance). The free weekly papers, notably *De Echo*, should also be closely scrutinised. Apartment-finding **agencies** advertise regularly in newspapers and are another useful source if you can afford the fee – normally one or two months' rent for finding a place – but beware of agencies that ask for money before they hand out an address since fly-by-night operators are common. Bear in mind, too, that whether you rent through an agency or not, an *overname* – illegal key-money paid to the previous tenant to cover furniture and accessories left behind – is often charged. This varies tremendously and can be exorbitant, but it's usually unavoidable and can only be recovered by charging it to the next tenant when you move out. Landlords also sometimes ask for a *borgsom*, a refundable security deposit.

When all's said and done though, a lot of housing is found by **word of mouth**. A remarkable grapevine springs up in the summer among the travelling community; people are constantly coming and going, looking for apartment-sharers or temporary house-sitters. Just let everyone you meet know you're homeless. It's also worth keeping an eagle eye on **notice boards** everywhere; the main public library at Prinsengracht 587 has a good one, as do bars and student eating-places such as the *mensas* and *Egg Cream* (addresses on pp.130 and 132). **Student dorms** have notice boards which often advertise temporary accommodation in students' rooms – not a bad short-term option since rooms are very cheap. Even **tobacconist's windows** should be perused, as the Dutch tend to take long summer holidays and often need house-sitters to take care of the cats and plants while they're away.

SQUATTING

The other way to solve your housing problem is to find a **squat** or *kraak*, though it's important to remember that the foreign squatter faces special problems – principally police harassment and deportation. If the police want you out, your rights as an EC citizen don't count for much, and being deported is an unpleasant and expensive experience. To avoid this it's essential to gain the support, and listen to the advice of, the local squatting group, although they aren't always terribly helpful to foreigners. Since Dutch squatters regard their own activities as community-oriented and politically motivated, they don't always welcome people whom they suspect are looking for a short rent-free stay in Holland. Become involved with a local group, get to know the people and keep looking for an empty place yourself – don't expect it all to be done for you.

A **short-term** squat of an empty flat in blocks due for demolition within about six months is probably the best solution for the temporary visitor. For a variety of reasons, these are likely to dry up in the future but, for the moment at least, they do exist. You have to be quick and get in before the wreckers, though, who are sent in by the council to make places uninhabitable. Lately this has become more important than ever, since in response to the city's heroin problem and the resultant colonies of junkies, the council is amazingly efficient about trashing the premises first. You really need to be tipped off or actually see people moving out and get in that evening; local squatters may be able to provide information. Once you're in, chances are there won't be any trouble, but again, your local squatting group or MAIC (see below) can clarify your legal position. Having established a claim on the property, your next problem is lack of furniture, gas and electrical appliances, etc. These are surprisingly easy to pick up – often off the street on rubbish-collection night – and a place can be made habitable in a couple of weeks with next to no cash outlay.

Long-term squats are much more complicated: they have to be observed for some time and thoroughly investigated before being attempted; the help of a squatters' group is imperative. The main aim of this type of squatting is to get a licence from the local council, and the best chance of success is in a place that is already in an unrentable condition.

The big **community squats** are much more than just a way of alleviating the housing problem. They are overtly political in nature and present a challenge to the establishment by opposing the activities of property developers in a very practical way. Most of the larger premises used for squatting were abandoned factories, hotels or warehouses – destined to be demolished and replaced by luxury apartments or office complexes, or simply left until land prices rose, enabling resale at a profit. Large groups of squatters moved in and set about creating a complete environment from nothing, building living spaces, workshops, studios and often even shops, cheap cafés, day-care centres, etc. These communities house hundreds of people and try to provide services which are lacking in inner city areas. Living in one entails quite a commitment – you have to be prepared to participate fully in the community and spend a lot of time and energy on

the squat – and they shouldn't be seen as a solution to the short-term housing problem of someone just passing through.

ADDRESSES

Aliens' Police (*Vreemdelingendienst*), Waterlooplein 9 (☎559 9111). Open Mon–Fri 9am–12.30pm , or ring between 2 and 4pm for an appointment.

Bevolkings Register, Stadhuis/Muziektheater complex, Waterlooplein (☎55 19 911). Mon–Fri 8.30am–3pm.

Bureau voor Rechtshulp, Spuistraat 10 (☎26 44 77). Free legal advice centre.

MAIC 14 Hartenstraat (☎24 09 77). Information on courses, accommodation and social benefits, as well as a general advice and legal centre for those new to the city. Mon–Fri noon–5pm.

Openbare Bibliotheek (Public Library), Prinsengracht 587 (☎26 50 65).

Student Housing Office, Oude Turfmarkt 139 (☎52 52 386). Individual **student halls** are listed under *Studenthuis* in the telephone directory.

Volksuniversiteit, Herenmarkt 93 (☎26 16 26). They run cheap and basic courses in Dutch – good for getting a toehold in the language early on.

DIRECTORY

ADDRESSES These are written, for example, as Haarlemmerstraat 15 III, which means the third-floor apartment at number 15 Haarlemmerstraat. The ground floor is indicated by h/s (*huis*) after

the number. The figures 1e or 2e before a street name are an abbreviation for Eerste and Tweede respectively – first and second streets of the same name. Dutch zip codes can be found in the directory kept at post offices (p.9), or by taking the number in purple on a large-scale *Falkplan* and putting "10" in front (note that complete codes have a two-letter indicator as well).

AIRPORT TAX Isn't charged when leaving The Netherlands.

AIRLINE OFFICES *Aer Lingus*, Heiligweg 14 (☎23 95 89); *Air UK* (☎74 77 47); *British Airways*, Stadhouderskade 4 (☎85 22 11); *British Midland* Strawinskylaan 1535 (☎06 022 24 26); *Canadian Pacific*, Stadhouderskade 2 (☎85 17 21); *KLM*, Leidseplein 1 (☎64 93 633); *NLM City Hopper*, Schipol Airport (☎64 92 227); *PanAm*, Leidseplein 29 (☎26 20 21); *Qantas*, Stadhouderskade 6 (☎83 80 810); *Transavia* ,Schipol Airport (☎60 46 518); *TWA*, Singel 540-4 (☎26 22 27).

BABIES When booking rooms, remember that some hotels don't accommodate babies, or will only do so during the low season. Check our listings and verify information with the hotel. For **babysitting services** and recommended **nurseries** see p.104.

BEACHES The Netherlands has some great beaches, though the weather is unreliable and the water often murky and full of jellyfish. For swimming or sunbathing, the nearest resort is **Zandvoort**, a short bus ride from easy-to-reach Haarlem – though beware of heavy crowds in season. Otherwise, there are resorts and long sandy beaches all the way up the dune-filled western coastline: **Katwijk** and **Noordwijk** are reachable by bus from Leiden, **Castricum-aan-Zee**, **Bergen-aan-Zee**, and **Egmond-aan-Zee** by bus from Alkmaar; or, with your own vehicle, it's possible to find any number of deserted spots in between.

BIKE HIRE See p.26.

BRING Toiletries, film and English-language books, all of which are expensive in Amsterdam. Also antihistamine cream if you react badly to mosquitoes – it can be hard to find in Amsterdam.

CARPARKS *Parking Prinsengracht*, Prinsengracht 540–2 (☎25 98 52) f3 per hour, around f20 per day. Others: *De Bijenkorf*, on Beursplein, and *Europarking*, at Marnixstraat 250. There are also underground garages under the Muziektheater and Museumplein.

CAR PROBLEMS See p.27.

CHURCHES Services in English at the *English Reformed Church*, Begijnhof (☎24 96 65), Sun at 10.30am; the *Anglican Church*, Groenburgwal 42 (☎24 88 77), Sun at 10.30am and 7.30pm; English Catholic Mass at the church of *St John and Ursula*, Begijnhof (☎22 19 18), on Sun at 12.15pm, May–Aug. For details of other religious services, consult the *VVV*.

CONSULATES/EMBASSIES *British Consulate General* Koningslaan 44 (☎76 43 43); *Eire Embassy* Willemskade 23 3016 DM Rotterdam (☎010/14 33 22); *Australian Embassy* Koninginnegracht 23, 2514 AB The Hague (☎070/61 41 11); *American Consulate General*, Museumplein 19 (☎66 45 661); *Canadian Embassy*, Sophialaan 7 2514 JP, The Hague (☎070/61 41 11); *New Zealand Embassy* Mauritskade 25, 2514 HD The Hague (☎070/46 93 24).

CONTRACEPTIVES Condoms are available from *drogisterij* or the *Condomerie* (p.101), but to get the pill you need a doctor's prescription – see p.14.

DIAMONDS The industry was founded here in the late 16th century by refugee diamond workers from Antwerp, but since World War II it has depended on tourists for a livelihood. Currently around twenty diamond firms operate in Amsterdam. All are working factories, but many open their doors to the public for viewing the cutting, polishing, and sorting practices, and (most importantly) for buying. City tours often include diamond factories (see p.30), but a few can be visited individually. Among them: *Coster*, Paulus Potterstraat 2–6 (☎76 22 22); *Bonebakker*, Rokin 88 (☎23 22 94); *Van Moppes*, Albert Cuypstraat 2–6 (☎76 12 42); and *Amsterdam Diamond Centre*, Rokin 1 (☎24 57 87). Admission is free.

DISABLED VISITORS Though Amsterdam's public transportation system has no facilities for disabled passengers, most of the city's major museums, concert halls, theatres, churches and public buildings are accessible to visitors in wheelchairs. Either of the *VVV* offices, themselves accessible, will provide lists of those that have ramps and lifts, or where staff are trained to escort disabled visitors. *NS* (Dutch Railways) offers a comprehensive service for disabled travellers, including a timetable in braille, free escort service and assistance at all stations. Get more details by calling ☎030/33 12 53 (Mon–Fri 8.30am–4pm), or from The Netherlands Board of Tourism leaflet, *Holland for the Handicapped*, which also describes hotel and camping facilities throughout the country. There is also a desk in the Schipol Arrivals Hall (North), open 6am–11pm, to help disabled people through the airport. Last but not least, paper currency has dots in the corner to indicate its value to the visually impaired.

DOG SHIT Step carefully when walking the streets as Amsterdam dog-owners have yet to train their mutts to use the gutters – something the council seems unwilling (or unable) to do anything about.

DRUGS Amsterdam has a liberal attitude to the consumption of soft drugs, for details of which see p.11.

ELECTRIC CURRENT 220v AC – effectively the same as British; American apparatus requires a transformer; both will need new plugs or an adaptor.

EMERGENCIES Police ☎22 22 22; **Ambulance** ☎55 55 555; **Fire** ☎21 21 21.

ICE SKATING See p.108.

ISIC CARDS Student ID won't help gain reduced admission to anything in the city – for this you need a museumcard or *CJP* (see p.71).

LAUNDERETTES *The Clean Brothers* is the best, at Jakob Van Lennepkade 179, Westerstraat 26 and Rozengracht 59 (daily until 9pm). Other launderettes at: Warmoesstraat 30, Oude Doelenstraat 12 and Herenstraat 24. Otherwise look under *Wassalons* in the Yellow Pages.

LEFT LUGGAGE See p.25.

LIBRARIES No one will stop you from using any of the *Openbare Bibliotheeken* for reference purposes, but to borrow books you'll need to show proof of residence. The main branch at Prinsengracht 587 (Mon 1–5pm and 7–10pm, Tues–Fri 10am–5pm and 7–10pm, Sat 10am–5pm) has English newspapers and magazines, photocopiers, and a cheap snack bar.

LOST PROPERTY For items lost on the **trams, buses, or metro** *GVB* Head Office, Prins Hendrikkade 108–114 (☎551 4911). For property lost on a **train** go to the *Verloren Voorpwerpen* at the nearest station. Amsterdam's is at the Centraal Station (☎557 8544); after ten days, all unclaimed property goes to Concordiastraat 70, Utrecht. If you lose something in the **street** or a park, try the police lost property at Waterlooplein 11 (Mon–Fri 11am–3.30pm; ☎55 98 005).

MOSQUITOES These thrive in Holland's watery environment, and bite their worst at the campsites. An antihistamine cream such as *Phenergan* is the best antidote.

NEWSPAPERS There's no difficulty in finding **British newspapers**, on sale just about everywhere the same day they come out (the Centraal Station shop has a good selection). For those wanting to practise their Dutch, *De Volkskrant* is the progressive, leftish daily, while *De Telegraaf* is a right-wing scandal sheet reminiscent of *The Sun*. The fashionable *Het Parool* ('The Password') and news magazine *Vrij Nederland* are the successors of underground printing during the Nazi occupation. *Algemeen Daagsblad* is a right-wing broadsheet, whose competitor, *NRC Handelsblad*, is centre-left and favoured by the city's intellectuals. The Protestant *Trouw* (Trust) covers the middle ground.

NOTICEBOARDS Most "brown cafés" have noticeboards with details of concerts, events and the like, occasionally displaying personal notices too. Both *Egg Cream* (see p.132) and the main library (see above) have noticeboards useful for apartment- and job-hunting, sharing lifts, etc. Try also the supermarkets, most of which have noticeboards.

PHOTO BOOTHS Scattered around town, but most reliably at Centraal Station.

RADIO (ENGLISH LANGUAGE) It's possible to pick up BBC Radio 4 on 1500m longwave and the World Service on 463m medium wave and short-wave frequencies between 75m and 49m at intervals throughout the day and night.

TAMPONS On sale at all *drogists* (sundries shops), though generally cheaper in supermarkets.

TELEPHONE HELPLINES In **English**: *Legal Hotline* (☎548 2611); *Mental and Social problems* (☎16 16 66); *Tram, Bus, and Metro Information* (☎27 27 27). In **Dutch**: *Road Conditions* (☎070/31 31 31); *Time* (☎002); *Weather* (☎003).

TIME One hour ahead of Britain, six hours ahead of Eastern Standard Time.

TIPPING Don't bother, since restaurants, hotels, taxis, etc., must include a fifteen percent service charge by law. Only if you're somewhere *really* flash is it considered proper to round up the bill to the nearest guilder.

TRAVEL AGENTS *NBBS* at Dam 17 (☎20 50 71), Leidsestraat 53 (☎38 17 36) and Ceinturbaan 294 (☎79 93 37), is the Amsterdam branch of the nationwide student/youth travel organisation and the best source of *BIJ* tickets, discount flights for anyone, etc. Also worth checking out are: *Nouvelles Frontières*, Van Baerlestraat 3 (☎66 44 131); *Budget Bus*, Rokin 10 (☎27 51 51); *Budget Air*, Rokin 34 (☎27 12 51); *Magic Plane*, Rokin 38 (☎26 48 44).

TV If you're staying somewhere with cable TV it's possible to tune in to BBC1 and BBC2; *Superchannel* (which offers reruns of British sitcoms, drama and documentaries); the Rupert Murdoch-owned *Sky Channel* (similar plus pop videos); *MTV* (24-hour pop videos); or *CNN New International* (an American-based cable news channel). Other Dutch TV channels, cable and non-cable, regularly run American and British movies with Dutch subtitles.

WINDMILLS There is today only one windmill in Amsterdam, De Gooyer in the Eastern Islands district. But the best place to see windmills is **Kinderdijk** near Rotterdam; they're also still very much part of the landscape in the polderlands north of Amsterdam. Also, some have been moved and reassembled out of harm's way in the open-air museums at **Zaanse Schans** (Zaandam) and **Arnhem**.

CLOTHING AND SHOE SIZES

Dresses

British	8	10	12	14	16	18		
Continental	36	38	40	42	44	46		

Women's Shoes

British	3	4	5	6	7	8	9	10
Continental	35	36	37	38	39	40	41	42

Men's Shoes

British	5	6	7	8	9	10	11	12
Continental	39	40	41	42	43	44	45	46

Sweaters

British	32	34	36	38	40	42	44	46
Continental	38	40	42	44	46	48	50	52

Shirts and Collars

British	14	14½	15	15½	16	16½	17	17½
Continental	36	37	38	39	40	41	42	43

PART TWO

THE

GUIDE

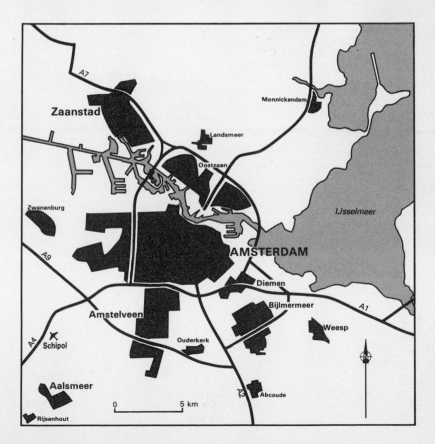

POINTS OF ARRIVAL

BY AIR

Amsterdam has only one international airport, **Schipol**. This is connected by train with Amsterdam's **Centraal Station**, a fast service leaving every fifteen minutes during the day, every hour at night; the journey takes twenty minutes and costs f4.40 one way. There are also trains to **Amsterdam RAI** and **Amsterdam Zuid** – useful if you know you'll be staying nearby.

As for Schipol itself, its claim to be the businessperson's favourite airport is well founded: it's compact enough to keep walking to a minimum, directional signs are clear and plentiful, and the duty-free shop is the cheapest in Europe. There are *bureaux de change* in the arrivals hall, as well as a *GWK* money exchange office in the railway station (Mon–Sat 7am–11pm, Sun 10am–6pm), and a *post office* in the departures lounge (daily 7am–11.30pm). *Left-luggage* is open from 6am to 11pm and costs f2 per item per day for this or a locker.

Flight enquiries and arrivals **information:** ☎60 10 966.

BY TRAIN OR BUS

Amsterdam has a number of suburban **train stations**, but all major internal and international traffic is handled by **Amsterdam Centraal**.

Arriving here leaves you at the hub of all bus and tram routes and just five minutes' walk from Dam Square. The station's facilities include a *GWK* bank and money-changing office (open 24 hours), *left-luggage* (Mon–Fri 5am–1am, Sat–Sun 6am–1am; f1.25 per item, bikes f1.65, lockers f1.50 for 30 hours), as well as the usual array of shops, newsstands, and restaurants (including a gourmet French restaurant – see p.134). For enquiries, bookings, and passenger information phone ☎20 22 66 for international travel, ☎06 899 1121 for travel within The Netherlands.

Almost all **buses** arrive at **Centraal Station** too, except for Hoverspeed's *City Sprint* service, which calls at **Stadionplein**, before terminating at **Leidseplein**, linked to the city centre by trams #1, #2 and #5.

BY CAR

Coming in on either highway **A4** or **A2** from the south, you should experience no traffic problems, and as soon as you approach Amsterdam's southern reaches, signs clearly direct you to the city centre. For the western portions of the city follow the Einsteinweg and watch the signs for the best exit for your destination; for other parts of the city follow the Ringweg-Zuid and get off at either the Olympic Stadium or the RAI exhibition centre exits.

ORIENTATION

There's no problem orienting yourself in Amsterdam. Centraal Station, where you're likely to arrive, lies on the northern edge of the city centre, on the banks of the river IJ: on the far side lies Amsterdam North, an area almost entirely outside your range of interest unless you're camping; in the other direction, the city fans south in a cobweb of canals surrounded by expanding suburbs.

The city is small enough not to have any really distinct neighbourhoods: it's easier just to distinguish between the central core and its artery, Damrak, and the main canals that encircle it. The neighbourhoods outside this broad half-circle are residential for the most part, and – aside from some museums, the Heineken brewery, and the occasional street market – won't be top of most people's travel agendas.

Public transport is good, and quick hops by tram are easy. But the best way to get around is to walk: you'll see more (remember, this is a city built around canals) and virtually everything of interest is within walking distance.

As a broad reference, it takes at most three-quarters of an hour to stroll from Centraal Station to the Rijksmuseum, which is about the longest walk you'd ever need to take.

GETTING AROUND THE CITY

By European capital standards Amsterdam is small, its public transport excellent, and most of the things you might conceivably want to see can be found in the city's compact centre: getting around couldn't be easier.

BUSES, TRAMS AND THE METRO

Apart from walking, **trams** – and, to a lesser extent, **buses** – offer the easiest transport alternative: the system is comprehensive and not at all expensive. Your first stop should be the main *GVB* (city transit) office in front of Centraal Station (next door to the *VVV*; Mon–Fri 7am–10.30pm, Sat & Sun 8am–10.30pm) where you can pick up a free route map and an English guide to the **ticketing** system.

This needs explaining. *Dagkaarten* (**day tickets**) are valid for as many days as you need – prices currently start at f8.85 for one day, going up to f17.25 for four, and f2.75 for each additional day. Or you can buy a *strippenkaart*. These are valid nationwide and work on a zonal arrangement whereby you cancel two strips for one zone, three strips for two and so on, when you board the tram or bus (the driver will do it for you on a bus; on trams you're trusted to do it yourself). The most economical *strippenkaart* has fifteen strips (currently f8.85), and can be purchased ahead of time at any *GVB* office (the others are in the Scheepvaarthuis at the corner of Prins Hendrikkade and Binnenkant, and there is sometimes a portacabin parked outside the Stadsschouwburg on Leidseplein), post office,

selected tobacconists, or at railway station ticket counters. Otherwise two-, three-, and ten-strip tickets are available from the driver – though they work out considerably more expensive. You'll rarely need to travel outside the central zone, so most of the time cancelling two strips is sufficient. Also, don't forget that the stamp made on the *strippenkaart* is timed and valid for an hour: you don't need to cancel it again if you change trams or buses within that time.

Of course, this system is wide open to abuse. But lately the city has been eager to crack down on those who don't pay (known as *zwartrijden* – "black riders"), and wherever you're travelling, at whatever time of day, there's a good chance you'll have your ticket checked. If caught, you're liable for a f26 fine, due on the spot, so it pays to be honest. Those planning to stay for some time might consider investing in a *sterabonnement* or **season ticket**, valid weekly, monthly, or yearly and available from the same outlets as a *strippenkaart*. A one-star weekly pass (valid for one zone only) currently costs around f12.50, and you need a photograph and your passport to buy one.

The *strippenkaart* system also works on the city's **metro**, which starts at Centraal Station and connects with the building complexes of Bijlmermeer to the east. It's clean, modern and punctual, although it can be a bit hairy at night, and apart from a couple of stops in the eastern reaches of the centre, most of the stations are in the suburbs and used mainly by commuters.

All of the above services stop running around 12.30am, when a wide network of **night buses** rolls into action, roughly hourly until 4am from Centraal Station to most parts of the city; the *GVB* offers a leaflet detailing all the routes.

BIKES AND CANAL BIKES

Another possibility, and a practical one, is to go native and opt for a **bicycle**: the city's well-defined network of bicycle lanes (*fietspaden*) means that this can be a remarkably safe way of getting around. If you haven't brought your own, it's possible to **hire a bike** from *Centraal Station* (f7 a day, f28 a week plus f200 deposit), or from a number of similarly priced bike hire firms scattered around town, most of which ask for smaller deposits or accept a passport instead: try *Rent-a-Bike*, Pieter Jacobsdwarsstraat 17, off Damstraat

(☎25 50 29), f9 a day plus f50 deposit and a passport – they also do tandems for f25 a day; *Heja*, Bestevaerstraat 39 (☎12 92 11), who also have mopeds; *Zijwind*, Ferdinand Bolstraat 168 (☎73 70 26); or *Koenders*, Utrechtsedwarsstraat 105 (☎23 46 57) and 880–900 Amsterdamse Bos (☎44 54 73). Also, if you're camping, it's usually possible to hire bikes from the campsite.

As for the **rules of the road**, remember that you are legally obliged to have reflector bands on both wheels, and that even in bike lanes (denoted by a white circle on a blue background or a small, black, oblong sign) it is illegal to ride two abreast. Also, a **word of warning**: lock up your bike at *all times*. (see Basics p.10) Bike theft is rife in Amsterdam, and it's not unusual to see the dismembered parts of bicycles still chained to their railings, victims of sharp-eyed gangs armed with bolt cutters who roam the streets hawking their prizes at suspiciously low prices. Ironically, this is often the cheapest way to pick up a bike – and you can always sell it (often at a profit) when the time comes to go home. Should you want to buy a bike legally, however, see p.92 for a listing of shops.

More for fun than for serious transport are the **canal bikes**, pedalboats that can be picked up (and dropped off) at one of four central locations — Leidseplein by the American Hotel, on the Singelgracht between the Rijksmuseum and the Heineken Brewery, Prinsengracht at the Westerkerk, and Keizersgracht near Leidsestraat. You're given a map to plan a route, and hire (f18.50 for a two-seater, f27.50 for four, plus f50 deposit) is by the hour; pick-up points are open from 9am to 11pm. For further information phone ☎26 35 35. In addition, *Roell Watersport* on Mauritskade (behind the Amstel Hotel, ☎92 91 24) hires out machines for f18 per hour for two people, f26 for four. They have two jetties: one at the intersection of Leidsestraat and Prinsengracht, the other outside the *Hans & Grietje* café on the corner of Speigelgracht and Lijnbaansgracht.

TAXIS AND CAR HIRE

Taxis are plentiful but expensive, and found in ranks on main city squares (Stationsplein, Dam Square, Leidseplein, etc.) or by phoning ☎77 77 77 – you can't hail them. Taxis aside, it's generally unwise to travel **by car**: parking is either difficult or expensive, and even if you have

brought your own car it won't make any difference to the zealous traffic police, who will clamp you or tow you away whatever the registration plate says. Reclaiming a car from the pound costs at least f250; a clamp is cheaper – you're only charged for the excess meter time – but you have to present yourself personally at the nearest clamp office to get it removed. If you get caught and don't know what to do, call ☎27 58 66.

Even when you're mobile, the abundance of trams and bikes makes driving hazardous, to say the least. If you do **bring your own car**, an ordinary driver's licence is acceptable, and the Dutch automobile organisation, ANWB, offers reciprocal repair/breakdown services to *AA* and *RAC* members; they can be contacted in Amsterdam at ☎26 82 51 (emergency number ☎06 08 08; main office ☎070/ 14 71 47). If you're not an *AA/RAC* member you can either pay for this service or, for a small fee, become a temporary member.

For just getting out of town, it's better to **hire a vehicle** by the day or week. All the major agencies are represented in Amsterdam: *Budget*, Overtoom 121 (☎12 60 66) or *Europcar*, Overtoom 51–53 (☎83 21 23) are slightly less expensive than *Hertz* and *Avis*, but the cheapest are such local operators as *Diks*, Gen. Vetterstraat 51–55 (☎17 85 05); van Ostadestraat 278–280 (☎66 23 366), whose prices start at around f47 a day plus a charge per kilometre over 100km. **Rules of the road** again the maximum speed limit within the city is normally 50 kph (31 mph.), and seatbelts must be worn by all drivers and front-seat passengers.

CANAL TRANSPORT AND CITY BUS TOURS

One way of getting orientated is to take a **canal trip** on one of the glass-topped boats that jam the major canals during the summer season. While not exactly riveting, these trips are the best way to see canal houses, and have a soporific charm if you're feeling lazy. Of the many to choose from, *P.Kooij* (☎23 38 10) runs hour-long tours for f8, which leave from the corner of Rokin and Lange Brugsteeg and have (atypically) a live commentary that's just about bearable.

If you want to combine a canal tour with real transportation, there is a **canal bus** service, which runs from Weteringschans opposite the Rijksmuseum to Centraal Station, with stops at Leidseplein, Leidsestraat/Keizersgracht and the

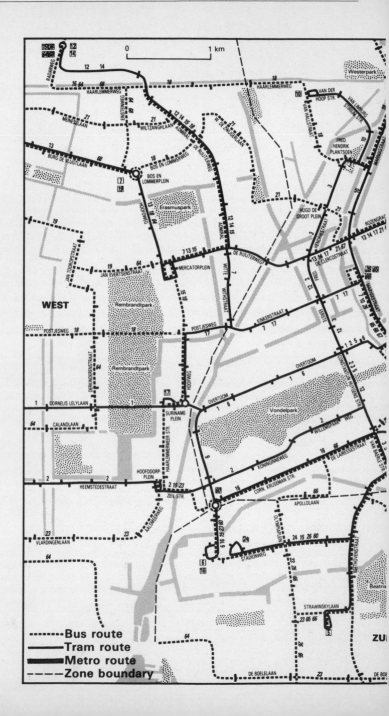

· · · · · ·Bus route
————Tram route
▬▬▬▬Metro route
— — —Zone boundary

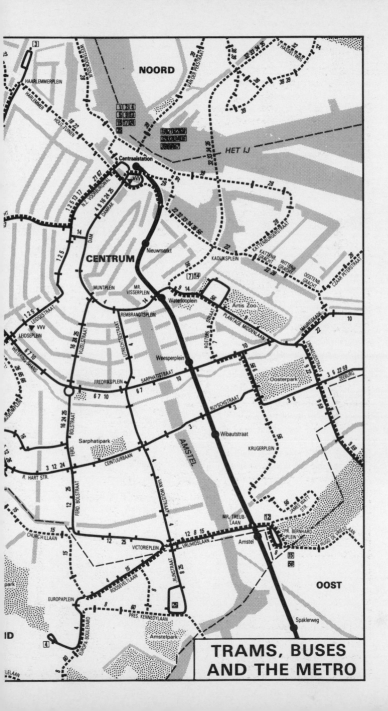

TRAMS, BUSES AND THE METRO

Westerkerk on the way. The whole journey takes about an hour, and boats leave the Rijksmuseum ever fifteen minutes – pick them up at any stop. A day ticket costs f12.50, a two-day ticket f20; more details on ☎23 98 86.

For the seriously moneyed, there are also **canal taxi** services. *Water Taxi*, outside Centraal Station (☎75 09 09), charge a f54 booking fee and f1.50 per minute inside Amsterdam; maximum seven people per boat; *Roell Watersport* (see above; ☎91 91 24), are slightly cheaper and can carry up to ten people. Both organisations can also provide drinks and snacks for the incredibly rich, but give them plenty of advance warning.

. Otherwise, as far as **city tours** go, plenty of people are willing to guide you around by road: the *GVB* offers a seventy-minute tour by *tourist tram*, which takes in the main sights of the immediate centre; or operators like *Lindbergh* (the cheapest), Damrak 26 (☎22 27 66), *Keytours*, Dam 19 (☎24 73 10), and *Holland International*, Damrak 7 (☎22 25 50), offer three–hour tours with stop-offs and, again, live commentary for f30–34.

The same organisations also offer a range of **excursions** into the outlying regions of Holland – pick up a leaflet for details and prices, and see our warnings on p.153.

FINDING A PLACE TO STAY

Unless you're camping, accommodation in Amsterdam is a major expense: even hostels are pricey for what you get, and hotels are among the most expensive in Europe. The city's size means that you'll inevitably end up somewhere central, but you'll still need to search hard to find a bargain.

At peak periods throughout the year (July–August, Christmas) it's advisable to book ahead of time – rooms can be swallowed up alarmingly quickly, especially during the summer. The *VVV* (addresses and opening times on p.7) will make advance bookings and book rooms on the spot for a f3.50 fee, or sell you a comprehensive accommodation list for f1.

Note: all tram line directions given below are from the Centraal Station.

HOSTELS

The bottom-line for most travellers is taking a dormitory bed in a **hostel**, and there are plenty to

choose from – official (YHA), unofficial, and Christian; in fact you'll probably be accosted outside the train station with numerous offers of beds. Most hostels expect you to provide your own sleeping bag (bed linen is often available for a small fee) and many, for security reasons, lock guests out of the dormitories for a short period each day and set some kind of nightly curfew – though it's usually late enough not to be a problem. The cheapest deal you'll find is around f11 per person a night (at the *Sleep-In* – see below); prices rise sharply at better-furnished and more central hostels to an average of about f17. If you want a little extra privacy, many of these also offer triples, doubles and singles for much less than you'd pay in a regular hotel, though their rates rarely include breakfast as hotel rates generally do.

OFFICIAL YOUTH HOSTELS

Vondel Park, Zandpad 5 (☎83 17 44). For facilities, the better of the two official hostels, with a bar, restaurant, TV rooms and kitchen for use of guests, and well-located for the summer events in the park. Rates f18 per person, including use of secure lockers, f5 extra for non–YHA member. f35–50 for double rooms. Curfew 2am. Tram #1, #2, #5.

Stadsdoelen, Kloveniersburgwal 97 (☎24 68 32). Nearer to the station (on the edge of the Red Light district) and with slightly more inviting dorms. Although no double rooms, prices and curfew are the same. Restaurant serves good value, though very basic, food. Tram #4, #9, #16, #24, #25.

CHRISTIAN YOUTH HOSTELS

Eben Haezer, Bloemstraat 179 (☎24 47 17). Don't be put off: though you may be given a booklet on Jesus, and the slogans on the walls may not be the ones you'd put up on yours, Amsterdam's two Christian youth hostels aren't evangelical, but simply provide neat, clean dormitories for rock bottom prices – f14 per person including bed linen and a hearty breakfast. Curfew 1am on weekends; age limit 35 – though this is negotiable. Tram #13, #14, #17.

The Shelter, Barndesteeg 21 (☎25 32 30). Smack in the middle of the Red Light district, this is much the less appealing of the two – though it's within walking distance of the station. Rates, curfew, and age limit are the same as *Eben Haezer*. By public transportation, subway stop Nieuwmarkt. Can take wheelchairs.

OTHER HOSTELS

Sleep-In, 's-Gravesandestraat 51 (☎94 74 44). A little way out of the centre but easily the city's cheapest accommodation with beds at f11 per person. Dorms are enormous, facilities minimal, but the atmosphere is great, and there are regular weekly films and musical and theatre performances. Also, around 600 beds mean you're unlikely to be turned away. No curfew, but open June to mid-Sept only. Weesperplein metro station or tram #6.

Arrive, Haarlemmerstraat 65 (☎22 14 39). A recently spruced-up hostel which has dorm beds for f23.50 and double rooms for f57 – approaching real hotel prices. Bed linen included but breakfast f5.75. 10-min walk from Centraal Station.

Adam and Eva, Sarphatistraat 105 (☎24 62 06). Outside the centre but virtually opposite Weesperplein metro and tram stops #6 or #10. Dorm beds f17.

Amstel, Steiger 5, De Ruijterkade (☎26 42 47). The only survivor of a number of barge hotels which used to be moored behind Centraal Station – now closed due to fire risks. This was always the largest and best-known, and still makes for a cheap and central place to stay. Prices range from f25 per person in a four-bed dormitory to f36 per person in a double room with private shower and toilet. All private rooms have phone and TV; all prices include breakfast.

Bob's Youth Hostel, N. Z. Voorburgwal 92 (☎23 00 63). An old favourite of backpackers, this has small, clean dorms for f18 per person including breakfast, in the coffee shop on the ground floor; the curfew 3.30am. A short walk from Centraal Station.

Hans Brinker, Kerkstraat 137 (☎22 06 88). Another well-established Amsterdam hostel, though more upmarket than Bob's, with dorm beds going for f27, doubles for f84 upwards. The facilities are good, but at these prices, why not go for a real hotel. . ? Tram #1, #2, #5.

International Student Centre, Keizersgracht 15 (☎25 13 64). Terrific location close to the station, with dorm beds for f19, doubles for f75 and up, and a good mixture of triples and four-bedded rooms from f25 per person. Spotless rooms, too; breakfast is extra.

Kabul, Warmeosstraat 38–42 (☎23 71 58). Doesn't really justify its higher (f25) dorm rates, but the doubles are quite reasonable at f55–75, and triples and four-bedded rooms are also available. There's no lockout or curfew, it's an easy walk from the station, and the late-opening Kabul bar next door has regular live bands. Breakfast f6 extra. Wheelchair access.

HOTELS

Amsterdam's **hotels** start at around f60 for a double, absolute minimum, and although a filling Dutch breakfast is normally included at all but the most expensive places, many middle-range hotels give the barest value for the money. There are exceptions, and don't be afraid to ask to see the room first – and to refuse it if you don't like it.

The hotels here are divided by price and listed alphabetically; we've also included a list of gay hotels – many of which cater for both gays and non-gays alike. **Prices** quoted are for the cheapest rooms in high season (ie, with a shared bath) including breakfast unless otherwise stated; most places have cheaper off-season prices.

INEXPENSIVE TO MODERATE (UNDER f100)

Abba, Overtoom 122 (☎18 30 58). Well-worn but clean rooms above a garage on the very busy Overtoom. Doubles f85, one quadruple f145. Tram #2, #6.

Acacia, Lindengracht 251 (☎22 14 60). Amicable hotel run by a young married couple. Doubles from f80. Tram #3.

Acro, Jan Luykenstraat 44 (☎66 20 526). Excellent, modern hotel which has been completely refurbished with stylish rooms and a plush bar and self-service restaurant. Doubles from f90 (slightly more if you stay only one night) but well worth the money. Tram #2, #3, #5, #12.

De Admiraal, Herengracht 563 (☎26 21 50). Friendly hotel just off Rembrandtsplein. Doubles from f80, breakfast an extra f7.50. Tram #4.

Adolesce, Nieuwe Keizersgracht 26 (☎26 39 59). Nicely situated just off the Amstel, with a choice of doubles at f75. A cheaper option than the *Fantasia* a few doors down. Curfew 2am. Bus #31, #150.

Bema, Concertgebouwplein 19b (☎79 13 96). Very small but a friendly place handy for concerts and museums. Doubles f85.

Beursstraat, Beursstraat 9 (☎26 37 01). Nestling behind Berlage's Stock Exchange, a basic but cheap hotel with doubles from f60, not including breakfast. A short walk from Centraal Station.

Brian; Singel 69 (☎24 46 61). Cheap at f30 per person including breakfast, and with equally inexpensive triple and quadruple rooms available too. But if you're after something peaceful, this ain't the place. Tram #1, #2, #5, #13, #17.

Casa Cara, Emmastraat 24 (☎66 23 135). Homey hotel five minutes from the Concertgebow and major museums. Doubles from f65. Tram #2.

Centralpark West, Roemer Visscherstraat 27 (☎85 22 85). With large, nicely furnished rooms, the Centralpark West is particularly good value. From f90 for a double. Tram #2, #3, #5, #12.

Clemens, Raadhuistraat 39 (☎24 60 89). One of a number of inexpensive hotels situated in the art nouveau crescent of the Utrecht Building. Clean, neat and good value for money, with doubles at f70. As this is one of the city's busiest streets, you should ask for a room at the back. Tram #13, #14, #17.

Cok, Koningslaan 1/Koninginneweg 34–36 (☎66 46 111). Actually three hotels on two sites – Student Class, with dorm beds for f35; Tourist Class, with double rooms for f90; and First Class, with doubles for considerably more. Packed with facilities, but rather a soulless place to stay. It's often fully booked too. Tram #2.

Continental, Damrak 40–41 (☎22 33 63). Though on the noisy tourist drag of Damrak, a clean and friendly hotel with doubles for f90 and up, breakfast f6.50. A short walk from Centraal Station.

Fantasia, Nieuwe Keizersgracht 16 (☎23 82 59). Large, popular, and welcoming hotel, with neat if unspectacular rooms and a large dining room and bar. From f90. Tram #1, #2, #5.

Fita, Jan Luykenstraat 37 (☎79 09 76). Mid-sized hotel in a quiet spot on the far side of the Vondelpark. Doubles from f80.

De Harmonie, Prinsengracht 816 (☎22 80 21). Small rooms, but a nice central setting just down from the Amstel and within easy reach of Rembrandtsplein. Doubles from f85. Tram #4.

Hegra, Herengracht 269 (☎23 78 77). On the expensive side at f90 for a double including breakfast, but relatively cheap for the location.

Pension Kitty, Plantage Middenlaan 40 (☎22 68 19). A little bit out from the centre, but decent-sized rooms for around f75 a double, including as much breakfast as you can eat. Good value. Tram #9, get off at the zoo.

De Lantaerne, Leidsegracht 111 (☎23 22 21). An elegant hotel for its price – around f85 for a double. But its location, just shouting distance from the *Melkweg* and a canal's breadth from the main police station, means it can get noisy. Tram #1, #2, #5.

De Leydsche Hof, Leidsegracht 14 (☎23 21 48). Stately canal house on one of the smaller and quieter canals. Doubles f75, no breakfast. Tram #1, #2, #5.

Mikado, Amstel 107–111 (☎23 70 68). Pleasantly unstuffy hotel whose best rooms are at the rear. Often group booked. f95 a double. Weesperplein metro.

Museumzicht, Jan Luykenstraat 22 (☎71 29 54). Conveniently located for the main museums, with plain rooms from f85. Tram #2, #3, #5, #12.

Van Ostade, Van Ostadestraat 123 (☎79 34 52). Friendly, family-run hotel near the Albert Cuyap market. Basic but clean rooms for f65 a double – which includes free laundry service and an extra-large breakfast. Tram #12, #25.

Piet Hein, Vossiusstraat 53 (☎66 27 205). Calm, low-key and clean, tucked away behind the Concertgebouw. Doubles for around f90.

Prinsenhof, Prinsengracht 810 (☎23 17 72). Tastefully decorated hotel with doubles from f85. Best rooms at the back. Tram #4.

Ronnie, Raadhuistraat 41 (☎24 28 21). Recently taken over by the American cousins of the *Clemens'* owners, and with equally good prices and facilities. Friendly and helpful, with doubles from f60 including breakfast. Three-, four-, and five-person rooms, too. Tram #13, #14, #17.

Seven Bridges, Reguliersgracht 31 (☎23 13 29). One of the city's most beautiful and best-value hotels both inside and out, with doubles starting at f75. Tram #4.

Smit, P. C. Hooftstraat 24–26 (☎76 63 43). Slightly iffy, with variable rooms. But if it's late and you haven't anywhere booked, they usually have space. From f80. Tram #2, #3, #5, #12.

Utopia, N. Z. Voorburgwal 132 (☎26 12 95). Doubles for f70, self-catering studios for f40 per person. Also (for guests) an all-night coffee shop and bar. Tram #1, #2, #5, #13, #17.

Verdi Sachiko, Wanningstraat 9 (☎71 19 41). Small and simple hotel near the Concertgebouw with double rooms starting at f85.

Vullings, P. C. Hooftstraat 78 (☎71 21 09). Small, elegantly-located hotel with (only) doubles from f85. Tram #2, #3, #5, #12.

Westertoren, Raadhuisstraat 35 (☎24 46 39). Welcoming and clean, with doubles from f75. Very good value for the this price-range, with breakfast served in your room. Tram #4.

MODERATE TO EXPENSIVE (OVER f100)

Acca, Van de Veldestraat 3a (☎66 25 262). *The* place to go if you've got money to burn: an intimate luxury hotel with double rooms starting at around f250. Tram #2, #3, #5, #12.

Agora, Singel 462 (☎27 22 00). Nicely located, small, amicable hotel near the flower market, with doubles from f125, three- and four-bedded rooms for proportionately less. Tram #1, #2, #5.

Amstel, Prof. Tulpplein 1 (☎22 60 60). If you can afford one night of ultimate class, this is the place to spend your f475 minimum.

Canal House, Keizersgracht 148 (☎22 51 82). Magnificently restored seventeenth-century building, centrally located on one of the principal *grachten*. American family-run with a friendly bar and cosy rooms. f160–180. Tram #13, #14, #17.

Estherea, Singel 305–307 (☎24 51 46). Pleasant middle-of-the-road hotel in a blandly converted canal house, with doubles from about f150. Tram #1, #2.

De Gouden Kettingh, Keizersgracht 268 (☎24 82 87). Rambling old canal house popular with British/business clientele. The fanciest and best

rooms overlook the canal; doubles go for f160, breakfast included. Tram #13, #14, #17.

Het Leidseplein, Korte Leidsedwarsstraat 79 (☎27 25 05). Smart, mid-sized hotel sandwiched between the calm of Leidsegracht and the frenetic Leidseplein. Doubles from f175.

Jan Luyken, Jan Luykenstraat 58 (☎76 41 11). Elegant hotel with doubles starting at f230.

Maas, Leidsekade 91 (☎23 38 68). Recently renovated, with clean and nicely decorated rooms for f100 a double without bath, around f150 with. Tram #1, #2, #5.

Museum, P. C. Hooftstraat 2 (☎83 18 11). Large and luxurious hotel next door to the Rijksmuseum. Doubles for around f230, all with private bath. Tram #6, #7, #10.

De La Poste, Reguliersgracht 3–5 (☎23 71 05). Slightly shabby rooms from f110 for a double. Tram #4.

Prinsen, Vondelstraat 38 (☎16 23 23). Affable hotel on the edge of the Vondel Park. Doubles from around f120. Tram #2, #3, #5, #12.

Titus, Leidsekade 74 (☎26 57 58). Variable rooms from f100. One of several similarly priced hotels to be found in this area. Tram #1, #2, #5.

Toren, Keizersgracht 164 (☎22 60 33). Fine example of a seventeenth-century canal house and once the home of a Dutch prime minister. Doubles from f115. Tram #13, #14, #17.

Vondel, Vondelstraat 28–30 (☎12 01 20). Overpriced and unfriendly hotel, with doubles at f160 plus. Tram #2, #3, #12, #15.

Weichmann, Prinsengracht 328–330 (☎26 89 62). Run by an engaging Dutch-American couple, a modern, comfortable hotel in two restored canal houses – excellent value for the price. Doubles from f105, triples and quads also available from f200–225. Tram #13, #14, #17.

GAY HOTELS

Many hotels in Amsterdam are run by gays, and the following are those particularly popular with a gay clientele and/or situated in the main gay areas. By no means are all exclusively gay.

Aero, Kerkstraat 49, second floor (☎22 77 28). In the middle of Amsterdam's main gay street, an almost exclusively gay hotel with sixteen rooms, many of which have shower and/or toilet. Prices ranges from f110 for a double, f135 triple, including breakfast. Tram #1, #2, #5.

Anco, Oudezijds Voorburgwal 55 (☎24 11 26). Small and basic exclusively gay male leather hotel in the Red Light district. Doubles f85. A short walk from the station.

Centralpark West, see *Inexpensive to moderate* above.

Gerstekorrel, Damstraat 22–34 (☎24 13 67). Small, simple hotel which is located about as centrally as it's possible to get. Doubles for around f125. Tram #4, #9, #16, #24, #25.

ITC (International Travel Club), Prinsengracht 1051 (☎23 02 30). Close to the major gay areas and perhaps the least expensive gay hotel of this quality. Singles from f58, doubles f98, off-season 7 nights for the price of 6. Tram #4.

John's Place, Beulingstraat 19 (☎24 16 03). Formerly the Queen's Head, now owned and revamped by an Englishman, with five rooms in English country style. Prices range from f75 to f150 a night, and John's not fussy about guests.

Monopole, Amstel 60 (☎24 62 71). Overlooking the Amstel, very close to the Musiektheater, and right next door to the Monopole Taveerne. Singles from f95, doubles from f130. Tram #4.

New York, Herengracht 13 (☎24 30 66). Exceptionally popular exclusively gay hotel, noted for its high standards and consisting of three modernised seventeenth-century houses – a short walk from Centraal Station. Singles from f75, doubles f100.

Quentin, Leidsekade 89 (☎26 21 87). Not a gay hotel but gays (especially women) made welcome. Singles at f50–60 and doubles from f80–125. Tram #1, #2, #5.

Toff's English-Style Apartments, Ruysdaelkade 167 (☎73 85 29). Self-catering apartments scattered all over the city that sleep two for f110. Toff's also runs personalised guided tours of Amsterdam's gay scene – see p.14.

Unique, Kerkstraat 37 (☎24 47 85). A convenient and exclusively gay hotel with singles at f70, doubles around f120. Tram #1, #2, #5.

Waterfront, Singel 458 (☎23 97 75). Recently opened smart hotel, handy for the gay bars but on the pricey side, with doubles at f100–140.

West End, Kerkstraat 42 (☎24 80 74). Another conveniently located hotel for the Kerkstraat area, with the Cosmo Bar as its main attraction; f50 single, f120 double, but prices may go up after the current renovation is completed. Tram #1, #2, #5.

Witz Apartments, Reguliersdwarsstraat 33 (☎27 91 78). Exclusively gay furnished apartments with kitchen facilities. Prices start from around f55 per night. Tram #1, #2, #5.

CAMPING

There are several **campsites** in Amsterdam, most of which are easily accessible by public transport or by car. The *VVV* directs most visitors to the "youth campsites" of *Vliegenbos* and *Zeeburg*, open April to September, while grownups and those with caravans or campers are advised to use one of the other sites.

YOUTH CAMPSITES

Vliegenbos, Meeuwenlaan 138 (☎36 88 55). A relaxed and friendly site, just a ten-minute bus ride from the station. Facilities include a general shop and bike hire. f4.50 a night per person without car, f5.75 if you're over 30; f7.50 with car, f6.50 with motorbike. Hot showers f1.25. Bus #32, from Centraal Station, night bus #77.

Zeeburg, Zuider Ijdijk 34a (☎94 44 30). Slightly better equipped than the *Vliegenbos*, in that it has a bar. But more difficult to get to and a little more expensive: f5.50 per person plus f1 per tent, f2.50 per car, f1 per shower, f2 per motorbike. Tram #3 or #10 to Muiderpoort Station, then bus #37, then a ten-minute walk; also served by night bus #76.

OTHER CAMPSITES

Amsterdamse Bos, Kleine Noorddijk 1, Amstelveen (☎41 68 68). Many facilities but a pretty long way out. Open April–Nov f10.35 for one person alone, all inclusive of showers, car or campervan per person, f6.60 if you're travelling in a group of two or more people. Yellow bus #171 or #172 and a short walk.

Amsterdam Ijsclub, Ijsbaanpad 45 (☎62 09 16). Vast campsite situated near the Olympic Stadium: aside from *Vliegenbos*, the closest to the city centre. Camping shop and canteen. Rates f4.25 per person, f3 per tent, parking f2.50. Trams #16 or #24, night bus #73 or #74.

Gaasper Camping, Loosdrechtdreef 7 (☎96 73 26). Amsterdam's newest campsite, just the other side of the Bijlmermeer housing complex, f4.50 per person, f3–f4 per tent, plus a charge for showers (f1.25). Metro to Gaasperplas station and a three-minute walk; night bus #75.

CHAPTER ONE

THE CITY

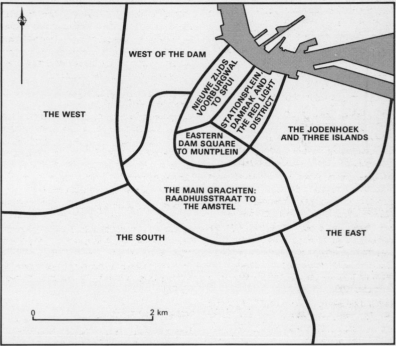

WEST OF THE DAM

NIEUWE ZIJDS VOORBURGWAL TO SPUI

STATIONSPLEIN, DAMRAK AND THE RED LIGHT DISTRICT

THE WEST

EASTERN DAM SQUARE TO MUNTPLEIN

THE JODENHOEK AND THREE ISLANDS

THE MAIN GRACHTEN: RAADHUISSTRAAT TO THE AMSTEL

THE SOUTH

THE EAST

0   2 km

A msterdam is a small city: its centre is compact, its buildings restrained, and, although the concentric canal system can initially be confusing, finding your bearings is straightforward. We've divided Amsterdam into the headings which follow for convenience; because of the nature of the city they don't always refer to uniform areas and are certainly not itineraries to be followed slavishly. Amsterdam is a city of low-key attractions and charms, and aimlessly wandering its streets and canals is as good a way as any to explore.

The centre of the city – along with the main canals, the area in which you'll spend most of your time – is the old **medieval core**, which fans south from Centraal Station, taking in the main artery of Damrak, Dam Square and Rokin. This, Amsterdam's commercial heart, boasts the best of its bustling street life, and is home to shops, many bars and restaurants and, not least, the infamous **Red Light district**. The area is bordered by the Singel, first of the **big canals**, on the far side of which curl Herengracht, Keizersgracht and

Prinsengracht. These canals are part of a major seventeenth-century urban extension and, with the radial streets of Leidsestraat, Vijzelstraat and Utrechtsestraat, create Amsterdam's distinctive cobweb shape. This is the Amsterdam you see in the brochures: still, dreamy canals, crisp reflections of seventeenth-century townhouses, railings with chained bicycles – an image which even today is not far from authentic.

Further out, the **Jordaan** grew up as a slum and immigrant quarter and remains the traditional heart of working-class Amsterdam, though these days there is a firm yuppie edge to the area. On the other side of town, the **Jodenhoek** was, as its name suggests, once home to the city's Jewish community. Now it's probably Amsterdam's most visibly changed district, and, since the construction of the Muziektheater and metro, the principal source of squabbles over the city's future.

Across the Singelgracht, which marks the outer limit of today's centre, lie the largely residential districts of **Amsterdam South**, **West** and **East**, in themselves not of great interest, though with attractions (principally the main museums) that could tempt you out that way. Amsterdam **North**, on the other hand, remains a quite distinct, though nondescript, entity, which most people visit for its campsite – though it is good cycling country. The *VVV* has details of routes, best of which are those along the Buiten IJ.

> *At the end of each section you will find listings of bars, coffee shops, restaurants, and hotels arranged alphabetically for cross-referencing with the* Drinking and Eating *chapter and the* Finding a Place to Stay *section.*

Stationsplein, Damrak and the Red Light District

This is the heart of the city and where you'll almost certainly arrive. It's a small area, but a varied one, ranging from the vigour of Stationsplein – the city's major traffic junction and home of the *VVV* (tourist) office – to the strategic tourist trap of Damrak and the studied (though real enough) sleaze of the Red Light district, not surprisingly one of Amsterdam's biggest tourist attractions.

Stationsplein and down Damrak

The neo-Renaissance **Centraal Station** is an imposing prelude to the city. When built late in the last century, this was a controversial structure, as it obscured the views of the port that brought Amsterdam its wealth. Since then, however, shipping has moved out to more spacious dock areas to the west and east, and the station is now one of Amsterdam's most resonant landmarks and a natural focal point for urban life. Stand here and all of Amsterdam, with its faintly oriental skyline of spires and cupolas, lies before you.

Stationsplein, immediately outside, is a messy open space, fragmented by ovals of water and dotted with chip stands and "M" signs indicating the city's spanking new (but quickly ageing) metro. Come summer, though, there's no livelier part of the city, as street performers compete for attention with the careening trams that converge dangerously from all sides. It's without a doubt a promising place to arrive, and with that in mind the municipal authorities are cleaning up the area's image, notably in the southeastern corner, where they're building a luxury hotel and encouraging development along the once-notorious Zeedijk (see p.40).

Just down the street from Zeedijk, the dome of the **St. Nicolaaskerk** catches the eye: despite a dilapidated exterior, it's the city's foremost Catholic church, having replaced the clandestine Amstelkring (see p.85) in 1887. Even if you manage to coordinate your visit with the limited open hours (April–Oct Tues–Fri 11am–4pm, Sat 2–4pm), you'll find that there's not much of note inside – except, on the high altar, the crown of Austro-Hungarian Emperor Maximilian, very much a symbol of the city and one you'll see again and again (on top of the Westerkerk and on much of the city's official literature). Amsterdam had close ties with Maximilian: in the late fifteenth century he came here as a pilgrim and stayed on to recover from an illness. The burghers funded many of his military expeditions; in return, he let the city use his crown in its coat of arms, which gave the upstart port immediate prestige in the eyes of the rest of the world.

Above all, though, Stationsplein acts as a filter for Amsterdam's newcomers, and from here **Damrak**, an unenticing avenue lined by tacky, over-priced restaurants and the bobbing canal boats of Amsterdam's considerable tourist industry, storms south into the heart of the city. Just past the boats is the Stock Exchange, or **Beurs** (sometimes known as the "Beurs van Berlage"), designed at the turn of the century by the leading light of the Dutch modern movement, H. P. Berlage. With its various styles from Romanesque to Neo-Renaissance interwoven with a minimum of ornamentation, it is something of a seminal work. Slip inside the entrance on Beuresplein and take a look at the main hall, where exposed ironwork and shallow-arched arcades combine to give a real sense of space. These days it's no longer used as an exchange; not surprisingly, the Beurs often hosts visiting theatre groups and exhibitions.

Opposite is one of Amsterdam's best boookshops, **Allert de Lange**, the contemporary outlet of a pioneering Jewish publisher who, in the 1930s, made available much of the work of refugee authors from Nazi Germany, such as Berthold Brecht and Max Brod. The **De Bijenkorf** department store building, facing the Beurs and extending as far as Dam Square, was another successful Jewish concern – so much so that during the occupation the authorities, fearing altercations with the Jewish staff, forbade German soldiers to shop on the ground floor. Today *De Bijenkorf* is a nationwide chain; see *Shopping*, p.97.

Around the Red Light District

Had you turned left off Damrak before the Beurs, you would have found yourself in the **RED LIGHT DISTRICT** (known locally as the "Walletjes"), bordered by the oldest street in the city, Warmeosstraat, and stretching across two canals which marked the edge of medieval Amsterdam. The **prostitution** here is sadly, but perhaps inevitably, one of the real sights of the city – and one of its most distinctive draws. The up-front nature of the porno industry here makes Soho seem tame by comparison.

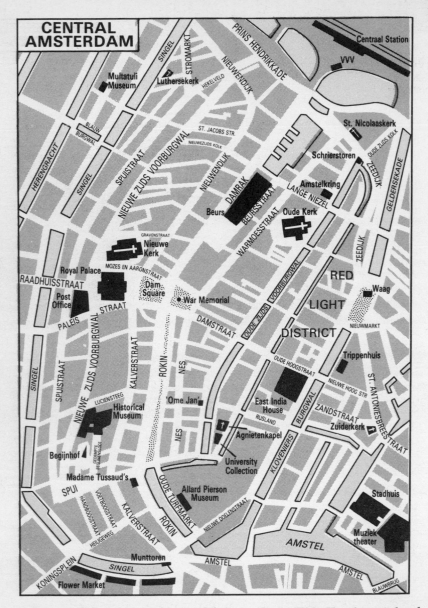

CENTRAL AMSTERDAM

Centraal Station

VVV

Multatuli Museum

Luthersekerk

St. Nicolaaskerk

Schrierstoren

Amstelkring

ST. JACOBS STR.

NIEUWEZIJDS KOLK

Beurs

Oude Kerk

LANGE NIEZEL

Nieuwe Kerk

GRAVENSTRAAT

Royal Palace

MOZES EN AARONSTRAAT

RAADHUISSTRAAT

Post Office

PALEIS

Dam Square

War Memorial

DAMSTRAAT

RED

LIGHT

DISTRICT

Waag

NIEUWMARKT

Trippenhuis

OUDE HOOGSTRAAT

NIEUWE HOOG STR

KALVERSTRAAT

ROKIN

NES

'Ome Jan'

East India House

RUSLAND

ZANDSTRAAT

Zuiderkerk

LUCIENSTEEG

Historical Museum

Agnietenkapel

University Collection

Begijnhof

Madame Tussaud's

Allard Pierson Museum

Stadhuis

SPUI

NIEUWE DOELENSTRAAT

KALVERSTRAAT

ROKIN

Muziek theater

AMSTEL

Munttoren

SINGEL

AMSTEL

AMSTEL

Flower Market

BLAUWBRUG

SINGEL

STROMARKT

PRINS HENDRIKKADE

NIEUWENDIJK

HEKELVELD

BLAUW BURGWAL

SPUISTRAAT

NIEUWE ZIJDS VOORBURGWAL

HERENGRACHT

SINGEL

DAMRAK

BEURSSTRAAT

WARMOESSTRAAT

OUDE ZIJDS KOLK

ZEEDIJK

GELDERSEKADE

OUDE ZIJDS VOORBURGWAL

VOORBURGWAL

BURGWAL

KLOVENIERS

ST. ANTONIESBREESTRAAT

NIEUWE ZIJDS VOORBURGWAL

SPUISTRAAT

SINGEL

VOETBOOGSTRAAT

HANDBOOGSTRAAT

HEILIGEWEG

KONINGSPLEIN

OUDE TURFMARKT

ZEEDIJK

Two canals form the backbone of the area: **Oude Zijds Voorburgwal** and **Oude Zijds Achterburgwal**. These, and the narrow connecting passages, are, most evenings of the year, thronged with people here to discover just how shocking it all is. The atmosphere is a festive one, with entertainment for all, as entire families titter and blush at the invitations to various kinds of illicit thrills. Men line the streets hawking the peep shows and "live sex" within, while the women sit bored behind glass, in shop windows that take their place among more conventional businesses on the same street. There's a nasty edge to the district too, oddly enough sharper during the daytime, when the pimps hang out in shifty gangs and drug addicts wait anxiously, assessing the chances of scoring their next hit.

Soliciting hasn't always gone on here however, and the rich facades of O. Z. Voorburgwal – known in the sixteenth century as the "Velvet Canal", because it was home to so many wealthy people – point to a more venerable past. As the city prospered, and the then-nearby docks grew busier, the area grew sleazier as more and more prostitutes were required to service the growing population of itinerant seamen. Today narrow **Warmoesstraat** is seedy and uninviting, but it was once one of the city's most fashionable streets, and home of Holland's foremost poet, **Joost van der Vondel**, who ran his seventeenth-century hosiery business from number 110 in between writing and hobnobbing with the Amsterdam elite. Vondel is a kind of Dutch Shakespeare: his *Gijsbrecht van Amstel*, a celebration of Amsterdam during its Golden Age, is one of the classics of Dutch literature, and he wrote regular, if ponderous, official verses, including well over a thousand lines on the inauguration of the new town hall alone. His house no longer stands, but a little way down on the right, by the wall of the city's stock exchange, a statue of the poet marks its site. After his son had frittered away the modest family fortune, Vondel lived out his last few years as doorkeeper of the pawn shop on O. Z. Voorburgwal (see below), dying at the age of 92 of hypothermia brought on by his advanced years. Unassuming to the end, his own suggested epitaph ran:

Here lies Vondel, still and old
Who died – because he was cold.

The **Oude Kerk** stands just off Warmoesstraat a little way up, its precincts offering a reverential peace after the excesses of the Red Light district – though even here some of the houses have the familiar *Kamer te huur* sign and window seat. There's been a church on this site since the late-thirteenth century, even before the Dam was built, but most of the present building dates from the fourteenth century. In the Middle Ages, many pilgrims flocked to Amsterdam – and specifically to this church – thanks to a mid-fourteenth-century miracle in which a dying man vomited the Host he had received at Communion, which was thrown on a fire yet did not burn. A chapel was originally erected somewhere between Nieuwe Zijds Voorburgwal and Kalverstraat, close to where the miracle happened, and when this burnt down and the host still didn't burn, a plaque was put up in the Oude Kerk to commemorate the event. In the manner of such tales, the Host began to turn up in different spots all over town, attracting pilgrims in droves. The faithful still come to take part in the annual commemorative *Stille Omgang*, a silent nocturnal procession on the Sunday closest to March 15.

Having been stripped bare during the Reformation and recently very thoroughly restored, the Oude Kerk is nowadays a survivor rather than an architectural masterpiece. Its handful of interesting features include – apart from a few faded vault paintings – some beautifully carved misericords in the choir, and the memorail tablet of Rembrandt's wife, Saskia van Uylenburg, who is buried here. It costs a guilder to get in and, in summer, another to ascend the tower. (summer Mon–Sat 11am–5pm; winter Mon–Sat 1–3pm; ring vestry bell for attention; tower June–Sept Mon & Thurs 2–5pm, Tues & Wed 11am–2pm.)

There's little else along Oude Zijds to stop for; only the clandestine **Amstelkring**, at the Zeedijk end of O. Z. Voorburgwal, is of real interest, once the principal Catholic place of worship in the city and now a museum (see p.85). Just past here, **Zeedijk** itself, though much cleaned up, provides evidence of more urban blight; until recently, you had to run the gauntlet of Surinamese heroin dealers trying to fast-talk you into a quick sale while idle groups of policemen looked on. The police claim to have the area under control now – part of the city-wide push to polish up Amsterdam's tarnished reputation as a tourist centre – and certainly this narrow street is considerably less intimidating than it once was, a process hastened by the recent completion of the luxury Barbizon Plaza Hotel nearby. But for the moment there's a long way to go: Zeedijk is still terribly dilapidated, and the heroin dealers – albeit much depleted in number – are creeping back to shoot up in doorways and hustle passers-by for small change.

For the moment, then, the best thing to do is hurry through. Zeedijk opens out on to **Nieuwmarkt** and the top end of **Gelderskade**, which together form the hub of Amsterdam's tiny **Chinese quarter**, consisting of a handful of oriental supermarkets and a couple of bookshops. As its name suggests, Nieuwmarkt was once one of Amsterdam's most important markets, first for fish, later for the cloth traders from the adjacent Jewish quarter, and nowadays for antiques on Sunday. During the last war it was surrounded by barbed wire behind which Jews were penned while awaiting deportation.

The main focus of the square, the turreted **Waag**, or old **St. Antoniespoort**, has played a variety of roles over the years. Originally part of the fortifications that encircled Amsterdam before the seventeenth-century expansion, it later became the civic weighing-house, and for a time was used by a number of the city's guilds, including the Surgeons' – the young Rembrandt's *Anatomy Lesson of Dr. Tulp* was based on the activities here. After a spell as the Amsterdam Jewish Museum, the Waag is now being put to use as a community media centre and TV studio, re-enacting its former role as a meeting place and contributing toward the area's much-needed facelift.

Kloveniersburgwal, which leads south from Nieuwmarkt, was the outer of the three eastern canals of sixteenth-century Amsterdam. Although not among the more attractive waterways, it does boast, on the left, one of the city's most impressive canal houses. Built for the Trip family in 1662, and large enough to house the Rijksmuseum collection for most of the nineteenth century, the **Trippenhuis** is a huge overblown mansion, its Corinthian pilasters and grand frieze providing a suitable reflection of the owners' importance among the Amsterdam *Magnificat* – the name given to the clique of families (Six, Trip, Hooft, Pauw) who shared power during the Golden Age. Directly opposite, on the right bank of the canal, there's another, quite different, house which gives an idea of the sort of resentment such ostentatious displays of wealth engendered. Mr Trip's coachman was so taken aback by the size of the new family residence that he exclaimed he would be happy with a home no wider than the Trips' front door. Which is exactly what he got, and 26 Kloveniersburgwal is known as the **House of Mr Trip's Coachman** – not surprisingly, at a yard or so across, the narrowest house in town.

Further up the canal, on the corner of Oude Hoogstraat, the red-brick former headquarters of the **Dutch East India Company** is a monumental building, built in 1606 shortly after the founding of the company. It was from here that the Dutch organised and regulated the trading interests in the Far East which made the country so profitable in the seventeenth century. Under the greedy auspices of the East India Company, The Netherlands (especially its most prosperous provinces, Holland and Zeeland) exploited the natural resources of the group of islands now known as Indonesia for several centuries, satisfying the whims of Amsterdam's burghers with shiploads of spices, textiles and exotic woods.

For all that, the building itself is of little interest, occupied these days by offices. It's better to continue on towards the southern end of Kloveniersburgwal, to where the **Oudmannhuispoort** passage leads through to O. Z. Achterburgwal. This was once part of an almshouse for elderly men, but is now filled with second-hand bookstalls and a group of buildings serving Amsterdam University. On O. Z. Achterburgwal you look across to the pretty **Huis op de Drie Grachten**, "House on the Three Canals", on the corner of Grimburgwal, which runs alongside more university buildings. A little way down O. Z. Voorburgwal on the right, through an ornate gateway, is the **Agnietenkapel**, also owned by the university and containing exhibitions on academic life through the ages (see p.84). Roughly opposite, the building at O. Z. Voorburgwal 300 has for years been known as "**ome Jan**" ("Uncle John's") for its function as central Amsterdam's pawn shop, established 350 years ago in a typically enlightened attempt to put a stop to the crippling activities of moneylenders who were making a killing among the city's poor. The poet Vondel ended his days working here, and a short verse above the entrance extols the virtues of the pawn shop and the evils of usury.

At the corner a passage cuts through to **Nes**, a long, narrow street, once home to the philosopher Spinoza; or you can make your way back up Oude Zijds past the **Galerie Mokum**, named after the old Jewish nickname for the city, now in general use. From here it's just a few yards to Rokin and, beyond, Kalverstraat. Alternatively, sink into one of the terrace seats of *'t Gasthuys* café, a popular student haunt and excellent for either a quick drink or a full lunch.

BARS *Anna Dodo*, *Argos* (gay), *Bern, Blincker, Club Jacques* (gay), *Cul de Sac, Eagle* (gay), *De Engelbewaarder, Frascati, 't Gasthuys, Hard Rock Cafe, De Hoogte, Café K. Appel, Kabul, Lokaal 't Loosje, Madame Arthur* (gay), *De Pieter, De Pieterspoort, De Pool, Stopera, Tapvreugd.*

COFFEE SHOPS "Smoking" *Extase, Goa, Roma, Rusland.* **"Non-smoking"** *De Eenhorn, Karbeel.*

RESTAURANTS Mensas *Atrium.* **Dutch** *De Bijenkorf.* **Pancakes** *Bredero.* **Vegetarian and health food** *Sisters.* **Chinese, Japanese and Thai** *Lana Thai.* **French** *Grand Café Restaurant First Class.* **Indonesian** *Mr. Moto.* **North, Latin and South American** *Café Pacifico.*

HOTELS/HOSTELS *Amstel* (barge), *Anco* (gay), *Baltic IV* (barge), *Beursstraat, Continental, Damhotel, The Dutch Cockney* (barge), *Kabul, Lucia* (barge), *The Shelter, Stadsdoelen, Sunrise* (barge).

Dam Square to Muntplein

Dam Square gives the city its name: in the thirteenth century the river Amstel was dammed here, and the small fishing village that grew around it became known as "Amstelredam". Boats could sail right into the square and unload their imported grain in the middle of the rapidly growing town, and the later building of Amsterdam's principal church, the Nieuwe Kerk, along with the Royal Palace, formally marked Dam Square as Amsterdam's centre.

Though robbed a little of its dignity by the trams that scuttle across it, the square is still the hub of the city, with all the main streets zeroing in on the maelstrom of buskers, artists and dope dealers who find an instant and captive clientele in the passers-by. At the centre there's a **War Memorial**, an unsightly stone tusk filled with soil from each of The Netherlands' eleven provinces and Indonesia. It serves as a gathering place for the square's milling tourists who seem to be wondering if, among the musicians and drug pushers, they've really found the heart of liberated Amsterdam.

Across the square, the **Royal Palace** (July–Aug 12.30–4pm; Sept–June guided tours Wed 1.30pm; f2.50, no museumcards) seems neither Dutch nor palatial – understandably so since it was originally built from imported stone as the city's town hall. The authorities of Europe's mercantile capital wanted a grandiose declaration of civic power, a building that would push even the Nieuwe Kerk into second place, and Jacob van Campen's then startlingly progressive design, a Dutch rendering of the classical principles revived in Renaissance Italy, did just that. At the time of its construction in the mid-seventeenth century, it was the largest town hall in Europe, supported by 13,659 wooden piles driven into the Dam's sandy soil; poet Constantyn Huygens called it "the world's Eighth Wonder/with so much stone raised high and so much timber under". It's the magisterial interior that really deserves this praise, though; the *Citizen's Hall* proclaims the pride and confidence of the Golden Age, with the enthroned figure of Amsterdam looking down at the world and heavens at her feet, the whole sumptuously inlaid in brass and marble. A good-natured and witty symbolism pervades the building: cocks fight above the entrance to the *Court of Petty Affairs*, while Apollo, god of the sun and the arts, brings harmony to the disputes. On a more sober note, death sentences were pronounced at the *High Court of Justice* at the front of the building, and the condemned immediately executed on a scaffold outside.

Otherwise, the Palace's interior is dull, darkened with the grand but uninspired paintings of the period. Rembrandt, whose career was waning, had his sketches for the walls rejected by the city fathers; today's city council must bemoan their predecessors' lack of judgement, since there's a good chance they'd now be sitting on one of Europe's major art treasures. The building received its royal monicker in 1808 when Napoleon's brother Louis commandeered it as the one building fit for an installed king. Lonely and isolated, Louis briefly ruled from here, until forced to acquiesce to Napoleon's autocratic demands. Upon his abdication in 1810 he left behind a sizeable amount of Empire furniture, most of which is exhibited in the rooms he converted.

Vying for importance with the Palace is the **Nieuwe Kerk** (daily 11am–4pm, Sun noon–2pm and 4–5pm) – despite its name, a fifteenth-century structure rebuilt several times after fires. Though impressive from the outside, the Nieuwe Kerk has long since lost out in rivalries with the Oude Kerk and the Royal Palace (it was forbidden a tower in case it outshone the new town hall), and is now used only for exhibitions, organ concerts and state occasions; Queen Beatrix was crowned here in 1980. The interior is neat and orderly, its sheer Gothic lines only slightly weighed down by seventeenth-century fixtures such as the massive pulpit and organ. Of the catalogue of household names from Dutch history, Admiral de Ruyter, seventeenth-century Holland's most valiant naval hero, lies in an opulent tomb in the choir, and the poet Vondel is commemorated by a small urn near the entrance.

Heading south from Dam Square, Damrak Street turns into the broad sweep of **Rokin**, which follows the old course of the Amstel River. Distinguished by the **Allard Pierson Archaeological Museum** (see p.88) and lined with grandiose nineteenth-century mansions – Amsterdam's *Sotheby's* is here, and, further down, the elaborate *fin de siècle* interior of the *Maison de Bonneterie* clothes store – Rokin gives trams running to and from Dam Square their single chance to accelerate in the city; cross with care.

Running parallel with Rokin, **Kalverstraat** has been a commercial centre since it hosted a cattle market in medieval times; now it has declined into a standard European shopping mall, an uninspired strip of monotonous clothes shops differentiated only by the varying strains of disco music they pump out. About halfway down the street, a lopsided and frivolous gateway forms an unexpected entrance to the former municipal orphanage that's now the **Amsterdam Historical Museum** (see p.83). The main way in is by the eye-catching Civil Guard Gallery, just around the corner off Sint Luciensteeg, which leads on to Gedempte Beginesloot and the **Begijnhof** (p.45).

Kalverstraat comes to an ignoble end in a stretch of ice-cream parlours and fast-food outlets before reaching **Muntplein**. Originally a mint and part of the old city walls, the **Munttoren** was topped with a spire by Hendrik de Keyser in 1620 and is possibly the most famous of the towers dotting the city, a landmark perfectly designed for postcards when framed by the flowers of the nearby floating *Bloemenmarkt* (flower market). From here, Reguliersbreestraat turns left toward the gay bars and loud restaurants of Rembrandtsplein, while Vijzelstraat heads straight out to the edge of the Amsterdam crescent.

BARS *De Drie Fleschjes, De Pilsener Club, De Pilsery, Wenteltrap, Wynand Fockinck, Zwart.*
COFFEE SHOPS **"Non-smoking"** *Lindsay's.*
RESTAURANTS Fish *Noordzee.* **Chinese, Japanese and Thai** *Roeng Warie.*
Indian *Mogul.*
HOTELS/HOSTELS *Gerstekorrel.*

Nieuwe Zijds Voorburgwal to Spui

Even before Amsterdam's seventeenth-century expansion, the town could be divided into old and new sectors; the outer boundaries were lined by a defensive wall, and it's this that gives **Nieuwe Zijds Voorburgwal** (New Sides Town Wall) its name. The wall itself disappeared as the city grew, and in the nineteenth century the canal that ran through the middle of the street was filled in, leaving the unusually wide swathe that runs from just below Prins Hendrikkade to Spui.

Nieuwe Zijds begins with a bottleneck of trams swinging down from the Centraal Station, and one of the first buildings you see is the **Holiday Inn**, built on the site of an old tenement building called **Wyers**. The 1985 clearance of squatters from Wyers ranks among the most infamous of the decade's anti-squatting campaigns, having involved much protest and some violence throughout the city. The squatters had occupied the building in an attempt to prevent another slice of the city from being handed over to a profit-hungry multinational and converted from residential use. Although widely supported by the people of Amsterdam, they were no match for the economic muscle of the American company, and it wasn't long before the riot police were sent in; construction of the hotel soon followed.

The fate of the **Luthersekerk**, directly west from here on Kattengat, hasn't been much better. With its copper-green dome, (which gives this area the label of *Koepelkwartier* or "Dome Neighbourhood"), it's been deconsecrated and acquired as a conference centre for the luxury Sonesta Hotel nearby. It's still possible, however, to look inside during the Sunday morning classical concerts. Across the water, the red-brick building at Singel 140–2 was once home of Captain Banning Cocq, the central character of Rembrandt's *Night Watch*. But more noticeable (and audible) is the quaintly named **Poezenboot** (cat boat), a refuge for the city's stray and unwanted cats, moored a little further along the Singel. Directly east, **Spuistraat** begins at a fork in N. Z. Voorburgwal, with a small red-light area edging around the St. Dominicus Kerk. These are the red lights the tourists miss, and the business here has the seamy feel of the real thing.

The trees that fringe Nieuwe Zijds conceal some good canal houses, and the specialised shops and private galleries try hard to preserve the refinement the street must have had before canal traffic gave way to trams. You need only compare it to the parallel **Nieuwendijk** to see how Nieuwe Zijds has retained some character. Nieuwendijk is a shabby, uninviting stretch of cheap shops and not-so-cheap restaurants, and the dark side streets have a frightening atmosphere of illicit dealings that hurries you back to the main roads. Things only improve as you approach the Nieuwe Kerk: there's a medieval eccentricity to the streets here, and all seediness vanishes as designer clothes shops appear in the old workshops clustered around the church. Walk down the wonderfully named *Zwarte Handsteeg* (Black Hand Alley) and you're back on Nieuwe Zijds. Just across the road, the **Post Office** manages to hold its own against the Nieuwe Kerk and Royal Palace. Built in 1899, its whimsical embellishments continue the town's tradition of sticking towers on things – here, as everywhere, purely for the hell of it.

Nieuwe Zijds broadens south of the post office, the streets running west, to Spuistraat and beyond, mostly filled with antique and stamp shops, and some of Amsterdam's oldest and most expensive restaurants. Both Spuistraat and Nieuwe Zijds culminate in **Spui**, a chic corner of town with a mixture of bookshops and packed bars centred around a small, rather cloying statue of a young boy – known as *'t Lieverdje* (Little Darling) – which was a gift to the city from a large cigarette company. Twenty years ago this was the scene of a series of demonstrations organised by the Provos, a left-wing group that grew out of the original squatters' movement. With the alternative culture then at its most militant, the Provos labelled 't Lieverdje a monument to tomorrow's addiction to capitalism and turned up in force every Saturday evening to preach to the Spui's assembled drinkers. When the police arrived to break up these small "happenings", they did little to endear themselves to the public – and much to gain sympathy for the Provos.

Spui's main attraction, though, is neither obvious nor signposted. Perhaps those who run the **Begijnhof** want it this way: enclosed on three sides, this small court of buildings is an enclave of tranquillity at once typically Dutch and totally removed from the surrounding streets. Most of the houses are seventeenth–century, but one, number 34, dates from 1475 – the oldest house in Amsterdam, and one built before the city forbade the construction of houses in wood, an essential precaution against fire. *Hofjes* (little courtyards) are found all over the Low Countries. Built by rich individuals or city councils for the poor and elderly, the houses usually turn inwards around a small court, their backs to the outside world. This sense of retreat suited the women who, without taking full vows, led a religious life in the *hofjes*, which often had their own chapel. Here the order was known as *Begijns*, and such was its standing in the city community that it was allowed to quietly continue its tradition of worship even after Catholicism was suppressed in 1587. Mass was inconspicuously celebrated in the concealed **Catholic Church**, a dark Italianate building with a breath-holding silence that seems odd after the natural peace outside. There's none of this sense of mystery about the **English Reformed Church** which takes up one side of the Begijnhof. Plain and unadorned, it was handed over to Amsterdam's English community when the Begijns were deprived of their main place of worship and, like the *hofje* itself, it's almost too charming, a model of prim simplicity. Inside are several old English memorial plaques, and pulpit panels designed by the young Piet Mondrian.

BARS *The American Bar, Carel's Café, Cuckoo's Nest* (gay), *Flying Dutchman, Harry's American Bar, Hoppe, De Koningshut, Luxembourg, La Strada, 't Packhuys, Scheltma, De Schutter, De Stope, Three Musketeers, de Verboden Vrucht, De Zwart.*

COFFEE SHOPS "Smoking" *Fancy Free, Grasshopper, Haussman, Prix d'Ami.* **"Non-smoking"** *Studio 2.*

RESTAURANTS Dutch *Dorrius, Haesje Claes, Keuken van 1870, Simon's, Sing Singel.* **Fish** *Lucius.* **Vegetarian and health food** *Egg Cream.* **French** *Cave Elvonne, Schransen bij Jansen.* **Italian** *Caprese, Casa di David, Tartufo.* **North, Latin and South American** *Curly's.*

HOTELS/HOSTELS *Bob's Youth Hostel, Utopia.*

The Main Grachten: from Raadhuisstraat to the Amstel

It's hard to pick out any particular points to head for along the **three main canals**. Most of the houses have been turned into offices or hotels, and there's little of specific interest apart from museums (for which see the following chapter). Rather, the appeal lies in wandering along selected stretches and admiring the gables while taking in the tree-lined canals' calm, so unusual in the centre of a modern European capital. For shops, bars, restaurants and the like, you're better off exploring the streets that connect the canals.

Apart from the Singel, which was part of Amsterdam's original protective moat, each of the canals was dug in the seventeenth century as part of a comprehensive **plan** to extend the boundaries of a city no longer able to accommodate its burgeoning population. The idea was that the council would buy up the land around the city, dig the canals, and lease plots back to developers on strict conditions. The plan was passed in 1607, and work began six years later, against a backdrop of corruption (Amsterdammers in the know bought up the land they thought the city would subsequently have to purchase). Increasing the area of the city from 450 to 1800 acres was a monumental task, and the conditions imposed by the burghers were tough ones. The three main waterways, Herengracht, Keizersgracht and Prinsengracht, were set aside for the residences and offices of the richer and more influential Amsterdam merchants, while the radial canals were left for more modest artisans' homes. Even the richest burgher had to conform to a set of stylistic rules when building his house, and taxes were levied according to the width of the properties. This produced the loose conformity you can see today: tall, narrow residences, with individualism restricted to heavy decorative gables and sometimes a gablestone to denote name and occupation. Even the colour of the front doors was regulated, with choice restricted to a shade that has since become known as "Amsterdam Green" – even now, difficult to find outside Holland. It was almost the end of the century before the scheme was finished – a time when, ironically, the demise of great Amsterdam had already begun – but it remains to the burghers' credit that it was executed with such success.

West to Vijzelstraat

Of the three canals, **Herengracht** ("Gentlemen's Canal") was the first to be dug, and so attracted the wealthiest merchants and the biggest, most ostentatious houses. The other two, **Keizersgracht** ("Emperor's Canal") and especially **Prinsengracht** ("Prince's Canal"), ended up with noticeably smaller houses – though both still hold some of the most sought-after properties in the city. Today, Herengracht remains the city's grandest stretch of water, especially between Leidsestraat and Vijzelstraat (see below), but you may find the older and less pretentious houses and warehouses of Prinsengracht more appealing. As in most cities, Amsterdam's wealthy seem to have had few scruples over the years in pulling down an older building if they thought they could erect something uglier.

One of the most imposing facades along **Herengracht** is the **Bijbels Museum**, which occupies a four-gabled, seventeenth-century stone house frilled with tendrils, carved fruit and scrollwork. Further along, **number 380** is even more ornate, an exact copy of a Loire château – stone again, with a main gable embellished with reclining figures, and a bay window stuck with cherubs, mythical characters, and an abundance of acanthus leaves. All of this is much more memorable than the stretch known as the "**Golden Bend**", between Leidestraat and Vijzelstraat, where the double-fronted merchant residences of the sixteenth and seventeenth centuries – principally numbers 441–513 and 426–480 – outdo each other in size if not in beauty. Most of the houses here date from the eighteenth century, with double stairways (the door underneath was the servants' entrance) and the slightly ornamented cornices that were fashionable at the time. The two-columned portal at 502 Herengracht indicates that this is the Mayor's official residence; and there are a couple of neat facades across Vijzelstraat, at number 539 and numbers 504–510, the second of which carries carved figures of dolphins on its crest. But otherwise the houses in this part of town are mainly corporate offices, and markedly less fascinating than the tourist authorities claim.

The one mansion you'll notice in your wanderings along **Keizersgracht** is that used in part by the experimental *Shaffy Theatre* group (see p.150) – the **Felix Meritis building** at Keizersgracht 324, a heavy neoclassical monolith built in the late eighteenth century to house the artistic and scientific activities of the society of the same name. For most of the nineteenth century this was very much the cultural focus of the city, at least for the very wealthy, and it aped the refined manners of the rest of "cultured" Europe in a way only the Dutch could: badly. It's said that when Napoleon visited the city the entire building was redecorated for his reception only to have him stalk out in disgust, claiming that the place stank of tobacco; and in spite of its use as a model for the later Concertgebouw, the concert hall was well known among musicians for its appalling acoustics. It used to be headquarters of the Dutch Communist Party; they sold it to the council who now lease it to the theatre – though recently there has been speculation over its closure.

On the corner of Keizersgracht and Leidsestraat, the designer department store, *Metz & Co.*, with its corner dome by Gerrit Rietveld, has a top-floor restaurant and tea room with one of the best views of the city. **Leidsestraat** itself is a long, slender passage across the main canals chiefly given over to airline offices and tourist boards, and to the trams that crash along the narrow thoroughfare, dangerously scattering passers-by. At its southern end, the street broadens into **Leidseplein**, hub of Amsterdam's nightlife but by day a none-too-attractive open space littered with sandwich boards touting the surrounding American burger joints. There's probably a greater concentration of bars, restaurants and clubs here than anywhere else in the city, and the streets extend off the square in a bright jumble of jutting signs and neon lights; around the corner, in a converted dairy, lurks the famous *Melkweg*(p.141). As for the square itself, on summer nights especially it can ignite with an almost carnival-like vibrancy, drinkers spilling out of cafés to see sword-swallowers and fire-eaters do their tricks, while the restaurants join in enthusiastically, placing their tables outside so you can eat without missing the fun. On a good night Leidseplein is Amsterdam at its carefree, exuberant best.

On the far corner, the **Stadsschouwburg** is the city's prime performance space after the Muziektheater, while behind, and architecturally much more impressive is the fairy-castle **American Hotel**. The hotel is the traditional meeting-place of Amsterdam media folk, though these days the renowned turn-of-the-century terrace room is mainly popular with tourists. Even if you're not thirsty it's worth a peek inside, the leaded stained glass, shallow brick arches, chandeliers and carefully coordinated furnishings as fine an example of the complete stylistic vision of Art Nouveau as you'll find.

Walking east from here, **Weteringschans**, and, running parallel, **Lijnbaansgracht**, ring the modern city centre. On the right the **Rijksmuseum** (p.74) looms large across the canal; left, Spiegelgracht and, further on, Nieuwe Spiegelstraat lead into the **Spiegelkwartier**, the focus of the Amsterdam antique trade. It's a small area, but there are around fifty dealers here – none, as you might expect, particularly inexpensive.

Kerkstraat, a narrow street featuring an odd mixture of gay bookshops and art galleries, leads east from here to connect with **Vijzelstraat** at the **ABN Building**, through which the street actually runs. The ABN, bland and plastic-looking on the whole, doesn't merit a second glance today – but its construction in the 1950s was the subject of one of Amsterdam's biggest property controversies. During that decade many canals had been filled in and large parts of the city torn down to make way for increased traffic. The tension between the conservationists and developers had been mounting for some time, and when the collapse of a building between Keizersgracht and Prinsengracht left this plot vacant, the scene was set for confrontation. There was immediate protest when it turned out that the *Algemene Bank Nederland* was to buy up the land for office use, and diverse groups of Amsterdammers joined together to keep the bank out. The architect had already defaced part of the city with the overbearing State Bank building on Fredericksplein, and many people felt he shouldn't be given the opportunity again – particularly not on the banks of one of the city's most beautiful canals. That the bank's offices stand now is proof enough that the conservationists lost, but it was an important early skirmish in the city's continuing struggles to keep the property barons at bay.

Looking towards Muntplein, the oversized **Nederladsche Handelmaatschapij Building** (now also owned by *ABN*) is another bank building totally unsympathetic with its surroundings. Though a much worthier work architecturally than the later bank, it would look more at home in downtown Manhattan than on the banks of a Dutch canal. In the other direction, Vijzelstraat becomes the filled-in **Vijzelgracht**, which culminates in a roundabout at **Weteringplantsoen**, and, on its southern side, one of Amsterdam's saddest spots. It was here, on April 3, 1945, that twenty people were shot by the Nazis – an example, in the last few weeks of their power, to anyone who might consider opposing them. An excerpt from a poem by Sjoerd on the wall recalls the incident with carefully levelled restraint:

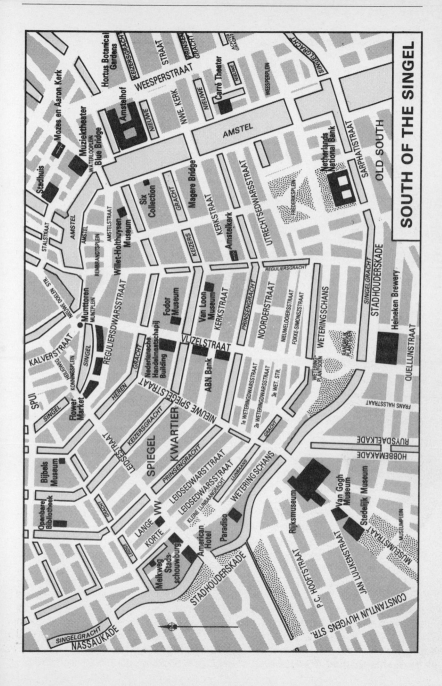

SOUTH OF THE SINGEL

When to the will of tyrants,
A nation's head is bowed,
It loses more than life and goods —
Its very light goes out.

In a wholly different vein, the **Heineken Brewery** (☎70 79 11) opposite, runs daily tours at 10am and 2pm. At a guilder a head these are a must: just be sure to arrive early, since tickets for both tours go on sale 9.30am and are normally gone by 9.45am. Though the brewery recently stopped production, and is in the process of being turned into a museum, it's still interesting to explore the old plant. Afterwards, you are given snacks and free beer, and the atmosphere is convivial – as you'd imagine when there are 200 people downing as much free beer as they can drink. Whether you have just one,0 or drink yourself into a stupor, it's a diverting way to get a lunchtime aperitif.

Rembrandtsplein and its environs

Towards the Amstel, the area cornered by Herengracht's eastern reaches is dominated by **Rembrandtsplein**, a dishevelled bit of greenery fringed with cafés and their terraces. This claims to be a centre of city nightlife, though the square's crowded restaurants are today firmly tourist-targeted; expect to pay inflated prices. Rembrandt's pigeon-spattered statue stands in the middle, his back wisely turned against the square's worst excesses, which include live (but deadly) outdoor music. Of the cafés, only the bar of the **Schiller Hotel** at number 26 stands out, with an original Art Deco interior reminiscent of a great ocean liner.

The streets leading north from Rembrandtsplein to the Amstel river are more exciting, containing many of the city's mainstream **gay bars** – accessible to all, and less costly than their upstart neighbours. **Amstelstraat** is the main thoroughfare east, crossing the river at the **Blauwbrug** (Blue Bridge), and affording views across of the new and unimaginative **Muziektheater** and **Town Hall** complex. Heading west, **Reguliersbreestraat** links Rembrandtsplein to Muntplein and, among slot-machine arcades and sex shops, houses the **Tuschinski**, the city's most famous cinema, with an interior that's a wonderful example of the Art Deco excesses of the 1920s. Expressionist paintings, coloured marbles, Persian carpets add to a general air of all-pervasive decadence. You can obviously see all this if you're here to watch a film (the Tuschinski shows all the most popular general releases); if you're not, guided tours are laid on during July and August on Sunday and Monday mornings at 10.30am (f5 per person).

The block of streets behind the Tuschinski was once known as *Duivelshoek* ("Devil's Corner"), and, though it's been tidied up and sanitised, enough of the back-street seediness remains to make it a spot most people avoid by night. To the south of Rembrandtsplein, **Thorbeckeplein** scores points for having a thinner concentration of clog and card shops, but is hardly a fitting memorial for Rudolf Thorbecke, a politician whose liberal reforms of the late nineteenth century furthered the city tradition of open-minded tolerance, and whose statue stands a short way from the topless bars and sex shows. **Reguliersgracht** flows south from here, a broad canal of distinctive steep bridges that was to have been filled in at the beginning of the century, but was saved when public outcry rose against the destruction of one of the city's more alluring stretches of water. The three great *grachten* nearby don't contain houses quite as grand as those to the west, but a handful of buildings can be visited: the **Van Loon House** at Keizersgracht 672 and the **Willet-Holthuysen House** at Herengracht 605 are both worthwhile examples of the seventeenth-century patrician canal house, and, best of all, the **Six Collection** at Amstel 218 has an easily absorbed group of paintings in a remarkably unspoiled mansion – though the current Baron Six, who still lives there, has a policy of actively discouraging visitors. For details of all three, see pp. 85, 84, and 87 respectively .

As the canals approach the Amstel, their houses become increasingly residential: even **Kerkstraat** is tamed of its bars and clubs, turning east of Reguliersgracht into a pleasant if unremarkable neighbourhood that lies beside the **Amstelveld**, a small square-cum-football pitch that few visitors happen upon. The **Amstelkerk**, a seventeenth-century graffiti-covered wooden church with a nineteenth-century Gothic interior marks the corner, and a Monday **flower market** here adds a splash of colour. **Utrechtsestraat**, the other artery that flows to and from Rembrandtsplein, is probably Amsterdam's most up-and-coming strip and contains most of the area's commercial activity, much of it in the shape of mid- to upper-bracket restaurants. It ends in the concrete wasteland of **Frederiksplein** – more a glorified tram stop than a square, presided over by the massive glass box of the **Netherlands Bank**. Leading off Frederiksplein, Sarphatistraat crosses the wide and windy reaches of the **Amstel River**, whose eastern side is stacked with chunky buildings such as the **Carré Theatre**, built as a circus in the early 1900s, but now more often a space for music and drama. Just beyond, the **Magere Brug**, ("Skinny Bridge") is (inexplicably) focus of much attention in the tourist brochures, and hence the most famous of the city's swinging bridges. More worthy of a serious look is the **Amstel Hof**, a large and forbidding former *hofje* that was one of a number of charitable institutions built east of the Amstel after a seventeenth-century decision to extend the major canals eastward towards the new harbour and shipbuilding quarter. Takers for the new land were few, and the city had no option but to offer it to charities at discount prices.

Move east from this part of the Amstel and you're heading toward the edges of the old Jewish area, though here, as in the Jodenhoek proper, there are scant traces of the community that thrived before World War II. The development of Weesperplein as a major traffic route (and the building of the metro beneath it) removed most of what little remained, but one painful reminder of the war years still stands at **Nieuwe Keizersgracht 58**. From 1940, this house was the headquarters of the *Judenrat* or Jewish Council, an organisation used by the Nazis to cover up the fact that Jews were being deported from the city to their deaths. The council helped implement the day-to-day running of the deportations, thereby furthering the belief among Jews that they were being taken to new employment in Germany. Just how much the council leaders knew isn't clear, but a good many workers within the organisation complied with Nazi orders in the belief that their own skins

BARS *Amstel Taveerne* (gay), *April* (gay), *Café Americain, Café Amstel 102* (gay), *De Balie, Chez Manfred* (gay), *Company* (gay), *Cosmo* (gay), *De Doffer, Eldorado* (gay), *Françoise's* (women's), *Gaiety* (gay), *H'88, Het Hok, De Komedie* (gay), *Huyschkaemer, Land van Walem, Morlang, Het Molenpad, Monopole Taveerne* (gay), *Mulliner's Wijnlokaal, Oblomow* (gay), *Oosterling, Open* (gay), *De la Paix, De Pels, Queen's Head Hotel* (gay), *Route 66* (gay), *Van Puffelen, Schiller, De Spijker* (gay), *De Tap, Taveerne de Pul* (gay), *Traffic* (gay), *Vivelavie,* (women's), *Wheels.*

COFFEE SHOPS "Smoking" *The Bulldog.* **Non-smoking** *Back Stage, 't Balkje* (gay), *Batôn, Berkhoff, Café Panini, Downtown* (gay), *The Eighties, Pompadour, De Utrechtsepoort.*

RESTAURANTS Dutch *De Blauwe Hollander, Sassafrass.* **Fish** *De Gouden Leeuw, De Oesterbar, Sluizer.* **Pancakes** *Welcome.* **Vegetarian and health food** *Baldur, De Bast, Golden Temple, Manou Macrobiotic Restaurant.* **Chinese, Japanese and Thai** *Dynasty, Yoichi.* **French** *Bistro de Vlier, 't Fornuis, Intermezzo, L. P. Jardin Parisien, Petra van Niftrik, Orient Express, Sluizer, De Smoeshaan, Het Tuinhuysch.* **Greek and Turkish** *Aphrodite, Filoxenia, Knossos.* **Indian** *The Tandoor.* **Indonesian** *Bojo, Tempo Doeloe, Yu and Mie.* **Italian** *Pizzeria Mimo.* **North, Latin and South American** *Alfonso's, Canecao Rio, Rose's Cantina, Sarita's Cantina.* **Spanish** *La Cacerola.*

HOTELS/HOSTELS *Adolesce, De Admiral, Aero* (gay), *Agora, Amstel, Brian, Canal House, Estherea, Fantasia, De Gouden Kettingh, Hans Brinker, De Harmonie, Hegra, ITC* (gay), *International Student Centre, John's Place* (gay), *De Lantaerne, Het Leidseplein, De Leydsche Hof, Maas, Mikado, Monopole* (gay), *New York Hotel* (gay), *De la Poste, Prinsenhof, Quentin* (gay), *Seven Bridges, Titus, Toren, Unique Hotel* (gay), *West End Hotel* (gay), *Witz Apartments* (gay).

would be saved. After the war the surviving leaders of the Jewish Council successfully defended themselves against charges of collaboration, stating that they effectively prevented far stricter deportation schemes. But the presence of the council office had already given this stretch of Keizersgracht a new name – *Nieuwe Martelaarsgracht*, the canal of the New Martyrs.

West from the Dam

Unlike the Jodenhoek, the area west of Amsterdam's immediate centre is one of the city's most untouched neighbourhoods – and one of its loveliest. The Prinsengracht here has a gentle beauty quite unlike its grander rivals, and holds the Anne Frank House as a specific draw; and the Jordaan, just beyond, with its narrow waterways spotted with tiny shops and bars, is as good (and as pretty) a place for idle strolling as you'll find.

The Westerkerk and the Anne Frank House
From behind the Royal Palace, **Raadhuisstraat** leads west across Herengracht and curves around the elegant nineteenth-century art nouveau **Utrecht Building** towards **Westermarkt**. Here, at Westermarkt 6, the seventeenth-century French philosopher René Descartes lived for a short

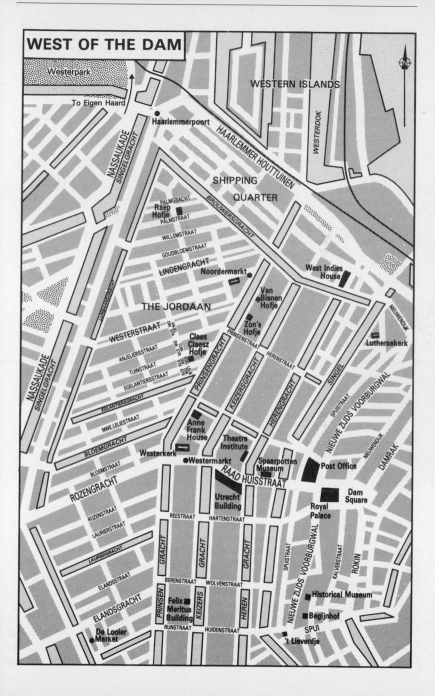

WEST OF THE DAM

Westerpark

To Eigen Haard

WESTERN ISLANDS

WESTERDOK

NASSAUKADE

SINGELGRACHT

Haarlemmerpoort

HAARLEMMER HOUTTUINEN

SHIPPING

QUARTER

PALMGRACHT

Raep
Hofje

PALMSTRAAT

BROUWERSGRACHT

WILLEMSTRAAT

GOUDBLOEMSTRAAT

LINDENGRACHT

Noordermarkt

West Indies
House

NIEUWENDIJK

THE JORDAAN

Van
Bienen
Hofje

WESTERSTRAAT

Zon's
Hofje

PRINSENSTRAAT

HERENSTRAAT

Luthersekerk

ANJELIERSSTRAAT

Claes
Claesz
Hofje

ANJEL
DW STR
1e STR

SINGEL

SPUISTRAAT

NIEUWE ZIJDS VOORBURGWAL

TUINSTRAAT

TUIN
DW STR
1e STR

PRINSENGRACHT

KEIZERSGRACHT

HERENGRACHT

NIEUWENDIJK

DAMRAK

EGELANTIERSSTRAAT

EGEL
DW STR
1e STR

EGLANTIERSGRACHT

NWE.LELIESTRAAT

Anne
Frank
House

BLOEMGRACHT

Theatre
Institute

Westerkerk

Spaarpotten
Museum

Post Office

BLOEMSTRAAT

Westermarkt

RAAD HUISSTRAAT

ROZENGRACHT

Utrecht
Building

Royal
Palace

Dam
Square

NASSAUKADE

SINGELGRACHT

LIJNBAANSGRACHT

ROZENSTRAAT

REESTRAAT

HARTENSTRAAT

SPUISTRAAT

NIEUWE ZIJDS VOORBURGWAL

KALVERSTRAAT

ROKIN

LAURIERSTRAAT

PRINSEN GRACHT

KEIZERS GRACHT

HEREN GRACHT

LAURIERGRACHT

ELANDSSTRAAT

BERENSTRAAT

WOLVENSTRAAT

ELANDSGRACHT

Felix
Meritus
Building

Historical Museum

Beginhof

De Looier
Market

RUNSTRAAT

HUIDENSTRAAT

SPUI

't Lieverdje

time, happy that the business-oriented character of the city left him able to work and think without being disturbed. As he wrote at the time, "Everybody except me is in business and so absorbed by profit-making I could spend my entire life here without being noticed by a soul".

It's the **Westerkerk** (daily 10am–4pm, closed Sun), though, which dominates the square, its tower – without question Amsterdam's finest – soaring graciously above the gables of Prinsengracht. On its top perches the crown of Kaiser Maximilian, a constantly recurring symbol of the city and an appropriate finishing touch to what was only its second place of worship built expressly for Protestants. The church was designed by Hendrik de Keyser (architect also of the Zuiderkerk and Noorderkerk) as part of the general seventeenth-century enlargement of the city, and completed in 1631. But while this is probably Amsterdam's most visually appealing church from the outside, there's little within of special note. Rembrandt, who was living nearby when he died, is commemorated by a small memorial in the north aisle. His pauper's grave can no longer be located; indeed, there's a possibility that he's not here at all, since many of the bodies were moved to a cemetery when underground heating was installed. The memorial is, however, close to where Rembrandt's son Titus is buried. Rembrandt worshipped his son – as evidenced by numerous portraits – and the boy's death dealt a final crushing blow to the ageing and embittered artist, leading to his own death just over a year later. During recent excavations, bones have been unearthed which could be those of Titus and even Rembrandt – something which has made the church authorities very excited about the resultant tourist possibilities. The only thing that can prove it one way or the other is the analysis currently taking place of the lead content of the bones, which in the case of an artist such as Rembrandt should be unusually high as lead was a major ingredient of paint. The church tower is open between June 1 and September 15, on Tuesday, Wednesday, Friday and Saturday from 2 to 5pm (guided tour only).

Directly outside the church stands a small, simple statue of **Anne Frank** by the Dutch sculptor Mari Andriessen – a careful and evocative site, since it was just a few steps from here, at Prinsengracht 263, that the young diarist used to listen to the Westertoren bells until they were taken away to be melted down for the Nazi war effort. The story of Anne Frank, her family and friends is well known. Anne's father, Otto, was a well-to-do Jewish businessman who ran a successful spice-trading business and lived in the southern part of the city. By 1942 the Nazi occupation was taking its toll: all Jews had been forced to wear a yellow star, and were not allowed to use public transport, go to the theatre or cinema or stray into certain areas of the city; roundups, too, were becoming increasingly common. As conditions became more difficult, and it looked as if the Franks themselves might be taken away, Otto Frank decided – on the advice of two Dutch friends and colleagues, Mr Koophuis and Mr Kraler – to move into their warehouse on the Prinsengracht, the back half of which was unused at the time. The Franks went into hiding in July 1942, along with a Jewish business partner and his family, the Van Daans, separated from the eyes of the outside world by a bookcase that doubled as a door. As far as everyone else was concerned, they had fled to Switzerland.

So began the two-year occupation of the *achterhuis*, or back annexe. The two families were joined in November of 1942 by a Mr Dussel, a dentist friend, and supplies and news of the outside world – which, for the Jews, was becoming daily more perilous – were brought regularly by Koophuis or Kraler, who continued working in the front office. In her diary Anne Frank describes the day-to-day lives of the inhabitants of the annexe: the quarrels, frequent in such a claustrophobic environment; celebrations of birthdays, or of a piece of good news from the Allied Front; and her own, slightly unreal, growing up (much of which, it's been claimed, was deleted by her father).

Two years later, the atmosphere was optimistic: the Allies were clearly winning the war, and it was thought it wouldn't be long before the fugitives could emerge. It wasn't to be. One day in the summer of 1944 the Franks were betrayed by a Dutch collaborator; the Gestapo arrived and forced Mr Kraler to open up the bookcase, whereupon the occupants of the annexe were all arrested and quickly sent to Westerbork – the northern Netherlands German labour camp where all Dutch Jews were processed before being moved to Belsen or Auschwitz. Of the eight from the annexe, only Otto Frank survived; Anne and her sister died of typhus within a short time of each other in Belsen, just one week before the German surrender.

Anne Frank's diary was among the few things left behind in the annexe. It was retrieved by one of the people who had helped the Franks and handed to Anne's father on his return from Auschwitz; he later decided to publish it. Since its appearance in 1947, it has been constantly in print, translated into 54 languages and has sold thirteen million copies worldwide. In 1957 the *Anne Frank Foundation* set up the **Anne Frank House** (July–Aug Mon–Sat 9am–7pm, Sun 10am–7pm; Sept–June Mon–Sat 9am–5pm, Sun 10am–5pm; closed Yom Kippur – Oct 9; f5, no museumcards; ☎26 45 33), one of the most deservedly popular tourist attractions in town; bearing this in mind, the best time to visit is early morning before the crowds arrive.

The rooms the Franks lived in for two years are left much the same as they were during the war, even down to Anne's movie star pin-ups in her bedroom and the marks on the wall recording the children's heights. A number of other rooms offer background detail on the war and occupation, one offering a video biography of Anne, from her frustrated hopes in hiding in the annexe up to her death in 1945, another detailing the gruesome atrocities of Nazism, as well as giving some up-to-date examples of fascism and anti-semitism in Europe which draw pertinent parallels with the war years. Anne Frank was only one of 100,000 Dutch Jews who died during that time, but this, her final home, provides one of the most enduring testaments to the horrors of Nazism.

The Jordaan and around

The Jews were by no means the only group who were oppressed by the Nazis: before being rounded up and deported, homosexuals were forced to wear pink cloth triangles on their jackets, a fact remembered by the pink triangle of the **Homo-Monument** on the corner of Keizersgracht and Westermarkt. The monument commemorates homosexuals who died in concentration camps, and known homosexuals who fought with the Allies and whose names were omitted from other remembrance monuments.

Across the Prinsengracht, on the northern side of Rozengracht, **THE JORDAAN**, is a likeable and easily explored area of narrow canals, narrower streets and simple, architecturally varied houses. The name is said to come from the French *jardin*, and many of the streets are named after flowers. Falling outside the seventeenth-century concentric-canal plan, the area was not subject to municipal controls, which led to its becoming a centre of property speculation, developing as a series of canals and streets that followed the original polder ditches and rough paths. In contrast to the splendour of the three main *grachten*, the Jordaan became Amsterdam's slum quarter, home of artisans, tradespeople, and Jewish or Huguenot refugees who had fled here to escape religious persecution at home. Though tolerated, the immigrants remained distinct minorities and were treated as such, living in what were often cramped and unsanitary quarters. Later, after much rebuilding, the Jordaan became the inner-city enclave of Amsterdam's growing industrial working class – which, in spite of increasing gentrification, it to some extent remains. The last couple of decades have seen the Jordaan gain a reputation as the home of young "alternative" Amsterdam, but there's a core population of residents, especially in the northern reaches, who retain long-standing roots in the district.

Other than a handful of bars and restaurants, some posh clothes shops and the odd outdoor market, there's nothing very specific to see (though it's a wonderful neighbourhood for a wander) apart from its *hofjes* – seventeenth-century almshouses for the city's elderly population. There were – and are – *hofjes* all over the city (most famously the Begijnhof, p.45), but there's a concentration in the Jordaan, and if you're passing through, it is worth looking in on a courtyard or two; many of them have real charm. Bear in mind, though, that most are still lived in, and be discreet.

Of those that warrant a specific visit, the **Van Bienen Hofje**, opposite the Noordermarkt at Prinsengracht 89–133, is the grandest, built in 1804, according to the entrance tablet, "for the relief and shelter of those in need". A little way down the canal at Prinsengracht 157–171, **Zon's Hofje** has a leafier, more gentle beauty; and, back in the main grid of the Jordaan, the **Claes Claesz Hofje** on 1e Egelantierdwarsstraat, a much earlier almshouse (built in 1616 for poor widows), is now noisily occupied by students of the Amsterdam Conservatory of Music. A little further north, look also at the buildings of **Raep Hofje**, Palmgracht 26–38, funded by the Raep family and sporting a carved *raep* (turnip) above the entrance. For more on *hofjes* – and an account of one of the country's most famous, the Frans Hals Museum in Haarlem – see p.157.

More general wanderings start on **Rozengracht**, the filled-in canal where, at number 184, Rembrandt once lived – though the house itself has long since disappeared and only a plaque marks the spot. Though not the Jordaan proper, the area south of this street is a likeable one, centring on the pretty Lauriergracht and including, at Elandsgracht 109, the **De Looier indoor antique market** – where a leisurely browse may unearth a bargain (see p.101). North of Rozengracht the Jordaan's streets and canals run diagonally off, bordering Prinsengracht. The main street of the district is **Westerstraat** (where there's a Monday general market), which runs down to join Prinsengracht at **Noordermarkt** and Hendrik de Keyser's **Noorderkerk**. This church, finished in 1623, is probably the architect's least successful creation in Amsterdam; nor is the square particularly attractive, part car park, part children's playground. It's the site of a Monday antiques market and the regular Saturday morning *Boerenmarkt* (farmers' market) during summer months – a lively affair full of avuncular ex-hippies selling organic produce, handicrafts, homemade wine and, rather cruely, a selection of exotic birds in very small cages. The next street over, **Lindengracht**, is home to another Saturday market, this time general. If you're interested in shopping, also check out **Tweede Anjelierdwarsstraat** and **Tweede Tuindwarsstraat** – two streets which hold the bulk of the Jordaan's ever-increasing trendy stores and clothing shops, and some of its liveliest bars and cafés for restorative sipping.

Brouwersgracht, just beyond, is one of Amsterdam's most picturesque and most photographed canals, marking what is in effect the northern boundary of the Jordaan and the beginning of a district loosely known as the **SHIPPING QUARTER**, which centres on the long arteries of **Haarlemmerstraat** and **Haarlemmerdijk**. In the seventeenth century this district was at the cutting edge of Amsterdam's trade: the warehouses along Brouwersgracht provided storage space for the spoils brought back from the high seas, and the building on Haarlemmerstraat at Herenmarkt, the **West Indies House**, was home of the Dutch West Indies Company, who administered much of the business. Today it's a good area for cheap restaurants and off-beat shops: the warehouses have been largely taken over and converted into spacious apartments, and the West Indies Company Building has a court-yard containing an overstated statue of Pieter Stuyvesant, governor of New Amsterdam (later named New York), and a swanky restaurant named after the seventeenth-century Dutch naval hero Piet Heijn.

At the far end of Haarlemmerdijk, the **Haarlemmerpoort** is an oversized and very un-Amsterdam–like former gateway to the city. Beyond this you can either walk on to the **Westerpark**, one of the city's smaller and more enticing parks, or duck under the railway lines to the **WESTERN ISLANDS** district, where ships were once unloaded and where there are more rows of gaunt warehouses – an atmospheric area, still largely deserted. The painter G. H. Breitner had his studio here – in the modern house beside the **Sloterdijkbrug** – and the area is still a favourite with artists, some of whom have moved in to exploit the space offered by the old warehouses. Across the Westerkanaal on Zaanstraat and Spaarndammerplantsoen, the **Eigen Haard** housing project is probably the most central example you'll see of the Amsterdam School of architecture. Designed by Michael de Klerk, this was one of a number of new schemes that went up in Amsterdam in the early part of this century, a result of legislation passed to alleviate the previously appalling housing conditions of the city's poor. Modern municipal architects – Dutch ones included – could learn a lot from the style, which is typical of the Amsterdam School. Rounded corners, turrets, and bulging windows and balconies lend individuality to what would otherwise be very plain brick residences. For more on the Amsterdam School see H. P. Berlage's *New South* (p.67) and Piet Kramer's *De Dageraad* estates, also in the South.

BARS *De Beiaard, Belhamel, Het Bruine Paard* (women's), *Chris, De Dwarsboom, Floor* (women's), *Gambit, Hegeraad, De Kalkhoven, De Kat in de Wijngaert, De Klepel, Laurier 33, 't Monumentje, Nol, Het Paleis, De Prins, De Prinses, De Reiger, Rum Runners, Saarein* (women's), *'t Smackzeyl, 't Smalle, Theo Ruiter, De Tuin, De Twee Heiligen, Twee Prinsen, De Twee Zwaantjes, De Vergulde Gaper, Winkel.*

COFFEE SHOPS "Smoking" *Biba, Bon Ami, Fairy Nuff, Just a Puff, Pie in the Sky, Siberië, So Fine.* **"Non-smoking"** *Arnold Cornelis, J.G. Beune, Cocky's, The Eighties, Dialoog.*

RESTAURANTS Dutch *De Bak, Claes Claesz, De Eenhuin, De Eetuin, Leto, Moeder's Pot, Rosereijn.* **Fish** *Albatros.* **Pancakes** *The Pancake Bakery.* **Vegetarian and health food** *Beit-Hamazon, Bolhoed, De Vliegende Schotel.* **Chinese, Japanese, Thai and Filipino** *Mango Bay.* **French** *Cafécox, De Gouden Reael, De Kikker, Robert & Abraham Kef.* **Greek and Turkish** *Plaka, Sultan Ahmet.* **Indian** *Koh-I-Noor.* **Indonesian** *Jaya, Kam–Wah, Speciaal.* **Italian** *Burger's Patio, Frappe, Mamma Mia, Pizzeria Collina, Pizzeria Pastorale, Toscana.* **North, Latin and South American** *Caramba, Mexico.* **Spanish** *Casa Tobio, Centra, Rias Altas.* **Surinamese and Caribbean** *Rum Runners.*

HOTELS/HOSTELS *Acacia, Arrive, Clemens, Eben Haezer, Ronnie, Westertoren, Weichmann..*

The Jodenhoek and Eastern Islands

Though there's hardly any visible evidence today, from the sixteenth century onward Amsterdam was the home of Jews escaping persecution throughout Europe. Under the terms of the Union of Utrecht, Jews enjoyed a tolerance and freedom unknown elsewhere, and they arrived in the city to practise the crafts of diamond processing, sugar refining and tobacco production – effectively the only trades open to them since the city's guilds excluded Jews from following any of the traditional crafts. This largely impoverished Jewish community lived in one of the least desirable stretches of the city, the old dock areas around Jodenbreestraat, which became known as the **JODENHOEK**. The docks moved east to Kattenburg, Wittenburg and Oostenburg – the **EASTERN ISLANDS**. By the early years of this century Jewish life was commercially and culturally an integral part of the city, the growing demand for diamonds making Jewish expertise invaluable and bringing wealth to the community for the first time.

In the 1930s the community's numbers swelled with Jews who had fled persecution in Germany. In May 1940, however, the Nazis invaded, sealing off the Jodenhoek as a ghetto. Jews were not allowed to use public transport or own a telephone, and were placed under a curfew. Round-ups and deportations continued until the last days of the war: out of a total of 80,000 Jews in the city, 75,000 were murdered in concentration camps.

After the war the Jodenhoek lay deserted: those who had lived here were dead or deported, and their few possessions were quickly looted. As the need for wood and raw materials grew in post-war shortages, the houses were slowly dismantled and destroyed, a destruction completed in the 1970s with the completion of the metro that links the city centre to the outer suburbs.

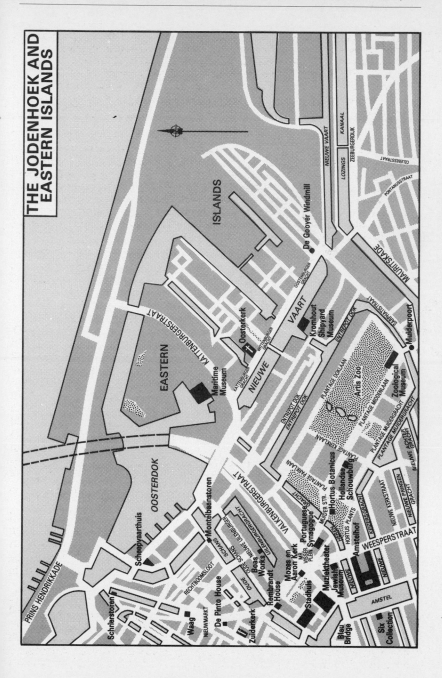

The Jodenhoek: Jodenbreestraat to Plantage Middenlaan

Nieuwmarkt signals the beginning of what was the Jodenhoek, and **St. Antioniesbreestraat** leads to its heart, an uncomfortably modernised street whose original old houses were demolished to widen the road for the heavy traffic that the Nieuwmarkt redevelopment (see below) would bring. Only the **De Pinto House** at number 69 survives, easily spotted by its creamy Italianate facade. Isaac De Pinto, a Jew who had fled Portugal to escape the Inquisition, was a founder of the East Indies Company and used some of the wealth he had accrued to decorate his house; today it's a branch of the public library, and worth dropping into for a glimpse of the elaborately painted ceiling. Nearby, the decorative landmark of Hendrik de Keyser's **Zuiderkerk** is similarly surrounded by new development: undergoing a major reconstruction, its tower is irregularly open in summer months, and the best place for an overview of this part of town.

St. Antioniesbreestraat runs into **Jodenbreestraat**, once the Jodenhoek's principal market and centre of Jewish activity. After the shipbuilding industry moved further east, this area (the small islands of Uilenburg and Marken) became the site of the worst living conditions in the city – cramped, dirty streets which housed the very poorest Jews, those who couldn't find employment in the diamond factories such as the **Boas Works**, whose empty buildings still stand on the southwest corner of Uilenburgergracht. It wasn't until 1911 that the area was declared a health hazard and redeveloped. Jodenbreestraat itself was modernised and widened in the 1970s and it lost much of its character as a result; only when you reach the **Rembrandt House** at number 6 (Mon–Fri 10am–5pm, Sun 1–5pm; f3.50) do you find any continuity with the past. Rembrandt bought the house at the height of his fame and popularity, living here for over twenty years and spending a fortune on furnishings – an expense that helped lead to his bankruptcy. An inventory made at the time details a huge collection of paintings, sculptures and art treasures he'd amassed, almost all of which went in the bankruptcy hearings, and in 1660 he was forced to move to a more modest house on Rozengracht in the Jordaan. The house itself is disappointing – mostly a reconstruction and with no artefacts from Rembrandt's life on exhibit – but you can view a great variety of the artist's engravings here. The biblical illustrations attract the most attention, though the studies of tramps and vagabonds are more accessible; a good accompanying exhibit explains Rembrandt's engraving techniques.

Jodenbreestraat runs parallel to its sibling development, the new **Muziektheater and Town Hall** on **Waterlooplein**, whose building occasioned the biggest public dispute the city had seen since the Nieuwmarkt was dug up in the 1970s to make way for the metro. The Waterlooplein, a marshy, insanitary area that rapidly became known as the poorest patch of the city, was the first neighbourhood settled by the Jews. By the late nineteenth century things had become so bad that the canals crossing the area were filled in and the shanty houses razed; the street markets then shifted here from St. Antioniesbreestraat and Jodenbreestraat. The Waterlooplein quickly became Amsterdam's largest and liveliest market, and a link between the Jewish community and the predominantly Gentile one across the Amstel. During the war it became infamous again, this time as a site for Nazi roundups; in the 1950s it regained some of its vibrancy with the establishment of the city's flea market here. Later, when the council announced the building of a massive new opera complex that would all but fill the square, opposition was widespread. People believed it should be turned into a residential area at best, a popular performance space at least – anything but an elitist opera house; the site (and anti-development campaign) was quickly dubbed the *Stopera*. Attempts to prevent the building failed, but since opening in 1986 the Muziektheater has successfully established itself with visitors and performers alike, and the **flea market** is beginning to drift back after being moved for a few years to nearby Valkenburgstraat – where some stalls remain. In the public **passageway** between the two buildings, a series of glass columns give a salutary lesson on the fragility of The Netherlands, one containing water indicating the sea levels in the Dutch towns of Vlissingen and Ijmuiden, and another recording the (much higher) levels during the 1953 flood disaster. Downstairs a plaque shows what is known as "Normal Amsterdam Level" (NAP), calculated in the seventeenth century as the average water level in the river IJ and still the basis for measuring altitude across Europe.

Just behind the Muziektheater, on the corner of Mr Visserplein, is the **Mozes en Aaron Kerk**, originally a small (clandestine) Catholic church that was rebuilt in rather glum neoclassical style in the mid-nineteenth century. The philospher Spinoza was born in a house on this site, and as a Jew, quickly came into conflict with the elders of the Jewish community over his radical views. When he was 23 the religious authorities excommunicated him, and he was forced to move to the Hague and take up work as a lens polisher.

The area around Mr Visserplein, today a busy and dangerous junction for traffic speeding towards the IJ tunnel, has the most tangible mementoes of the Jewish community. The brown and bulky **Portuguese Synagogue** (Mon–Fri 10am–noon, 1–4pm; Sun 10am–1pm; free) was completed in 1675 by Sephardic Jews who had moved to Amsterdam from Spain and Portugal to escape the Inquisition, and who prospered here in the seventeenth and eighteenth centuries. A glance inside gives you an idea of just how wealthy the community was, the high barrel vault emphasising the synagogue's size, the oak and jacaranda wood its riches. When it was completed the Portuguese Syhagogue was the largest in the world: today the Sephardic community has dwindled to thirty or forty.

Across the way from the Portuguese Synagogue the **Jewish Historical Museum** is cleverly housed in a complex of High German synagogues that date from the late seventeenth century. For many years after the war the buildings lay in ruins, and it's only recently that the museum has moved in. In addition to photos and mementoes from the holocaust, the museum gives a broad introduction to Jewish beliefs and life. For opening hours and a full description, see p.86.

Between the museum and the Portuguese Synagogue is **J. D. Meijerplein**, where a small statue marks the spot on which, in February 1941, 400 young Jewish men were rounded up, arrested, loaded on trucks, and taken to their eventual execution at Mauthausen in reprisal for the killing of a Nazi sympathiser in a street fight between members of the Jewish resistance and the Dutch Nazi party. The arrests sparked off the "February Strike", a general strike led by transport workers and dockers and organised by the outlawed Communist party in protest against the deportations and treatment of the Jews. Although broken by mass arrests after only two days, it was a demonstration of solidarity with the Jews that was unique in occupied Europe and unusual in The Netherlands, where the majority of people had done little to prevent or protest the actions of the SS. Mari Andriesson's statue of *The Docker* on Meijerplein commemorates the event, but a better memorial, tinged with Amsterdam humour, is the legendary slogan – "Keep your filthy hands off our filthy Jews".

Leaving Mr. Visserplein via Muiderstraat, with the prim **Hortus Botanicus** (botanical gardens) to the right (see p.89), you reach another sad relic of the war at Plantage Middenlaan 24. The **Hollandse Schouwburg**, a predominantly Jewish theatre before 1940, was the main assembly point for Dutch Jews prior to their deportation to Germany. Inside, there was no daylight and families were packed in for days in conditions that foreshadowed the camps. The house across the street, now a teacher training college, was used as a day nursery. Some, possibly hundreds, managed to escape through here and a plaque outside extols the memory of those "who saved the children".

The Hollandse Schouwburg is today little more than a shell. Its facade is still intact, but the roof has gone and what used to be the auditorium is now a quiet, grassy courtyard. A memorial – a column of basalt on a base in the form of a Star of David – stands where the stage once was. It seems understated, a failure to grasp the enormity of the crime. Off the beaten track and with few visitors, it is a temptation to the local kids, whose shouts bring an attendant from his office; a battered vending machine offers a leaflet and photographs. It's almost impossible now to imagine the scenes that went on here, but the sense of emptiness and loss is strong. If sometimes there seems to be a hollow ring to fun-loving Amsterdam, this place is why.

Prins Hendrikkade and the Eastern Islands

The broad boulevard that fronts the grey waters of the Oosterdok is **Prins Hendrikkade**, a continuation of the road that leads to Stationsplein in the west and goes on deep into the docks of eastern Amsterdam. Since the city emerged as a maritime power in the sixteenth century, this strip, along with its twin to the west, served as a harbour front to the ships which carried its riches: merchant vessels brought grain from the Baltic and took diamonds, fabric and wines to the north, vastly increasing the city's importance as a market and bringing about the prosperity of the Golden Age. Today Prins Hendrikkade is a major artery for cars flowing north via the IJ tunnel, and the only ships docked belong to the police or navy. But the road is lined with buildings that point to a more interesting nautical past. The first of these, the squat **Schrierstoren**, was traditionally the place where, in the Middle Ages, tearful women saw their husbands off to sea (the name could be translated as "weepers' tower") – though this is probably more romantic invention than fact. A sixteenth-century inlaid stone records the emotional leave-takings, while another much more recent tablet recalls the departure of Henry

Hudson from here in 1609 – the voyage on which he inadvertently discovered Manhattan. A little further along, the **Scheepvaarthuis** at Prins Hendrikkade 8 is covered inside and out with bas reliefs and other decoration relating the city's maritime history; it's also embellished with slender turrets and expressionistic masonry characteristic of the Amsterdam School of architecture that flourished early in this century.

Several of the houses along Prins Hendrikkade and the streets nearby have similarly impressive facades: **Kromme Waal**, opposite the Scheepvaarthuis, has a fussy collection of gables, and the building at Prins Hendrikkade 131 was once home of Amsterdam's greatest naval hero, Admiral de Ruyter; he's depicted in a stern frieze above the door. A little further along, the wide **Oude Schans** was the main entrance to the old shipbuilding quarter, and the **Montelbaanstoren** tower that stands about halfway down was built in 1512 to protect the merchant fleet. A century later, when the city felt more secure and could afford such luxuries, it was topped with a decorative spire by Hendrik de Keyser, the architect who did much to create Amsterdam's prickly skyline.

The chief pillar of the city's wealth in the sixteenth century was the **Dutch East India Company**. Its expeditions established links with India, Sri Lanka and the Indonesian islands, and later China and Japan, using the Dutch Republic's large fleet of vessels to rob the Portuguese and Spanish of their trade and the undefended islanders of their wood and spices. Dutch expansionism wasn't purely mercantile: not only had the East India Company been given a trading monopoly in all lands east of the Cape of Good Hope, but also unlimited military, judicial and political powers in the countries which it administered. Behind the satisfied smiles of the comfortable burghers of the Golden Age was a nightmare of slavery and exploitation.

The twin warehouses where the East India Company began its operations still stand at Prins Hendrikkade 176, but a better picture of the might of Dutch naval power can be found in the **Maritime Museum** on Kattenburgerplein, housed in a fortress-like former arsenal of the seventeenth century (p.83).

As the wealth from the colonies poured in, the old dock area to the southeast around Uilenburg was no longer able to cope, and the East India Company financed a major reclamation of, and expansion into, the marshland to the east of the existing waterfront, forming the three islands of **Kattenburg**, **Wittenburg**, and **Oostenburg**. A shipbuilding industry developed, and in time the Eastern Islands became the home of a large community working in the shipfitting and dockyard industries. The nineteenth century brought the construction of iron ships, and at a wharf at Hoogte Kadijk 147 an old shipyard is now the **Kromhout Museum** (p.83). The museum still patches up ancient boats and offers a slide show that's a useful introduction to the area's history.

In time, the shipyards of the Eastern Islands declined, the working-class neighbourhood shrank, and today there's not much to show of a once-lively community. The **Oosterkerk**, across the water from the Kromhout was, like the East India Company building and the Maritime Museum, designed by Daniel Stalpaert; now it functions as a social and exhibition centre, part of an attempt to give back this area some of its former identity; you'll see a local newspaper on sale, and the people here still refer to themselves as "Islanders". South of the Kromhout it's worth wandering through to the **Entrepot Dok**, a line of old warehouses, each bearing the name of a destination above its door. Recreated as hi-tech offices and apartments, and with weird gurglings coming from the **Artis Zoo** across the way, it seems an odd sort of end for the Eastern Islands' rich maritime tradition.

Keep going down Oostenburgergracht and you'll reach **"De Gooyer"**, a windmill that dates from 1814. Once mills were all over Amsterdam, pumping water and grinding grain; today only this old corn mill remains, now converted into a shop, though its sails still turn on the first Saturday of the month – wind permitting.

BARS *De Druif, 't Entré Pôtje, Tisfris.*
RESTAURANTS Mensas *De Weesper.* **Thai** *De Klaas Compaen.*
HOTELS/HOSTELS *Pension Kitty.*

The Outer Limits: South, West and East

Amsterdam is a small city and its residential outer neighbourhoods can be easily reached from the city centre. Of them, the **South** holds most interest, with all the major museums, the Vondelpark (a must on summer Sundays), the raucous "De Pijp" quarter and the 1930s architecture of the New South more than justifying the tram ride. As for the other districts, you'll find a good deal less reason for making the effort. The **West** is nothing special, aside from the occasional odd park and one lively immigrant quarter; nor is the **East**, although this does have one conceivable target in the Tropical Museum.

The Old South

During the nineteenth century, unable to hold its mushrooming population within the limits of its canals, Amsterdam began to expand, spreading into the neighbourhoods beyond the Singelgracht which now make up the district known as the **OLD SOUTH**. This large and disparate area includes the leafy residential quarters immediately south of Leidseplein as well as the working-class enclaves further east. **The Vondelpark,** lies at the centre of the former, these days the city's most enticing park. Named after the seventeenth-century poet Joost van der Vondel (see p.39), and funded by local residents, it was landscaped in the latter part of the last century in the English style, with a bandstand and an emphasis on nature rather than on formal gardens. Today it's a regular forum for drama and other performance arts in the summer, and at weekends young Amsterdam flocks here in force to meet friends, laze by the lake, buy trinkets from the flea markets that spring up in the area or listen to music – though the live bands that once formed the main focus here have since been banned due to pressure from local residents.

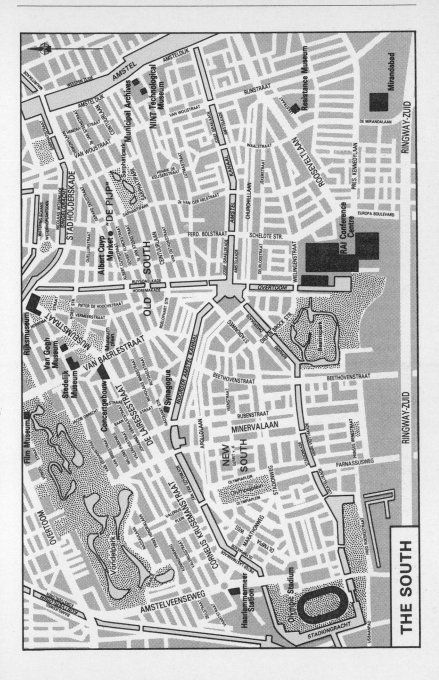

THE SOUTH

At the park's bottom right-hand corner there's a fine neo-Gothic church by Cuijpers, as well as the Netherlands Film Museum (p.88), housed in a pavilion near the Vondelstraat entrance. This is one of Amsterdam's better-heeled residential districts, with designer shops and delis along chic **P. C. Hooftstraat** and **Van Baerlestraat**, and some of the city's fancier hotels (and plenty of its cheaper ones, too) on their connecting streets. But what this area really means to the visitor is **museums**, a number of which – the **Rijksmuseum**, **Van Gogh** and **Stedelijk** (pp.74, 80, and 82) – are imposingly grouped around the grassy wedge of **Museumplein**. This fans back as far as the Concertgebouw at its southern end, and is a bare and rather windswept open space. But halfway across you'll come upon a group of slim steel blocks which commemorate the women of the wartime concentration camps, particularly Ravensbruck, where some 92,000 met their deaths through starvation, disease, or extermination. A "Vrouwen van Ravensbruck" committee organises annual anti-fascist events, and the text on the right reads: "For those women who until the bitter end refused to accept fascism".

At the bottom end of Museumplein, on sleek Van Baerlestraat, is the **Concertgebouw**, completed in 1883 and renowned for its marvellous acoustics and its famed – and much recorded – resident orchestra. The building has just been given a major £12 million facelift following the discovery that the wooden piles on which it rested were rotting, causing subsidence. The foyer has been moved around to the side, housed in a new, largely glass wing which contrasts nicely with the red-brick and stone of the rest of the building.

The Old South isn't all culture, however, and by no means is it all wealthy either. Walking east from Museumplein, across Hobbemakade, you enter the busy heart of the Old South, known as **"De Pijp"** (The Pipe) after its long, sombre canyons of brick tenements that went up in the nineteenth century as the city grew out of its canal-girded centre. The population here is dense and overcrowded, much of it made up of immigrants, and De Pijp has always been one of the city's closest-knit communities – and one of its liveliest. Recently, it has been forced to absorb some of the worst residue of Amsterdam's heroin-dealing trouble spots (those which have been "cleaned up" elsewhere by the police), and you'll see groups of policemen hanging around keeping a sharp eye out for any illicit trading. But it's still a cheerful area, its hub the long slim thoroughfare of **Albert Cuypstraat**, whose daily general market – which stretches for about a mile between Ferdinand Bolstraat and Van Woustraat – is the largest in the city, with a huge array of stalls selling meat, fish, cheeses, buckets of olives, cheap clothes, and anything else you're prepared to seek out. Watch, too, for the bargain-basement and ethnic shops which flank it on each side, and check out the Indian and Surinamese restaurants – they're often much cheaper than their equivalents in the city centre.

The New South
Aside from the small but pretty **Sarphatipark**, a few blocks south of the Albert Cuyp, there's little else to detain you in the Old South, and you'd be better off either walking or catching a tram down into the **NEW SOUTH** – a

real contrast to its neighbour and the first properly planned extension to the city since the concentric canals of the seventeenth century. The Dutch architect H. P. Berlage was responsible for the overall plan, but he died before it could be started and the design was largely carried out in the 1930s by two prominent architects of the Amsterdam School, Michael de Klerk and Piet Kramer. De Klerk and Kramer were already well known for their housing estates in west (p.57) and southeast Amsterdam, and Kramer had also been responsible for the distinctive lettering design on the city's bridges. Cutbacks in the city's subsidy led them to tone down the more imaginative aspects of the scheme, and most of the buildings are markedly more sober than previous Amsterdam School works (such as the Scheepvarthuis on Prins Hendrikade; p.63). But otherwise they followed Berlage faithfully, sticking to the architect's plan of wide boulevards and crooked side-streets (a deliberate attempt to achieve the same combination of monumental grandure and picturesque scale as the great seventeenth-century canals), and adding the odd splash of individuality to corners, windows and balconies.

Nowadays the New South is one of Amsterdam's most sought-after addresses. **Apollolaan**, **Stadionweg** and, a little way east, **Churchillaan**, especially, are home to luxury hotels and some of the city's most sumptuous properties, huge idiosyncratic mansions set back from the street behind trees and generous gardens. **Beethovenstraat**, main street of the New South, is a fashionable shopping boulevard, with high-priced, slightly staid stores catering for the district's wealthy residents. It's hard to believe that once there were few takers for the apartments down here, and that soon after it was finished the area had become a second ghetto for Jews fleeing the terror in Nazi Germany. The Frank family, for example, lived in the South, on Merwedeplein, and there's a whimsical brick **synagogue** on Jacob Obrechtplein, built in the Expressionist style of the 1930s.

If you can read Dutch, the Jewish novel *Tramhalte Beethovenstraat* by Grete Weil will give you a candid picture of the years of occupation in this part of the city. Otherwise, the New South still has plenty of reminders of the war period, when it was the scene of some of the Nazis' worst excesses. The bedraggled **trio** at the intersection of Apollolaan and Beethovenstraat was sculpted to commemorate the reprisal shooting of 29 people on this spot in 1944; the **school** on Gerrit van der Veenstraat, named after an Amsterdam resistance fighter who was shot for organising false identity papers for Jews and attacking Nazi strongholds in the city, was once headquarters of the Gestapo – and where the Frank family were brought after their capture; and the former **synagogue** on Lekstraat houses an excellent museum recording the activities of the resistance movement (see p.84).

The area achieved a brief period of notoriety in 1969, too, when John Lennon and Yoko Ono staged their week-long **Bed-In** for peace in the Amsterdam Hilton on Apollolaan. The press came from all over; fans crowded outside, hanging on the couple's anti-war proclamations, and the episode was seen as the beginning of John and Yoko's subsequent campaign for peace worldwide. At the opposite end of Beethovenstraat, dense trees and shrubs of the **Beatrixpark** flank the antiseptic surroundings of the adjacent **RAI exhibition centre**: a complex of trade and conference centres built a few years back as part of the city's plan to attract more business people to the city – along with their considerable expense accounts. It's of little general appeal (though one hall does sporadically host concerts), but if you're at a loose end you may find one of its many exhibitions interesting. The **Olympic Stadium**, built for the 1928 games, is a useful landmark; just north of it is the **Haarlemmermeer Station**, terminus of the summer museum tram which runs several times a day to the Amsterdamse Bos further south, technically outside the city limits in Amstelveen.

The **Amsterdamse Bos** is the city's largest open space, a 2000-acre woodland park planted during the 1930s in a mammoth project to utilise the wasted energies of the city's unemployed. Once a bleak area of flat, marshy fields, it combines a rural feel with that of a well-tended city park. The Bosbaan, a 1km-long canal in the north of the park, is used for boating and swimming; there are children's playgrounds and spaces for various sports, including ice skating; there's a reserve in the south containing bison and buffalo; or you can simply jog your way around a choice of fourteen planned trails. If it's out of season or you're not into old trams, take one of the buses (#170, #171, #172) which run directly from Stationsplein. Once there, the best way to get around is to hire a bicycle (March–Oct) from the main entrance on Van Nijenrodee-weg and follow the 27 miles of path. It's also possible to hire canoes, canal bikes and motor boats. Maps and basic information are available from the Bosmuseum (see p.89), a few kilometres along the Bosbaan from the main entrance.

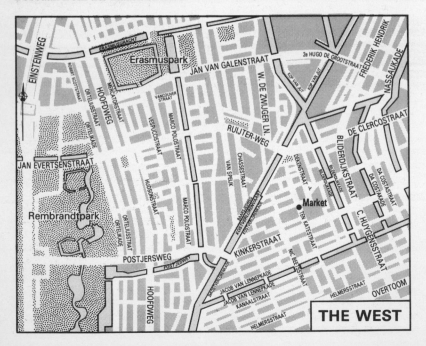

THE WEST

The West

Of all Amsterdam's outer central districts, Amsterdam **WEST** is probably the least appealing, primarily a residential area with only a couple of nondescript parks as possible destinations. There's the **OLD WEST**, whose busy Turkish and Middle Eastern immigrant-based streetlife can be worth checking out if you find yourself in the vicinity: **Kinkerstraat** is a good place to bargain-hunt if you're not after anything fancy, and there's also the vigourous **ten Katestraat market**, about halfway down the street on the right. But outside of this zone, in the districts of Bos en Lommer and Overtoomse Veld, there's little other than the large – but on the whole mediocre – **Rembrandtpark** to draw you out this far.

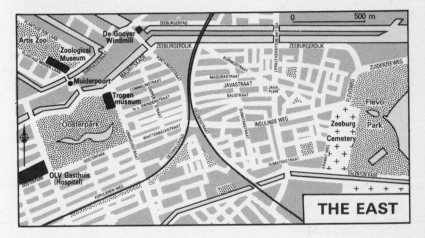

The East

A cupolaed box splattered with graffiti and topped with a crudely carved pediment, the sturdy **Muiderpoort** marks the boundary between Amsterdam's centre and the beginning of Amsterdam **EAST**. Across the canal the gabled and turreted **Royal Tropen Institute** – a more respectable label for what was once home of the Royal Colonial Institute – has a marble-and-stucco entrance hall which you can peek into, though the only part open to visitors is the excellent Tropenmuseum around the corner (see p.86).

Behind the Tropen Institute, the **Oosterpark** is a peaceful oblong of green, and a gentle introduction to the area, which extends south and east, a solidly working-class district for the most part, particularly on the far side of Linnaeustraat. There's a high immigrant presence here, and the street-names – Molukkenstraat, Madurastraat, Javaplein – reflect Holland's colonial past, an era which, after the war, ended in defeat and humiliation as the Dutch struggled to hang on to territories they were in no position to defend.

Today the housing is still relatively poor, though there's ambitious urban renewal going on, and many of the ageing terraced houses have been torn down to make way for new and better-equipped public housing. As in the Old

South, there's an underlying drug problem in this area, but while you're unlikely to need (or want) to come out here, it's by no means a forbidding district. Two things which may make you decide to visit (apart from the Zeeburg campsite, p.34) are the **Dapperstraat market** – a kind of Eastern equivalent to the Albert Cuyp – and, at the end of tram routes #3 and #10, the **Flevopark**, dull in itself but giving access to the Ijsselmeer and patches of Dutch countryside right out of Ruisdael. Just in front, the drab **Zeeburg Jewish cemetery** was once the city's major burial place for impoverished Jews, but few graves remain today. **Nieuwe Oosterbegraafplaats**, also in the East, is more significant: though not an exclusively Jewish cemetery, it holds an urn containing the ashes of some of those who died at Buchenwald, and a glass memorial – symbolically cracked – to the internees of Auschwitz, with an accompanying plate inscribed with the words of contemporary Dutch novelist, Jan Wolkers: "Auschwitz – Never again".

BARS *Keyser's, 't Orkestje, Welling, Wildschut.*

COFFEE SHOPS **"Non–smoking"** *Granny, The Sandwich Shop.*

RESTAURANTS **Chinese, Japanese and Thai** *New San Kong, Umeno.* **French** *Beddington's.* **Indian** *New Delhi, Rishi Roti Room.* **Indonesian** *Sama Sebo.* **North, Latin and South American** *Cajun Louisiana Kitchen.* **Surinamese and Caribbean** *Sin Doe, Warung Span Macaranda.*

HOTELS/HOSTELS *Abba, Acca, Adam and Eva, Bema, Casa Cara, Centralpark West, Cok Budget, Fita, Museum, Museumzicht, Van Ostade, Piet Hein, Prinsen, Sleep-In, Smit, Toff's Apartments* (gay), *Verdi Sachiko,Vondel, Vondel Park, Vullings.*

CHAPTER TWO

MUSEUMS AND GALLERIES

Slogging around museums isn't everyone's idea of fun, and you may find more than enough visual stimulation in Amsterdam's mansions and *grachten*. But the city has a superb concentration of galleries, of which three – the **Rijksmuseum**, the **van Gogh** and the **Stedelijk** – rank among the best in the world. Add to this over thirty small museums (including the **Anne Frank House**, an excellent **Jewish Historical Museum**, and the beautiful hidden church of the **Amstelkring**), and you get some idea of just how impressive that concentration is. The listings below, combined with the map on the following pages, should help you choose.

If you intend to visit more than a couple of museums it's advisable to buy a **museumcard**. Available from the *VVV* (f25 if you're under 26, f40 otherwise), this card is valid for a year and grants free entry to all state and municipally run museums, not only in Amsterdam but throughout the country. You need to take a passport photo along to get one, but considering it costs f6.50 to visit the Rijksmuseum alone, it's a bargain if you intend to visit more than a couple of museums; where museumcards *aren't* accepted we've said so. An alternative is the **Cultureel Jongeren Paspoort** or **CJP**, which for f25 gets you reductions in museums, and on theatre, concert and *filmhuis* tickets – though these can vary greatly, and are often not that substantial. Valid throughout the country and in Belgium, it's available only to those under 35 and can be bought from the *Uitburo* in the Stadsschouwburg on Leidseplein. Incidentally, **entry-prices for kids** are usually half that of the adult admission.

Opening times, particularly of state-run museums, tend to follow a pattern: closed on Monday, open from 10am to 5pm Tuesday to Saturday and from 1 to 5pm on Sunday and public holidays. Almost all the museums offer at least basic **information** in English or a written English guide. Most have temporary special exhibitions or *tentoonstelling*; the best way to find out what's showing is to pick up a free copy of the English *Museum Magazine*, available from any museum. "Museum Agenda" in *Uitkrant* and *What's On In Amsterdam* are also useful for up-to-the-minute listings.

Finally, if you like to take your museums the easy way, between April and October the *VVV* runs a **museum boat** from the Centraal Station: it stops at the Anne Frank House, Amsterdam Historical Museum, Rijksmuseum, van

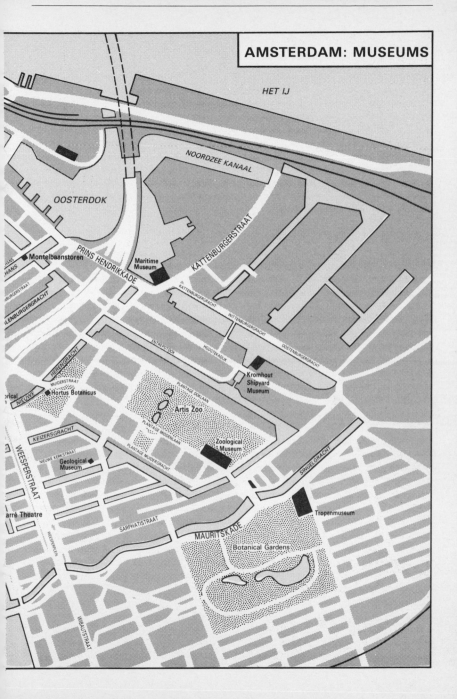

AMSTERDAM: MUSEUMS

HET IJ

NOORDZEE KANAAL

OOSTERDOK

KATTENBURGERSTRAAT

PRINS HENDRIKKADE

Montelbaanstoren

Maritime Museum

KATTENBURGERGRACHT

WITTENBURGERGRACHT

ENTREPOTDOK

NOORDERKADIJK

OOSTENBURGERGRACHT

HERENGRACHT

MUIDERSTRAAT

Hortus Botanicus

NIEUWE

PLANTAGE DOKLAAN

Artis Zoo

PLANTAGE MIDDENLAAN

Kromhout Shipyard Museum

KEIZERSGRACHT

NIEUWE KERKSTRAAT

PLANTAGE MUIDERGRACHT

Geological Museum

Zoological Museum

SINGELGRACHT

WEESPERSTRAAT

arré Theatre

WEESPERPLEIN

SARPHATSTRAAT

MAURITSKADE

Tropenmuseum

Botanical Gardens

WIBAUTSTRAAT

Gogh and Stedelijk Museums, Rembrandt House, Jewish Historical Museum and the Maritime Museum. Tickets cost around f10 and are valid all day, allowing gentle canal hops; the first of five boats leaves at 9.30am, Tuesday to Saturday only. There's also the **Canal Bus** service, which takes in the central museums all year round; see *Basics* for details.

THE MAJOR COLLECTIONS

The Rijksmuseum

Stadhouderskade 42. Tues–Sat 10am–5pm, Sun 1–5pm; f6.50. Tram #7, #10, #16, #24, #25. The Dutch paintings section is always open; if, however, you specifically want to see another department, phone ☎732 121 to check opening hours. Free half-hourly films give the background to the major paintings; for more on Dutch art and artists, see p.186.

Housed in a whimsical neo-Gothic structure built by P. J. H. Cuijpers in 1885, the **RIJKSMUSEUM** is the one museum you shouldn't leave Amsterdam without visiting, if only briefly. Its **seventeenth-century Dutch paintings** constitute far and away the best collection to be found anywhere, with twenty or so Rembrandts alone, as well as copious arrays of works by Steen, Hals, Vermeer and many other Dutch artists of the era – all engagingly displayed with the layperson in mind. There are, too, representative displays of all other pre-twentieth–century periods of Dutch and Flemish painting, along with treasures in the **medieval art** and **Asiatic** sections that are not to be missed. To do justice to the place demands repeated visits; if time is limited, it's best to be content with the core paintings and a few selective forays into other sections.

Paintings of the fifteenth to seventeenth centuries

Starting from the first floor shop, the eastern wing runs chronologically through the Rijksmuseum's collection of Low Countries painting. First off are works from the early **NETHERLANDISH PERIOD**, when divisions between present-day Holland and the Flemish south weren't as sharp as they are today. The canvases here are stylised, commissioned either by the church or by rich patrons who wanted to ensure a good deal come the Day of Judgement, and thus tended to illustrate religious themes. This means they're usually full of symbols and allusions, and often set against a suitably ecclesiastical backdrop – as with the *Madonna Surrounded by Female Saints*, painted by an unknown artist referred to (after this picture) as the Master of the Virgin Among Virgins. Of the artists here, though, the work of **Geertgen tot Sint Jans** is the most striking: his *Holy Kindred*, painted around 1485, is a skilfully structured portrait of the family of Anna, Mary's mother, that illustrates the symbolism of the period. The Romanesque nave represents the Old Testament, the Gothic choir the New; Mary and Joseph in the foreground parallel the figures of Adam and Eve in the altarpiece; lit candles on the choir screen bring illumination, and Joseph holds a lily, emblem of purity, over Mary's head. Alongside

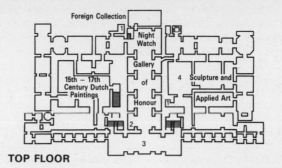

TOP FLOOR

THE RIJKSMUSEUM

1 Toilets
2 Information
3 Museum Shop
4 Auditorium / Film Theatre
5 Restaurant
6 Reading Room
7 Educational Services
8 Cloakroom

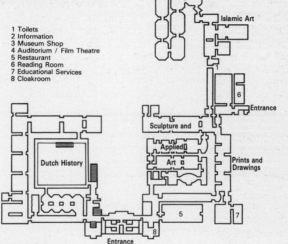

GROUND FLOOR

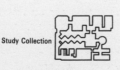

Study Collection

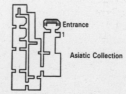

BASEMENT

are Geertgen's *Adoration of the Magi*, full of humility and with an engaging fifteenth-century backdrop of processions, castles and mountains, and his *Tree of Jesse*, crammed with tumbling, dreamlike medieval characters. An even clearer picture of the Low Countries in the Middle Ages comes across in *The Seven Works of Charity*, attributed to the **Master of Alkmaar**. Originally hung in St. Laurenskerk in Alkmaar, each of the panels shows the charitable acts expected of those with sufficient piety (and cash): alms are doled out to the poor against a toytown landscape of medieval Alkmaar.

The rooms move into the sixteenth century with the work of **Jan van Scorel**, represented here by a voluptuous *Mary Magdalen*, next to which is his pupil **Maerten van Heemskerck's** portrait of Master of the Mint *Pieter Bicker*, shiftily counting out the cash. Farther on, the gallery opens out to reveal soft, delicate compositions, most notably **Cornelis Cornelisz van Haarlem's** *Bathsheba* and *Fall of Man*, in which the artist (typically) is more concerned with the elegant and faintly erotic arrangement of his nudes than with the biblical stories that inspired them.

After this begin the classic paintings of the **DUTCH GOLDEN AGE**: portraits by Hals and Rembrandt, landscapes by Jan van Goyen and Jacob van Ruisdael, the riotous scenes of Jan Steen and the peaceful interiors of Vermeer and Pieter de Hooch. First, though, are some early seventeenth-century works, including **Frans Hals'** expansive *Isaac Massa and His Wife* and more sensational paintings such as **Dirck van Baburen's** *Prometheus in Chains* – a work from the Utrecht School, which used the paintings of Caravaggio as its model. Through a small circular gallery devoted to the miniatures of Hendrik Avercamp (skating scenes mostly) and Adriaen van Ostade (grotesque peasants) are a number of thoroughly Dutch works, among them the soft, tonal river scenes of **Salomon van Ruisdael** and the cool church interiors of **Pieter Saenredam**. Search out especially Saenredam's *Old Town Hall of Amsterdam*, in which the tumbledown predecessor of the current building (now the Royal Palace) is surrounded by black-hatted townsmen in a set piece of seventeenth-century daily life.

Beyond this is a mixed selection of canvases from the hands of **Jacob van Ruisdael** – Salomon's nephew but, though also a landscapist, quite different in style – and of **Rembrandt** and some of his better-known pupils. Perhaps the most striking is the *Portrait of Maria Trip*, but look, too, at Ferdinand Bol's *Portrait of Elizabeth Bas*, Govert Flinck's *Rembrandt as a Shepherd* – interesting if only for its subject – and the *Portrait of Abraham Potter* by **Carel Fabritius**, this last a restrained, skilful work painted by one of Rembrandt's most talented (and shortest-lived) students.

The next rooms take you into the latter half of the seventeenth century, and include works ranging from **Gerrit Berckheyde's** crisp depictions of Amsterdam and Haarlem, to the carousing peasants of **Jan Steen**. Steen's *Morning Toilet* is full of associations, referring either to pleasures just had or about to be taken, while his *Feast of St. Nicholas*, with its squabbling children, makes the festival a celebration of pure greed – much like the drunken gluttony of the *Merry Family* nearby. And the out-of-control ugliness of *After the Drinking Bout* leaves no room for doubt about what Steen thought of all this ribaldry.

It's in the last few rooms, though, that the Dutch interior really comes into its own, with a gentle moralising that grows ever more subtle. **Vermeer's** *The Letter* reveals a tension between servant and mistress – the lute on the woman's lap was a well-known sexual symbol of the time – and the symbolism in the use of a map behind the *Young Woman Reading a Letter* hints at the far-flung places her loved one is writing from. **Gerard ter Borch**, too, depicts apparently innocent scenes, both in subject and title, but his *Lady with a Mirror* glances in a meaningfully anxious manner at her servants, who look on with delicate irony from behind dutiful exteriors, and the innocently named *Interior Scene* is clearly taking place in a brothel. The paintings of **Pieter de Hooch** are less symbolic, more exercises in lighting, but they're as good a visual guide to the everyday life and habits of the seventeenth-century Dutch bourgeoisie as you'll find. So, too, with **Nicholas Maes**, whose *Woman Saying Grace* is not so much a moral tableau as a simple celebration of experience.

Mingling with these interior scenes are more paintings by **Hals** and **Rembrandt** – later works, for the most part, from the painters' mature periods. Hals weighs in with a handful of portraits, including the boisterous *Merry Toper*, while Rembrandt – at his most private and expressive best here – is represented by a portrait of his first wife *Saskia*, a couple of his mother, and a touching depiction of his cowled son, *Titus*. All are in marked contrast to studio-mate Jan Lievens' stiff though perceptive *Constantin Huygens* on the opposite wall, a commissioned work if ever there was one. There was some criticism of this painting among Huygens' high-ranking friends, though Huygens himself seemed pleased enough with it, claiming that the thoughtful expression accurately "reflected the cares of my heart".

A small room off to the side of the last one offers an introduction to the **GALLERY OF HONOUR** and one of the Rijksmuseum's great treasures – Rembrandt's *The Night Watch*, the most famous and most valuable of all the artist's pictures, recently restored after being slashed by a vandal in 1975. The painting is a so-called Civil Guard portrait, named after the bands of militia that got together in the sixteenth century to defend the home front during the wars with the Spanish. They later grew into social clubs for local dignitaries – most of whom would commission a group portrait as a mark of prestige. This, of the Guards of the Kloveniersdoelen in Amsterdam, was erroneously tagged *The Night Watch* in the nineteenth century – a result both of the romanticism of the age and the fact that for years the painting was covered in soot. There are other misconceptions about the painting, most notably that it was this work that led to the downward shift of Rembrandt's standing with the Amsterdam elite. In fact, there's no evidence that the militia group weren't pleased with the picture, or that Rembrandt's commissions flowed in any more slowly after he had completed it. Though not as subtle as much of the artist's later work, it's an adept piece, full of movement and carefully arranged – these paintings were collections of individual portraits as much as group pictures, and part of the problem in creating one was to include each individual face while simultaneously producing a coherent group scene. The sponsors paid for a prominent position in the painting, and the artist had also to reflect this.

The four surrounding paintings also depict various companies of the Kloveniersdoelen, and they make for interesting comparison. On the left, **Bartholomeus van der Helst's** portrait is probably the best of the lot: it's lively and colourful, but like the other three its arrangement and lighting are static. Van der Helst's painting also includes (as was usual) a self-portrait of the artist, here on the far left of the picture – as does that by **Govert Flinck**, on the top far right of this picture, and in both of his other portraits. It seems Rembrandt didn't bother with this, though art historians have been speculating for centuries about whether the pudgy face peering out from the back of the *Night Watch*, between the soldier and the gesticulating militiaman, could be the artist making a rare Hitchcockian appearance.

Elsewhere, the Gallery of Honour houses the large-scale works from the museum's collection of Dutch paintings. Some of these are notable only for their size – the selection of naval battles particularly – but a number do stand out, and would in any museum. Two of Rembrandt's better-known pupils crop up here: **Nicholas Maes**, with one of his typically intimate scenes in *Dreaming*, and **Ferdinand Bol**, both in his *Regents of the Nieuwe Zijds Workhouse* and the elegantly composed *Venus and Adonis*. The dashing *Self-portrait* is his too, a rich and successful character leaning on a sleeping cupid. By way of contrast, Rembrandt himself follows with a late *Self-portrait*, caught in mid-shrug as the Apostle Paul, a self-aware and defeated old man. Opposite, *The Stallmeesters* is an example of one of his later commissions and, as do so many of Rembrandt's later works, it demonstrates his ability to capture a staggering range of subtle expressions. Nearby is *The Jewish Bride*, one of his very last pictures, finished in 1665. No one knows who the people are, nor whether they are actually married (the title came later), but the painting is one of Rembrandt's most telling, the paint dashed on freely and the hands joining lovingly in, as Kenneth Clark wrote, a "marvellous amalgam of richness, tenderness and trust".

The Foreign Collection

Tucked away in a small gallery behind the *Night Watch*, the Rijksmuseum's collection of **FOREIGN PAINTINGS** is undoubtedly overshadowed by the quality of the surrounding homegrown works. Aside from a scattering of **Belgian** artists – lusty Jordaens and the bloated pink subjects of Rubens and van Dyck – **Italian** works are the collection's mainstay. These include a beautiful embossed *Mary Magdalen* by Crivelli, a dignified *Portrait of a Nobleman* by Paolo Veronese and a couple of *Portraits* by Pietro di Cosimo. A tiny collection, and one, not surprisingly, often overlooked.

Later Dutch Painting

To pick up chronologically where the Gallery of Honour left off, it's necessary to move down to the ground floor, where the **eighteenth- and nineteenth-century DUTCH PAINTINGS** collection begins with the work of **Cornelis Troost**, whose eighteenth-century comic scenes earned him the dubiously deserved title of the "Dutch Hogarth". More enduring are the later pictures, notably the pastels of Pierre-Paul Prud'hon & **Jan Ekels'** *The Writer* – small and simple, the lighting and attention to detail imitative of Vermeer.

After this, rooms follow each other in haphazard fashion, with sundry landscapes and portraiture from the lesser nineteenth-century artists. **Jongkind** is best of the bunch, his murky *River Landscape in France* typical of the Impressionism that was developing in the nineteenth century. The chief proponents of Dutch Impressionism originated from or worked in The Hague, and the handy label of the **Hague School** covers a variety of styles and painters who shared a clarity and sensitivity in their depiction of the Dutch landscape. Of the major Hague School painters, the Rijksmuseum is strongest on the work of **Jan Weissenbruch**, whose land- and seascapes, such as *View near the Geestbrug*, hark back to the compositional techniques of van Ruisdael, and that of the **Maris Brothers**. Jacob Maris' sultry landscapes are the most representative of the School, while the younger Willem Maris' work is more direct and approachable – his *Ducks* being a good example. **Anton Mauve** is similar, filling such pictures as *Morning Ride on the Beach* with shimmering gradations of tone that belie the initial simplicity of the scene.

While members of the Hague School were creating gentle landscapes, a younger generation of Impressionist painters working in Amsterdam – the **Amsterdam School** – was using a darker palette to capture city scenes. By far the most important picture from this turn-of-the-century group is **G. H. Breitner'**s *Singelbrug near Paleisstraat in Amsterdam*, a random moment in the street recorded and framed with photographic dispassion. Breitner worked best when turning his attention to rough, shadowy pictures of the city as in *Rokin* and *Damrak*, though splotchy colours give his beach scenes – *Donkey Rides on the Beach*, particularly – a movement lacking in the works of the Hague School. Isaac Israëls' work is both lighter in tone and mood, his canvases showing how close he was to the French Impressionists of the period.

Dutch History

The **Dutch history section** starts promisingly with exhibitions depicting aspects of life in the Golden Age, and not surprisingly focusses on the naval might that brought Holland its wealth. Fearsome **model ships** impress, but more revealing of everyday life are the maritime odds and ends from the *Witte Leeuw*, an East Indian vessel that sank in 1613 laden with a cargo of pepper and Chinese porcelain. The galleries off this room, however, are for the most part uninspired, filled with relics of Holland's naval and colonial past. The prize for the most conspicuous exhibit goes to **Willem Pieneman** for his painting of the *Battle of Waterloo*, a vast canvas that took six years to complete. All the big names of the battle are there (the artist spent two years on the portrait studies alone) but it's nevertheless a laboured, rather arid piece.

Sculpture and Applied Art

The Rijksmuseum has a huge amount of applied art, so unless your tastes are eclectic it's wise to restrict yourself to a single period: easily the most impressive is the first-floor collection of **Medieval and Renaissance applied art**. Beginning with a handful of Byzantine trinkets and Limoges enamels, the collection leads off the main hall with the magnificent *Ten Mourners*, sensitive fifteenth-century figures taken from the tomb of Isabelle de Brabant in Antwerp. Contemporaneous with these is the fifteenth-century **carving**, especially the work of **Adriaen van Wesel** of Utrecht, whose scenes, (for example, the *Meeting of the Magi)*, are packed with vigour and expression. Look out, too, for the *Anna te Drieën*, carvings of the infant Jesus with Mary and her mother Anna – a popular grouping in the Low Countries at this time.

Other galleries here are stuffed from floor to ceiling with **delftware**, the blue-and-white ceramics to which Delft gave its name in the seventeenth century. The original designs were stylised copies of Chinese ceramics imported by the Dutch East Indies Company, but the patterns quickly fell into the domestic traditions of landscapes, animals and comic figures. By the early years of the eighteenth century, Delft's craftspeople had become confident enough to create vases, jars and even musical intruments, in polychrome as well as the traditional blue and white. Examples of each and every period are here, but you'll need an inexhaustable interest to cope with so large a collection.

Of the rest, much of the ground floor is a warehouse of furniture, ceramics and textiles from the sixteenth century on: dull beyond belief, with only the **dolls' houses** providing diversion.

The Asiatic Collection

Holland's colonial connection with the East means that Asian art can be found in most of the museums' collections, but the **Asian collection** proper holds its most prized treasures. Of the different cultures, **China** and **Japan** are best represented: the striking twelfth-century *Statue of Avalokiteshvara* and graceful *Paintings* by Kao Ch'i-p'ei, drawn with his fingernails, are highlights of the Chinese collection, while the seventeenth-century **ceramics** and **lacquerwork** are the best of the Japanese. If you're interested, you'll find much more, from twelfth-century Indonesian gold jewellery to Cambodian carving. An excellent collection, and one to linger over.

Rijksmuseum Vincent van Gogh

Paulus Potterstraat 7. Tram #2, #3, #5, #12, #16. Tues–Sat 10am–5pm, Sun 1–5pm; f10. Informative cassettes are on hire to guide you around the highlights of the permanent collection. During summer there are sometimes also half-hour playlets on different aspects of the artist's life, roughly every hour in the downstairs auditorium, price f3.50. For information on courses, held in spring and autumn, and on the walk-in studio sessions (summer and winter), ask at the workshop.

Vincent van Gogh is arguably the most popular, most reproduced and most talked-about of all modern artists, so it's not surprising that the **RIJKSMUSEUM VINCENT VAN GOGH**, opened in 1973 and comprising the extensive collection of the artist's art-dealer brother Theo, is Amsterdam's top tourist attraction. Housed in an angular building designed by the aged Gerritt Rietveld, it's a gentle and unassuming introduction to the man and his art – and one which, due both to the quality of the collection and the building, succeeds superbly well.

The museum starts with a group of works by van Gogh's better-known friends and contemporaries, many of whom influenced his work – Gauguin, Emile Bernard, Adolph Monticelli and others. It moves on to the works of the man himself, for the most part chronologically. The first go back to the artist's **early years** in Nuenen, southern Holland, where he was born: dark, sombre works for the most part, ranging from an assortment of drab grey and brown *Still Lifes* to the gnarled faces and haunting, flickering light of *The Potato Eaters* – one of van Gogh's best-known paintings, and the culmination of hundreds of studies of the local peasantry.

Across the hall, the sobriety of these early works is easily transposed on to the **Parisian** urban landscape, particularly in his *View of Paris*, where the city's domes and rooftops hover below Montmartre under a glowering, blustery sky. But before long, under the sway of fellow painters and, after the bleak countryside of North Brabant and the sheer colour of the city itself, his approach began to change. This is most noticeable in the views of Montmartre windmills, a couple of self-portraits, and the pictures from Asnières just outside Paris, where the artist used to travel regularly to paint. Look also at *A Pair of Shoes*, a painting that used to hang in the house van Gogh shared with Gauguin in Arles, at *Woman in the Café Tambourin* (actually a portrait of the owner, with whom the artist was friendly), and at the dazzling movement of *Edge of a Wheatfield*.

In February 1888, van Gogh moved to **Arles**, inviting Gauguin to join him a little while later. With the change of scenery came a heightened interest in colour, and the predominance of yellow as a recurring motif: it's represented best in such paintings as *Van Gogh's Bedroom* and the *Harvest at La Crau*, and most vividly in *The Yellow House*. A canvas from the artist's *Sunflowers* series is justly one of his most lauded works, intensely, almost obsessively, rendered in the deepest oranges, golds and ochres he could find. Gauguin told of van Gogh painting these flowers in a near trance, and there were usually sunflowers in jars all over their house.

At the asylum in **St. Remy**, where van Gogh committed himself after snipping off part of his ear and offering it to a local prostitute, nature took a more abstract form in his work – trees bent into cruel, sinister shapes, skies coloured purple and yellow, as in the *Garden of St Paul's Hospital*. Van Gogh is at his most expressionistic here, the paint applied thickly, often with a palette knife, especially in the final, tortured paintings done at **Auvers**, including *Undergrowth*, *The Reaper*, or *Wheatfield with Crows*, in which the fields swirl and writhe under black, moving skies. It was only a few weeks after completing this last painting that van Gogh shot and fatally wounded himself.

On the second floor, the museum shows a revolving selection from its vast stock of van Gogh's **drawings**, notebooks and letters, and also affords space to relevant temporary exhibitions. The top floor is used as a **temporary exhibition space** year round, usually showing works loaned from other galleries that illustrate the artistic influences on van Gogh, or his own influence on other artists.

Stedelijk Museum

Paulus Potterstraat 13. Tram #2, #3, #5, #12, #16. Daily 11am–5pm; f7. For details of the museum's Sun performances of classical music, see p.146.

Despite its reputation as Amsterdam's number one venue for modern art, the **STEDELIJK** can be a bit of a disappointment. True, its temporary exhibitions are often of world renown, and worth catching if you happen to be in town, but the museum is primarily devoted to displays of contemporary art on loan. Should you want to see something of its extensive permanent collection (impressively complete from the nineteenth century onwards) you'll need to be here in the summer, when the museum's holdings are shown through much of July and August.

This said, the Stedelijk *is* the city's most important contemporary art exhibition space. The **ground floor** is usually given over to at least a couple of temporary exhibits, often by living European artists (some, though not all, from the museum's own stock), as is the bright two-storey **extension** at the back. Justifiably, current Dutch art often gets a thorough showing (as it does at the nearby *Museum Overland*), so keep an eye out for the work of such painters as Jan Dibbets, Rob Scholte, and Marlene Dumas – for more on whom, see p.193.

Of the museum's **permanent collection**, there's always a good (rotating) smattering hanging on the **first floor**. Briefly, and broadly, this starts off with drawings by Picasso, Matisse and their contemporaries, and moves on to paintings by major Impressionists – Manet, Monet, Bonnard – and Post-Impressionists: Ensor, van Gogh, and Cezanne. Farther on, Mondrian holds sway, from the early, muddy-coloured abstractions to the cool, boldly coloured rectangular blocks for which he's most famous. Similarly, Kasimir Malevich is well represented, his dense attempts at Cubism leading to the dynamism and, again, bold, primary tones of his "Suprematist" paintings – slices, blocks and bolts of colour that shift around as if about to resolve themselves into some complex computer graphic. You may also find a good stock of Marc Chagall's paintings (the museum owns a wide selection of his work), and a number of pictures by American Abstract Expressionists Mark Rothko, Ellsworth Kelly, and Barnett Newman. Jean Dubuffet, too, with his swipes at the art establishment, may well have a profile, and you might catch Matisse's large cut-out, *The Parakeet and the Mermaid*.

Two additional large-scale attractions are on the ground floor – Karel Appel's *Bar* in the foyer, installed for the opening of the Stedelijk in the 1950s, and the same artist's wild daubings in the museum's restaurant. But perhaps the single most interesting permanent exhibit is Ed Kienholz's *Beanery* (1965) in the basement of the museum: modelled on his local bar in Los Angeles, in this tableau the clock-faced figures, the hum of conversation, and the music create a nervous, claustrophobic background to the horror of the newspaper headline in the vending machine – "Children Kill Children in Vietnam Riots". For Kienholz, this is *real* time, and that inside the bar is "surrealist time . . . where people waste time, lose time, escape time, ignore time".

OTHER MUSEUMS

Municipal History

Amsterdam Historical Museum

Kalverstraat 92. Tram #1, #2, #4, #5, #9, #14, #16, #24, #25. Daily 11am–5pm; f3.50; guided tours on Wed and Sat at 3pm.

Housed in the restored seventeenth-century buildings of the Civic Orphanage, Amsterdam's Historical Museum attempts to survey the city's development with artefacts, paintings and documents from the thirteenth century onwards. Much is centred around the "Golden Age" of the seventeenth century: a large group of paintings portrays the city in its heyday and the good art collection shows how the wealthy bourgeoisie decorated their homes. Sadly, most of the rest of the museum is poorly documented and lacks continuity. Still, it's worth seeing for the nineteenth-century paintings and photos and, more notably, the play-it-yourself **carillion** and the **Regents' Chamber**, unchanged since the Regents dispensed civic charity there 300 years ago. Directly outside the museum, the glassed-in **Civic Guard Gallery** draws passers by with free glimpses of the large company portraits – there's a selection from the earliest of the 1540s to the lighter affairs of the seventeenth century.

Anne Frank House

Prinsengracht 263. Tram #13, #14, #17. July–Aug Mon–Sat 9am–7pm, Sun 10am–7pm; Sept–June Mon–Sat 9am–5pm, Sun 10am–5pm; f5, children f3; no museumcards.
See p.55.

Kromhout Shipyard Museum

Hoogte Kadijk 147. Bus #22, #28. Mon–Fri 10am–4pm; f2.50 (includes guided tour), no museumcards.

The Kromhout shipyard was one of the few survivors of the decline in shipbuilding during the nineteenth century. It struggled along producing engines and iron ships until it closed in 1969 and was saved from demolition by being turned into a combination of industrial monument, operating shipyard, and museum. Money is still tight, which means that little shipbuilding or restoring is going on at the moment, but the enthusiastic staff and good explanatory background material make this an up-and-coming place, and a useful adjunct to the Maritime Museum nearby.

Maritime Museum

Kattenburgerplein 1. Bus #22, #28. Tues–Sat 10am–5pm, Sun 1–5pm; f5, children f3.

A fortress-like building (see p.63) housing a well-presented display of the country's maritime past in an endless collection of maps, navigational equipment and weapons, though most impressive are the large and intricate **models** of sailing ships and men-of-war that date from the same period as the original ships. A detailed English guide book is available (necessary as all the labelling is in Dutch), and if ships and sailing are your passion you'll doubtless find the place fascinating; for the non-nautical it can be a little tedious. Best go for the highspots: a **cutaway outrigger** of 1840, the glitteringly ostentatious **Royal Barge**, and the museum's **periscope** for a seagull's eye view of the city.

Municipal Archives
Amsterdijk 67. Tram #3, #4. Mon–Fri 8.45am–4.45pm, Sat 9am–12.15pm; free.
Though the Municipal Archives holds regular exhibitions on subjects related to the city's past, extensive research facilities are its chief concern. Starting with Count Floris V's grant of toll privileges to the city in 1275 (the oldest document to mention Amsterdam by name), the Archives have a mass of material on the city; perhaps the most interesting is the photo collection, documenting changes to each of Amsterdam's streets from the nineteenth century on. All births, marriages and deaths on record from the early sixteenth century are here, and there's an extensive array of newspapers, posters, and Amsterdam-related ephemera.

Resistance Museum
Lekstraat 63. Tram #4, #12, #25. Tues–Fri 10am–5pm; Sat–Sun 1–5pm; f3.50.
Strikingly installed in a former synagogue, the Resistance Museum charts the rise of the resistance from the German invasion of The Netherlands in May 1940 to the country's liberation in 1945. The museum has a fascinating collection of contemporary material – photos, illegal newsletters, anti-Jewish propaganda and deportation orders – and it also generates interest by being interactive: slide shows and radio broadcasts start at the touch of a button, while mock-up hiding places and prison cells complete with piped-in prison sounds recreate some of the horrors faced by Dutch resistance fighters. The museum is primarily designed for those too young to have first-hand knowledge of the period, and though purists may balk at the gimmickry, its aim of revealing the brutality and thoroughness with which the Wehrmacht forces routed members of the resistance is forcefully achieved. The English guide to the exhibition, available for f1.50, is essential.

University of Amsterdam Historical Collection
O.Z.Voorburgwal 231. Tram #4, #9, #16, #24, #25. Mon–Fri 9am–5pm, but phone first for an appointment; ☎525 33 39/☎525 33 41; free.
Real specialist stuff: a collection of books, prints, letters, etc. related to the history of the city's university. Not everyone's cup of tea. . .

Canal Houses

Willet-Holthuysen Museum
Herengracht 605. Tram #4, #9, #14. Daily 11am–4pm; f1.75.
Splendidly decorated in Rococo style, this is more museum than home, containing Abraham Willet's collection of glass and ceramics. But, save for the basement kitchen, a well-equipped replica of a seventeenth-century kitchen, it's very much look-don't-touch territory. Out back there's an immaculate eighteenth-century garden – worth the price of the admission alone.

Van Loon Museum
Keizersgracht 672. Tram #4, #9, #14. Mon only, 10am–5pm; f5.
Less grand and more likeable than the nearby Willet-Holthuysen, with a pleasantly down-at-heel interior of peeling stucco and shabby paintwork. Built in 1672, the house's first tenant was the artist Ferdinand Bol; fortunately he didn't suffer the fate of many subsequent owners who seem to have been cursed with a series of bankruptcies and scandals for over two hundred years. The van Loon family bought the house in 1884, bringing with them a collection of family portraits and homely bits and pieces that stretch from 1580 to 1949.

Three other museums housed in buildings that offer a flavour of seventeenth-century Dutch interiors are the Amstelkring (see below), the Theatre Institute (p.88) and the Six Collection (p.87).

Ethnic and Religious

Amstelkring Museum
O.Z. Voorburgwal 40. Tram #4, #9, #16, #24, #25. Mon–Sat 10am–5pm, Sun 1–5pm; f3.50.
Seventeenth-century Holland was, by the standards of its contemporaries, a remarkably tolerant society: in Amsterdam many religions were accepted if not exactly encouraged, and most freedoms could be bought, either with hard cash or a proven popularity. Catholics, however, had to confine their worship to the privacy of their own homes – an arrangement which led to the growth of so-called clandestine Catholic churches throughout the city. Known as "Our Dear Lord in the Attic", this is the only one left; it occupies the loft of a wealthy merchant's house, together with those of two smaller houses behind it. The **church** itself is delightful, three balconied storeys high and reaching from the massive organ (which must have been heard all over the neighbourhood) to a mock marble altar decorated with a chubby *Baptism of Christ* by Jacob de Wit – one of three painted for the purpose. In addition, the **house** itself has been left beautifully untouched, its original furnishings (reminiscent of interiors by Vermeer or de Hooch) making the Amstelkring a tranquil and still relatively undiscovered escape from the excesses of the nearby Red Light district. One of the city's best and least demanding small museums.

Bijbels Museum
Herengracht 366. Tram #1, #2, #5. Tues–Sat 10am–5pm, Sun 1–5pm; f3, no museumcards.
A small but imaginative museum with engaging displays relating to Jewish daily life, religious ritual and the history of the Bible in Dutch. It's refreshingly eclectic, making connections across all faiths. The admission charge tends to limit its visitors to enthusiasts only, or those with time on their hands.

Jewish Historical Museum
J.D.Meijerplein. Metro to Waterlooplein, Tram #9, #14. Daily, except Yom Kippur, 11am–5pm; f5.

Housed in a former Ashkenazi synagogue complex in the old Jewish quarter of Amsterdam, the Jewish Museum is one of the most modern and impressive in western Europe; it won the 1988 European Museum of the Year award. Four synagogues, built during the seventeenth and eighteenth centuries, have been restored and linked together as a centre for the study of the history of the Jewish community that's designed to be of interest to all. The **Nieuwe Synagogue** of 1752 is the starting point of the exhibition, which includes memorabilia from the long – and, until the Nazi occupation, largely unoppressed – history of the Jews in The Netherlands. Inevitably, the most poignant part of the exhibition is from the war years, but the main focus of the display is the religious traditions of the Dutch community rather than the holocaust. As a lesson in how to combine ancient and modern, spiritual and historical, it's hard to beat.

Tropenmuseum
Linnaeusstraat 2. Tram #3, #6, #9, #10. Mon–Fri 10am–5pm, Sat–Sun noon–5pm; f6.

As part of the old Colonial Institute (now the less controversially titled Tropical Institute), this museum used to display only artefacts from the Dutch colonies. Since the 1950s, however, when Indonesia was granted independence, it has collected applied arts from all over and its holdings now cover the world. Most are on permanent exhibit and are imaginatively displayed through a variety of media – slides, videos and tapes. All of this makes for an impressively unstuffy exposition of contemporary Third World life and problems – both urban, covering the ever-expanding slum dwellings of cities such as Bombay, and rural, examining such issues as the dangerous wholesale destruction of the world's tropical rainforests. The best sections are those devoted to Africa, India and (not surprisingly) Indonesia, but it's really all worth seeing, even if you have little interest in ethnography. Also, look in on the *bookshop*, which has a good selection of books on Third World subjects, and the *Soeterijn Theatre* downstairs, which specialises in cinema, music and dance from a non-western or political angle (see p.145). Kids might be interested in the *TM Junior Museum*, detailed on p.106.

Art

Fodor Museum
Keizersgracht 609. Tram #16, #24, #25. Daily 11am–5pm; admission varies with exhibition, but normally f1. Phone ☎24 99 19 for exhibition details.

Rotating exhibitions of works by contemporary Amsterdam artists. There's an annual summer exhibition of art bought by the city council, and the museum arranges exchanges with other European capitals. Information printed in English is rare, but the museum's monthly magazine should help you keep in touch.

Overholland Museum
Museumplein 4. Tram #2, #3, #5, #12, #16. Tues–Sat 11am–5pm, Sun 1–5pm; f7.50, children f6.50.
Changing exhibitions of drawings, watercolours, and collages by contemporary (mainly European) artists. A worthy adjunct to the Stedelijk, though not really worth the steep admission charge.

Rembrandt House
Jodenbreestraat 4–6. Metro to Nieuwmarkt. Mon–Sat 10am–5pm, Sun 1–5pm; f2.
See p.60.

The Six Collection
Amstel 218. Tram #4. Apply first (with passport) at the Rijksmuseum for a note of introduction. This is essential; the house is still lived in and is extremely protective of its privacy. You most definitely won't get in without the letter. Open May 1–Oct 30 Mon–Fri 10am–noon and 2–4pm; Nov 1–April 30 Mon–Fri 10am–noon; Closed public holidays; free.
The Six Collection is deliberately underplayed in the city's tourist brochures, in part because only those with a little knowledge of Dutch art will find it rewarding, and, more importantly, because the current Baron Six, descendent of the seventeenth-century collector and burgomaster, still lives in the elaborately furnished canal house and doesn't encourage visitors – worth bearing in mind if you do come. **Rembrandt** was a friend of the burgomaster and his *Portrait of Jan Six* is the collection's greatest treasure. Painted in 1654, it's a brilliant work, the impressionistic treatment of the hands subtly focusing attention on the subject's face. Also here are Rembrandt's *Portrait of Anna Wijmer*, Six's mother, and **Hals's** portrait of another figure prominent in Rembrandt's oeuvre, *Dr. Tulp*, a great patron of the arts whose daughter married Jan Six. Other connections between the Six family and their collection are well explained by the staff, and the whole group of paintings is a must if you have any interest in seventeenth-century painting.

Film, Theatre and Literature

Multatuli Museum
Korsjepoortsteeg 20. Tram #1, #2, #5, #13, #17. Tues 10am–5pm, other times phone ☎24 74 27 for an appointment; free.
Just one large room, but an interesting one if you've even heard the man's name. Multatuli was the pen name of **Edward Douwes Dekker**, Holland's most celebrated nineteenth-century writer and a champion of freethinking. Disgusted with the behaviour of his fellow Dutch in their East Indies colonies, he returned home to get establishment backs up with his elegantly written satirical novel, *Max Havelaar*, now something of a Dutch literary classic. This is the house he lived in during his final years, filled with letters, first editions, and a small selection of original furnishings, including the chaise longue on which he breathed his last. No info in English but the attendant will keep you informed.

Netherlands Film Museum
Vondelpark 3, near the southern end of Roemer Visscherstraat. Tram #1, #2, #3, #5, #6, #12. Library and documentation centre open Tues–Fri 10am–5pm; f2.50; filmshows f8.50.

Essentially, the Netherlands Film Museum is a showcase for obscure films on a variety of subjects – not always Dutch and usually organised by theme. The library has a well-catalogued collection of books, magazines and journals, some in English, but the museum is really worth visiting only if the movies being shown seem appealing. Check *Uitkrant* or *Amsterdam This Week* for details, and look out for the Sunday market outside the museum – a dozen or so stalls selling books and posters about films past and present.

Netherlands Press Museum
International Institute for Social History, Cruquiusweg. Mon–Fri 9am–5pm, by appointment only , ☎52 53 991; free.

The history of the Dutch press since 1903, as revealed in newspapers, leaflets, posters and political cartoons. Of pretty specialised interest.

Netherlands Theatre Institute
Herengracht 168. Tram #13, #14, #17. Tues–Sun 11am–5pm; f2.50.

The Theatre Institute is one of the bolder exhibition spaces in Amsterdam, with lively, provocative recreations of contemporary stage sets alongside models that trace the earlier days of the theatre in The Netherlands. It's also a resource centre, with a library, bookshop and historical (including video) collections. If you're interested in getting to know or making contacts in the theatre, this could be the place.

Script Museum
University library, Singel 425. Tram #1, #2, #4, #9, #16, #24, #25. Mon–Fri 9.30am–1pm & and 2–4.30pm; free.

Offbeat collection of different alphabets from around the world. Thankfully the medium is often more interesting than the message – stones, snakeskins, and tree bark provide note pads for some weird hieroglyphs.

For museums specifically appealing to **kids**, see p.105.

Miscellaneous

Allard Pierson Museum
Oude Turfmarkt 127. Tram #4, #9, #14, #16, #24, #25. Tues–Fri 10am–5pm; Sat–Sun and holidays 1–5pm; f3.50, kids f1, no museumcards.

A small and excellent museum, the Allard Pierson manages to overcome the fatigue normally induced by archaeological collections by arranging high-quality exhibits in intimate galleries that encourage you to explore; also, simple background information personalises what might otherwise be meaningless objects. The museum's highlights include a remarkably well-preserved **collection of Coptic clothes** and artefacts from the sixth century, good Greek pottery and jewellery, and fine gold and precious stones from all periods.

Bos Museum
Koenenkade, Amsterdamse Bos. At the end of the Tram Museum's line, or bus #170. #171 or #172 from Centraal Station. Daily, 10am–5pm.
Information centre for visitors to the Amsterdamse Bos (see p.68), with maps and details on the park's facilities, as well as an exhibition on its history and its contemporary role.

Geological Museum
Nieuwe Prinsengracht 130. Tram #6, #7, #9, #10, #14. Mon–Fri 9am–5pm; free.
The geological collection of Amsterdam University: boring boulders, monotonous minerals and other assorted rubble. Rock fans only.

Hash Info Museum
O.Z. Achterburgwal 148. Tram #4, #9, #16, #24, #25. Daily, 10am–noon; f5.
Still going strong between intermittent battles with the police, this displays various types of dope and numerous ways to smoke it. Pipes, books, videos and plenty of souvenirs, though these days there are lots of open spaces where the police have removed the exhibits.

Hortus Botanicus
Plantage Middenlaan 2. Tram #7, #9, #14. April–Sept Mon–Fri 9am–5pm, Sat & Sun 11am–5pm; f5.
Pocket-sized botanical gardens whose 6000 plant species make a wonderfully relaxed break from the rest of central Amsterdam. Worth wandering in for the sticky pleasures of the hot houses, its terrapins, and for the world's oldest (and probably largest) potted plant. Stop off for coffee and cakes in the orangery.

Max Euwe Centre
Paleisstraat 1. Tram # 4, #9, #16, #24, #25. Mon–Fri 10.30am–4pm; free.
An interesting exhibition pertaining to the history of chess and the development of the competitive game, with a review of the career of Max Euwe – Holland's most famous chess player and only world champion to date. Chess sets are available if you feel so inspired, both the real thing and the computer variety. A good bet for chess freaks on a rainy afternoon.

Museum of Torture Instruments
Heiligweg 19, Monday-Saturday 10am–5pm.
Macabre, somewhat prurient collection of medieval punishment equipment, including a guillotine, a (used) garotte and that favourite of the Inquisition, the chair of nails. Good English info, well documented with contemporary posters.

CHAPTER THREE

SHOPS AND MARKETS

Unless you come from a very small town or do all your shopping in *Harrods*, you'll be able to find much of what's available in Amsterdam's shops at home – and often more cheaply. Where Amsterdam scores, however, is in some excellent, unusual **speciality shops** (designer clocks, rubber stamps, Indonesian arts, condoms, to name just a few), a handful of good **markets**, and its shopping convenience – the city's centre concentrates most of what's interesting within its tight borders.

There are few specific **shopping areas**. But broadly, **Nieuwendijk**, **Kalverstraat**, and **Leidsestraat** are where you'll find mass-market clothes and mainstream department stores; **Rokin**, running parallel, is more pricey; the **Jordaan**, west of the centre, is home to more specialised, more adventurous clothes shops; while to the south, **P. C. Hooftstraat**, **Van Baerlestraat**, and **Beethovenstraat** play host to designer clothiers, upmarket ceramics stores, confectioners and delicatessens. There's also the **Spiegelkwaartier**, centre of Amsterdam's antique trade, which cuts through the main canals near the Rijksmuseum. Many of the most interesting, and more specialised shops are scattered among the small streets which connect the main canals.

As for **open hours**, most shops take Monday morning off, and open from 9.30am to 5.30 or 6pm the rest of the week except Sunday; they stay open late on Thursday and close early Wednesday afternoon. Larger shops will accept **payment** with a major credit card (*American Express, Visa, Access*, etc.), but never by travellers' cheque. Most shops will, however, take Eurocheques.

Art and Design

Amsterdam is full of private **commercial art galleries**. Not confined to any specific areas, they're scattered all over the city centre, though often, because of the space the older houses offer, you'll find them along the major canals. *What's On In Amsterdam* carries selective listings of major shows, as does (with more adventurous entries, but in Dutch) *Agenda*. For an overall picture of what each gallery is about, it's best to supplement our brief listings with a current edition of *Museum Magazine*, or perhaps the *Amsterdam Art Guide*.

Since original art may be out of your price range, we've included listings of places to pick up **prints**, **posters and cards**, as well as a couple of shops selling **artists' materials**.

Galleries

Amazone, Singel 270 (☎27 90 00). Women's art and related exhibitions.

Amsterdamse Beeldhouwers Kollektief, Zeilmakersstraat 15 (☎25 63 32). Permanent exhibit of Dutch sculptors.

Art & Project, Prinsengracht 785 (☎22 03 72). Contemporary sculpture and painting from home and abroad. One of the country's major galleries.

Arti et Amicitae, Spui 1a (☎23 35 08). Impressive nineteenth-century exhibition space showing art by the members of the society of the same name. Another, more internationally-slanted space at Rokin 112.

E. H. Ariens Kappers, Nieuwe Spiegelstraat 32 (☎23 53 56). Old prints and engravings, often affordable, covering a wide range of subjects.

Elisabeth den Bieman de Haas, Nieuwe Speigelstraat 44 (☎26 10 12). Twentieth-century paintings and graphics; focus on the Cobra group.

Espace, Keizersgracht 548 (☎24 08 02). Paintings and drawings from the 1960s and 1970s.

Barbara Farber, Herengracht 340 (☎27 63 43). American avant-garde and graffiti art.

Galerie Amsterdam, Warmoesstraat 101 (☎24 74 08). Exhibitions relating to Amsterdam and environs.

Galerie d'O, Weteringstraat 39 (☎24 19 45). Erotic art by Dutch artists.

Hans Gieles, Spuistraat 3 (☎23 72 92). New developments in Dutch art.

Jurka, Singel 28 (☎26 67 33). Up-to-the-minute paintings and photographs.

C. M. Kooring-Verwindt, Speigelgracht 14–16 (☎23 65 38). Twentieth-century Dutch art. A wide selection.

Living Room, Laurierstraat 70 (☎25 84 49). Trends in Dutch art.

Mokum, OZ Voorburgwal 334 (☎24 39 58). Surrealism.

Montevideo, Buiksloterweg 5 (☎23 71 01). Video arts.

Nieuw Perspectief, Amstel 43 (☎26 39 52). Contemporary art and photography.

Nova Zembla, Korte Leidsedwarsstraat 143 (☎25 15 89). Contemporary art and art books.

Stov, Lange Leidsedwarsstraat 208 (☎23 09 67). Centre for textile art and design.

Taller, Keizersgracht 607 (☎24 67 34). Group of Latin American artists who work and exhibit in this converted coach house.

Torch, Prinsengracht 218 (☎26 02 84). Exhibitions of new photography.

Fons Welters, Palmdwarsstraat 36 (☎22 71 93). Recent sculpture and other 3-D work.

Wonen, Leidsestraat 5 (☎23 09 84). Exhibitions on architecture.

Posters, Prints and Art Supplies

Albracht-Singers, Kalverstraat 73 (☎23 18 74). Art and general stationery supplies.

Art Unlimited, Keizersgracht 510 (☎24 84 19). Enormous card and poster shop. Good for communiqués home that don't involve windmills.

Cards for Days, Huidenstraat 26 (☎24 87 75). A good bet for silly cards.

Van Beek, Stadhouderskade 63–64 (☎66 21 670). Long-established outlet for artists' materials.

Van Ginkel, Warmoesstraat 145 (☎23 89 85). Supplier of artists' materials, with the emphasis on print making.

Paper Moon, Singel 417 (☎26 16 69). Well-stocked card shop.

Bikes

Bikes can be **hired** from Centraal Station or a number of private outlets all over town – see p.26. And you may well be approached on the street by someone offering you a bike to **buy**. For a legal purchase, try either of the shops listed below, or one of the railway stations, which sell, repair and store (*stalling*) bikes.

R. P. van Heel, Hofmeijerstraat 15 (☎65 68 68). Bike repairs.

G De Flart, Overtoom 272 (☎85 09 44). Cycle sales and repairs.

P. Jonker, Spiegelgracht 12 (☎23 25 42). Good selection of used bikes.

Laut, Oude Hoogstraat 17 (☎27 92 89). Bikes, both second-hand and new.

Lohman, De Clercqstraat 70–76 (☎18 39 06). New and used bikes.

C. Markenstein, Nieuwe Hoogstraat 23–25 (☎24 61 37). Every bike part you could need.

Tweewielercentrum, Haarlemmerstraat 30 (☎25 15 81); Linnaeuparkweg 142 (☎92 81 66). New and used bikes, sales, and repairs.

Books and Magazines

Though prices are upped, virtually all Amsterdam bookshops stock at least a small selection of **English-language books**, and in the city centre, at least, it's possible to pick up most English **newspapers** the day they come out; English-language **magazines**, too, are available from newsstands and bookshops.

English Language/General

Allert de Lange, Damrak 62 (☎24 67 44). Perhaps Amsterdam's best bookshop, with a great stock of Penguins, a marvellous travel section, and an informed staff.

American Discount Book Centre, Kalverstraat 158 (☎25 55 37). As the name suggests, entirely English-language, and with especially good gay and pulp-fiction sections.

Athenaeum, Spui 14–16 (☎22 62 48). Excellent all-round bookshop, with the most complete stock of English-language magazines in the city.

De Bijenkorf, Damrak 90 (☎21 80 80). Best of the department stores for English-language books.

Bruna. A nationwide chain, and a safe bet for popular paperbacks and mainstream newspapers and magazines. Branches all over town; for the nearest, look in the phone book under *Bruna*.

The English Bookshop, Lauriergracht 71 (☎26 42 30). Exclusively English-language bookshop with a small but quirky collection of titles, many of which you won't find elsewhere.

Scheltema Holkema Vermeulen, Koningsplein 20 (☎26 72 12). One of Amsterdam's biggest and best bookshops. Five floors of everything from fiction to philosophy. Top floor has remaindered and bargain books.

Discount/Second-hand

N. C. Berg, 8–10 Oude Schans (☎24 08 48). Delightfully untidy old bookshop.

The Book Exchange, Kloveniersburgwal 58 (☎26 62 66). Good on fairly up-to-date paperbacks. See also another, unnamed, bookshop down the canal at Kloveniersburgwal 44.

The English Open Book Exchange, Prinsengracht 42 (☎27 93 37). Buys, sells, and lends used English paperbacks.

Van Gennep, N.Z. Voorburgwal 330 (☎26 44 48). Excellent discount bookshop; many bargains if you're prepared to look.

Island International, 2e Tuindwarsstraat 14a (☎26 85 09). Mainly remaindered English books. A small selection, but worth a visit.

A. Kok, Oude Hoogstraat 14–18 (☎23 11 91). Large and well-stocked second-hand bookshop. Loads of bargains, and prices down to a guilder.

Lorelei, Prinsengracht 495 (☎23 43 08). Women's/feminist second-hand books. Open Wed–Sat from noon.

De Omslag, Warmoesstraat 155 (☎24 47 08). Good fiction selection.

De Slegte, Kalverstraat 48–52 (☎22 59 33). The Amsterdam branch of a nationwide operation specialising in used and new books at a discount.

Vrouwenindruk, Westermarkt 5 (☎24 50 03). Second-hand feminist books.

Special Interest

Art/Architecture

Architectura & Natura, Leliegracht 44 (☎23 61 86). Books on architecture and interior design.

Art Book, Prinsengracht 645 (☎25 93 37). The city's best source of high-gloss art books. Keep in mind, also, the shops of the main museums, particularly the Stedelijk.

Premsela, Van Baerlestraat 78 (☎66 24 266). Slightly snooty art book specialists.

Comics

Lambiek, Kerkstraat 78 (☎26 75 43). The city's largest comic bookshop and gallery.

Stripwinkel Capitein Rob, 2e Egelantiersdwarsstraat 8 (☎22 38 69). Cartoon books, old and new.

Cookery

Kookboekhandel, Runstraat 26 (☎22 47 68). Cookery books in a variety of languages, including English, also some out-of-print treasures.

Gay and Lesbian

Intermale, Spuistraat 251–253 (☎25 00 09). Gay men's bookshop.

Vrolijk, Voetboogstraat 7 (☎23 51 42). Gay and lesbian bookshop.

Kids

De Kinderboekwinkel, 1e Bloemdwarsstraat 23 (☎22 47 61); N.Z. Voorburgwal 344 (☎22 7741). Children's books, some of which are in English. See also *Comics*, above.

Languages

Intertaal, Van Baerlestraat 76 (☎71 53 53). Teach-yourself books and dictionaries in every language you could think of.

Religion, Occult/Astrology/Mind and Body

Arcanum, Reguliersgracht 54 (☎25 08 13). Specialists in the occult.

Au Bout de la Monde, Singel 313 (☎25 13 97). Astrology, psychology, mysteries, mysticism. With record shop downstairs.

Dawn Horse, Prinsengracht 719 (☎27 52 20). Mysteries, New Age, and Aquarian books.

Het Martyrium, Va Baerlestraat 170 (☎73 20 92). Enormous selection of books on religious subjects.

Theatre

Theatre Bookshop, Leidseplein 26a (☎22 64 89). Theatre books, magazines, and cards.

Politics and Third World

Milieuboek, Henri Polaklaan 42 (☎24 49 89). Opposite Artis zoo, this store specialises in books on environmental issues.

Tropenmuseum Bookstore, Linnaeusstraat 2 (☎568 82 00). Books on Third-World politics and culture, many in English. See also *De DerdeWinkel,* listed under "Miscellaneous Shops".

Tweede Wereld Centrum, Raadhuisstraat 44 (☎27 94 91). Books, records, posters, etc, from Eastern Europe.

Travel

A la Carte, Spui 23 (☎25 06 79). Travel guides and maps.

Pied à Terre, Singel 393 (☎27 44 55). Hiking guides and maps.

Women

Xantippe, Prinsengracht 290 (☎23 58 54). Women's and feminist books and literature.

See also **Lorelei** and **Vrouwenindruk** (above), both specialists in second-hand feminist books.

Clothes

When it comes to **clothes**, Amsterdam is in many ways an ideal place to shop: prices aren't through the roof, you're not overwhelmed by the selection, and the city is small enough that a shopping trip doesn't have to destroy your feet.

But don't expect a huge selection. The city's department stores tend to be conservative, and the big international designers appear to have boycotted Amsterdam altogether. What you will find are good-value mainstream styles along Kalverstraat and – south of Dam Square – Nieuwendijk, and more upmarket stuff along the parallel Rokin and down in the south of the city on P. C. Hooftstraat, Van Baerlestraat and Beethovenstraat.

More interestingly, there's a fair array of one-off, individually-run places, youth-orientated clothes shops and/or **second-hand clothing** stores in the Jordaan, on Nieuwe Hoogstraat (a handful), or along the narrow streets that connect the major canals west of the city centre. The Waterlooplein flea market (see p.100) can also be a good hunting ground for second-hand clothes.

What follows is a brief rundown of the more exciting outlets:

New and Designer Clothes

Agnes B, Rokin 126 (☎27 14 65). Shop of the French designer.

Columbine Instant White, Nieuwe Hoogstraat 6 (☎23 15 99). Exciting designer outfits; well worth a look, especially during sale times.

Diversi, 1e Leliedwarsstraat 6 (☎25 07 73). Small but inspired collection of reasonably priced, mainly French clothes for women.

Exota, Nieuwe Leliestraat 32 (☎20 91 24); Nieuwe Hartenstraat 10 (☎23 18 88). Good, fairly priced selection of new and used clothing.

Fiorucci, Kalverstraat 128 (☎25 29 61). Amsterdam branch of the Italian clothes chain.

Hobbit, Van Baerlestraat 44 (☎66 40 779). High prices but a good, varied selection of women's clothes. Watch for sales.

Kenzo, Van Baerlestraat 66 (☎66 26 253). Outlet for one of the city's few world-renowned designers.

Mac and Maggie, Kalverstraat 53 and 172 (☎26 10 39 & 24 10 00). A rare find on the downscale reaches of Kalverstraat. Unusual colours, nice cuts, decent prices. Men and women.

Martyn van Kesteren, Reestraat 25 (☎25 63 71). Mainly Italian separates for men.

Laetitia, Nieuwe Hoogstraat 21 (☎27 39 40). Stylish – and expensive – young designs.

Pauw, Leidsestraat 16 (☎26 56 98). Mainstream, largely unexceptional separates for exceptional prices. Branches all over town.

Raymond Linhard, Van Baerlestraat 50 (☎79 07 55). Cheerful, well-priced separates.

Local Service, Keizersgracht 400–402 (☎26 68 40). Men and women's fashions. Ultra-trendy and expensive.

Look Out, St. Luciensteeg 22 (☎27 76 49); Utrechtsestraat 91 (25 50 32). Colourful coats and knits – not cheap.

De Mof, Haarlemmerdijk 107–111 (☎23 17 98). Basically an industrial clothier, selling heavy-duty shirts, baggy overalls and the like for rock-bottom prices.

Sissy Boy, Van Baerlestraat 15 (☎71 51 74). Ridiculous prices, but stunning clothes.

Edgar Vos, P. C. Hooftstraat 132–134 (☎62 63 36). Amsterdam shop of the Dutch designer.

Western House, Lealverstraat 154 (☎22 32 29). Jeans, jackets, leathers, hats, jewellery, and accessories.

Second-hand clothes

Bop Street, 1e Bloemdwarsstraat 14 (☎22 08 49). 1950s clothes and memorabilia.

Empathy, Berenstraat 16 (☎22 96 83). Vintage clothes. On the expensive side, but some very nice stuff.

The End, Nieuwe Hoogstraat 26 (☎25 31 62). Unspectacular but inexpensive.

Jojo, Huidenstraat 23 (☎23 34 76). Particularly good for trench coats and Fifties jackets.

Lady Day, Hartenstraat 9 (☎23 58 20). Good-quality second-hand women's clothes at reasonable prices.

Puck, Nieuwe Hoogstraat 1 (☎25 42 01). Vintage secondhand clothes.

Second Best, 2e Anjelierdwarsstraat 8 (☎27 52 15). More Jordaan cast-offs.

Zipper, Huidenstraat 7 (☎23 73 02); Nieuwe Hoogstraat 10 (☎27 03 53). Mainly used clothes selected for style and quality – or so it says on the door. Prices start high.

Accessories: Shoes, Hats, Jewellery

Dr. Adam's, Oude Doelenstraat 5–9 (☎22 37 34); P. C. Hooftstraat 90 (☎62 38 35). One of the city's broadest selections of shoes.

Big Shoe, Leliegracht 12 (☎22 66 45). Specially commissioned Italian shoes for larger-sized feet.

Body Sox, Keizersgracht 35 (☎27 65 53). Socks, tights and stockings in every conceivable colour and design.

Bonnier, Haarlemmerstraat 58 (☎22 16 41). Very reasonably priced bag and umbrella shop.

The English Hatter, Heiligeweg 40 (☎23 47 81). Hats and classic menswear.

Hoeden M/V, Herengracht 422 (☎26 30 38). Hats, from felt Borsalinos to straw Panamas.

Ice & Lemon, 2e Tuindwarsstraat 7 (☎23 06 60). Shoes, unusual styles. Opposite the aptly-named *Gin and Tonic*, which sells rather less interesting clothes.

Elles Portland, Keizersgracht 473. Stylish handmade jewellery.

Meijer's Schoenhandel, Nieuwendijk 96 (☎24 11 81); P. C. Hooftstraat 45 (☎64 33 55). Flamboyant men's and women's shoes.

Shoebaloo, Koningsplein 7–9 (☎26 79 93). Unisex shoes, trendy styles. See also *Bagbaloo* around the corner.

Sieradam, Hartenstraat 22 (☎26 07 49). Handmade women's jewellery: wild styles.

Tulips, 1e Leliedwarsstraat 25 (☎27 55 95). Tights and socks – a vast array.

Williams, Nieuwe Hoogstraat 5. Small range of affordable and very stylish shoes.

D. Zaal, Oude Hoogstraat 6 (☎23 01 10). Good selection of bags and suitcases.

For children's clothes see p.107.

Department Stores

Amsterdam's **department stores**, like many of the city's shops, err on the side of safety. Venture inside if you have an unfulfilled shopping urge; otherwise save them for specifics.

De Bijenkorf, Damrak 90 (☎21 80 80). Dominating the northern corner of Dam Square, this is the city's top shop, a huge bustling place that has an indisputably wide range and little of the snobbishness of a place like *Harrods* – or even *Metz* (see below).

HEMA, Nieuwendijk 174 (☎23 41 76); Reguliersbreestraat 10 (☎24 65 06). A kind of Dutch Woolworth's, and as such good for stocking up on toiletries and other essentials.

Maison de la Bonneterie, Kalverstraat 183 (☎26 21 62). Apart from the building, which rises through balustraded balconies to a high central dome, nothing special: very conservative and, on the whole, extremely expensive.

Metz & Co., Keizersgracht 455 (☎24 88 10). By far the city's swishest store, with the accent on Liberty prints, stylish ceramics and designer furniture of the kind that gets exhibited in modern art museums: just the place to pick up a Rietveld chair. If your funds won't stretch quite that far, settle for a cup of coffee in the top floor Rietveld restaurant, which affords great views over the canals.

Peek & Cloppenberg, Dam 20 (☎23 28 37). Less a department store than a multi-floored clothes shop with some painfully middle-of-the-road styles. Nonetheless, an Amsterdam institution.

Vroom & Dreesman, Kalverstraat 201–221 & 212–224 (☎22 01 71). The main Amsterdam branch of the middle-ground nationwide chain. Again, useful for essentials.

Food and Drink

Below are listings of **speciality food shops**, together with a selection of **wine and spirits shops** noted for their centrality, speciality, or sheer value, and **night shops**, which sell provisions and (often) hot meals to take away and are open 4pm–1am.

For home cooking and economical eating and drinking, the most central **supermarkets** are those of the *Mignon* chain, which has branches at Nieuwendijk 175 (☎24 40 78); Leidsestraat 76 (☎27 19 00); and Reguliersbreestraat 19 (☎24 29 94). The outlets of the larger *Albert Heijn* and *Dagmarkt* groups are listed in the Yellow Pages under *Supermarkten*.

Speciality Food Shops

Bread

Paul Année, Runstraat 25 (☎23 53 22); Bellamystraat 2–4 (☎18 31 13). The best wholemeal bread in town; also try the *speculaas* and fruit and nut loaf.

Van Muyden, Leidsestraat 18 (☎27 77 61). Specialises in different types of bread, plain and filled; a good option, too, for a cheap on-your-feet lunch.

Cheese

Robert & Abraham Kef, Marnixstraat 192 (☎26 22 10). A wide range of French cheeses and facilities for tasting. Otherwise, for ordinary Dutch *Goudas*, etc., central cheese shops include **Kaasland**, Haarlemmerdijk 1; **Arxhoek**, Damstraat 23; **Say Cheese**, Herenstraat 23; **De Waag**, Nieuwemarkt 6.

Coffee and Tea

Geels & Co., Warmoesstraat 67 (☎24 06 83). Oddly situated among the porno shops of Warmoesstraat, this is the city's oldest and best-equipped specialist in coffee and tea.

Keyser, Prinsengracht 180. Beautiful old-fashioned interior and friendly service.

't Zonnetje, Haarlemmerdijk 45 (☎23 00 58). Tea and coffee dealer, and herbalist.

Delis

Dikker & Thijs, Leidsestraat 82 (☎25 88 76). The city's best-known gourmet shop, with an unrivalled selection of fine wines, fish, cooked meats, cheeses and hors d'oeuvres. The prices are, to say the least, sobering.

Eichholtz, Leidsestraat 48 (☎22 03 05). Smaller and cheaper than *Dikker & Thijs*.

Fish

Dikker & Thijs (above) are good for fish, and for both lunchtime snacks and take-away meals there are centrally located fish and seafood **stalls** on Nieuwmarkt; Westermarkt; Utrechtsestraat at Herengracht; Raadhuisstraat at Singel; and on Stadhouderskade near Leidseplein. And a good central **shop**, *De Kreeft*, on Muntplein at Vijzelstraat 3.

Health Food

De Bast, Huidenstraat 11 (☎23 04 50). Health food shop with a sister restaurant up the street (see p.132).

De Belly, Nieuwe Leliestraat 174 (☎24 52 81). Small and very friendly shop stocking all things organic.

Manna, Spui 1 (☎25 37 43); Ferdinand Bolstraat 122 (☎71 65 14); Lijnbaansgracht 119 (☎27 72 97). Largest and best of the city's health food shops, and with a small café upstairs.

De Zonnebloem, Haarlemmerdijk 174 (☎26 63 10). Small, adequately stocked health food shop. Now owned by *Manna*; see above.

Pastries and Sweets

Berkhoff, Leidsestraat 46. Elegant handmade pastries and chocolates.

J. G. Beune, Haarlemmerdijk 158 (☎24 83 56). Handmade cakes and chocolates in an old-style interior.

Arnold Cornelis, Van Baerlestraat 93 (☎66 21 228); Elandsgracht 78 (☎25 85 85). The apple tart is a treat.

Kwekkeboom, Reguliersbreestraat 36 (☎23 68 47); Damstraat 20 (☎24 83 65). One of the city's most famous pastry shops, showered with awards for its goods. Not cheap, but you're paying for the *chocolatier*'s equivalent of Gucci.

Landskroon, Singel 385 (☎23 77 43). Amsterdam's best pastry shop, with a small area for on-the-spot consumption.

Wines and Spirits

Chateau P. C. Hooft, Honthorststraat 1 (☎6649 371). Extensive but expensive off-licence on the corner of the chic P.C. Hooftstraat.

Hart's Wijnhandel, Vijzelgracht 3 (☎23 83 50); Nieuwe Spiegelstraat 41 (☎23 40 21); Koninginneweg 143 (☎66 25 250). Beer, wine and spirits from the cheap to the pocket-stinging.

Het Karbeel, Warmoesstraat 58 (☎27 49 95). Wine and cheese shop with a small mezzanine café for lunch and regular exhibitions of contemporary art. Open Thurs until 9pm.

J. G. Kievit, Haarlemmerstraat 7 (☎22 27 81). Central and well-stocked wine and spirits shop.

1001 Bieren, Huidenstraat 21 (☎23 77 11). International beer shop.

De Vergulden Poort, Brouwersgracht. Wine warehouse with wine by the bottle or case.

H. P. de Vreng, Nieuwendijk 75 (☎24 45 81). Nine thousand miniature bottles on sale in a celebrated wine and spirits store.

Night Shops

Baltus, Vijzelstraat 127 (☎26 90 69).

Big Bananas, Leidsestraat 76 (☎27 19 00).

Dolf's, Willemstraat 79 (☎26 75 10).

Doorneveld Avondverkoop, De Clercqstraat 1 (☎18 17 27).

Markets

Amsterdam's markets are more diverting than its shops. There's a fine central **flea market** on Valkenburgerstraat, vibrant **street markets** such as the Albert Cuyp, emphasising food and cheap clothing, and smaller **weekly markets** devoted to everything from stamps and flowers to (somewhat cruelly) birds.

General and Flea Markets

Albert Cuyp, Mon–Sat 9am–4.30pm. Amsterdam's best-known – and best – general market.

Boerenmarkt (Noordermarkt). Sat 10am–1pm. Organic produce, handicrafts – and exotic birds.

Dapperstraat, Mon–Sat 9am–4pm. Daily general market.

Lindengracht, Sat 9am–4pm. General market.

Waterlooplein Mon–Sat 10am–4pm. New and second-hand clothes, antiques, junk, books and bikes. Amsterdam's best and most enjoyable browse.

Westerstraat, Mon 7.30am–1.30pm. General market.

Specialised Markets

Antiques

Nieuwmarkt, May–Sept Sun 10am–5pm . Good-quality antiques.

Noordermarkt, Mon 7.30am–1.30pm. More junk than antiques.

"De Looier", Elandsgracht Mon–Thurs 11am–5pm, Sat 9am–5pm. Indoor antiques stalls, selling a wide variety of goods.

Books

Oudemannhuispoort, Mon–Sat 10am–4pm.

Flowers

Bloemenmarkt, on the Singel between Muntplein and Koningsplein. Mon–Sat 9am–4.30pm. Plants and flowers, pots and bulbs, sold from stalls on floating barges. Very reasonable.

Amstelveld, Kerkstraat at Reguliersgracht Mon 10am–3pm.

Stamps

N. Z. Voorburgwal, between Dam Square and Spui. Wed & Sat 10am–4pm.

Miscellaneous and Ethnic

Perhaps more than any other place in Europe, Amsterdam is a great source for shops devoted to one particular product or interest. What follows is a selection of favourites:

Akkerman, Kalverstraat 149 (☎23 16 49). Vast array of pens, inks and writing implements.

Baobab, Elandsgracht 128 (☎26 83 98). Textiles, jewellery and ceramics from Indonesia and the Far East.

Jan Best, Keizersgracht 357 (☎23 27 36). Famed antique lamp store.

Centro Jose-Marti, Herengracht 259 (☎26 95 90). Latin American culture, particularly books.

Clockwitz, Herengracht 305 (☎24 27 06). Designer clocks in all shapes and sizes.

Condomerie Het Gulden Vlies, Warmoesstraat 141 (☎27 41 74). Condoms of every shape, size and flavour imaginable. All in the best possible taste.

De Derde Winkel, Huidenstraat 16 (☎25 22 45). Crafts from – and books about – developing countries.

D. Eberhardt, Damstraat 16 (☎24 07 24). Chinese and southeast Asian crafts, ceramics, clothes and jewellery.

Electric Lady, 2e Leliedwarsstraat 4. Pungently 1970s collection of psychedelia of all kinds, most of it luminous.

Flying Objects, 2e Tuindwarsstraat 8 (☎26 84 25). Beautiful kites.

Gerda's Bloemenwinkel, Runstraat 16 (☎24 29 12). Amsterdam is full of flower shops, but this is its most imaginative and sensual. An aesthetic experience.

P. G. C. Hajenius, Rokin 92–96 (☎23 74 94). Old, established tobacconist selling its own (and other brands of) cigars, tobacco, smoking accessories and every make of cigarette you can think of.

The Head Shop, Kloveniersburgwal 39 (☎24 90 61). What it says.

Jacob Hooij, Kloveniersburgwal 12 (☎24 30 41). Homeopathic chemist with an ancient interior and a huge stock of *drop* – Dutch licorice.

't Japaanse Winkeltje, N.Z. Voorburgwal 175 (☎27 95 23). Japanese arts and crafts.

Joe's Vlieger en Frisbeehandel, Nieuwe Hoogstraat 19 (☎25 01 39). Kites, frisbees, etc. More down-to-earth than its Jordaan rival.

Donald E. Jongejans, Noorderkerkstraat 18 (☎24 68 88). Hundreds of spectacle frames, none of them new, some of them very ancient. Supplied the specs for Bertolucci's *The Last Emperor*.

't Klompenhuisje, Nieuwe Hoogstraat 9a (☎22 81 00). Amsterdam's best and brightest array of clogs.

Knopenwinkel, Wolvenstraat 14 (☎24 04 79). Buttons in every conceivable shape and size.

Old Prints, Spiegelgracht 27, below the *Hans en Grietje* bar (☎28 88 52); Singel 496 (☎25 55 78). Old prints of Amsterdam and much else besides, at discount prices.

1001 Kralen, 1e Bloemdwarsstraat 38 (☎24 36 81). "Kralen" means "beads", and 1000 would seem a conservative estimate in this place, which sells nothing but.

Out of Africa, Herengracht 215 (☎23 46 77). African arts and crafts.

Le Petit Marchand, Kerkstraat 155 (☎26 59 52). In the heart of the pricey Spiegelkwaartier antique district, a refreshingly downmarket mixture of junk and items of genuine value.

Poppendoktor, Reestraat 20 (☎26 52 74). Candles on one side, soft toys, dolls, and puppets on the other. Exhaustive collections of both.

Posthumus, St. Luciensteeg 15 (☎38 13 82). Posh stationery, cards and, best of all, a choice of hundreds of rubber stamps.

't Winkeltje, Prinsengracht 228 (☎25 13 52). Jumble of cheap glassware and crockery, candlesticks, antique tin toys, kitsch souvenirs, old apothecaries jars and flasks. Perfect for browsing.

Witte Tanden Winkel, Runstraat 5 (☎23 34 43). Wacky toothbrushes and just about every dental hygiene accoutrement you could ever need.

For general toy shops see Kid's Amsterdam, p.107.

Records

Record prices in Amsterdam don't differ much from Britain, but the selection tends to be more limited. Still, the city does have one or two specialised dealers – particularly strong in jazz and in reggae, second-hand and used – who may be able to turn up something you couldn't find back home.

Boudisque, Haringpakkersteeg 10–18 (☎23 26 03). New wave, reggae and black music.

Concerto, Utrechtsestraat 58–60 (☎23 52 28). New and used records, pop, jazz and classical. Perhaps the best all-round selection in the city.

Free Record Shop, Kalverstraat 32 and 230 (☎26 58 08); Ferdinand Bolstraat 79 (☎71 60 74). One of the city's better pop/rock chains.

Get Records, Utrechtsestraat 105 (☎22 34 41). Emphasis on new wave.

Golden Age Records, N.Z. Voorburgwal 51–53 (☎25 22 81). Jazz and blues specialists.

Jazz Inn, Vijzelgracht 9 (☎23 56 62). Just jazz.

Richter, P. C. Hooftstraat 121 (☎66 21 184). Classical music specialists.

The Sound of the Fifties, Prinsengracht 669 (☎23 97 45). 1950s/1960s pop and jazz, second-hand and new.

CHAPTER FOUR

KIDS' STUFF AND SPORT

There's plenty more to do in Amsterdam than drag yourself around canals and press your nose up against shop windows: if you're travelling with **kids**, attractions include tram rides, circuses and a great zoo. For **sporting activities**, both indoor and out, participatory and for spectators, the city's facilities are second to none.

MAINLY FOR KIDS

Amsterdam's attractions are aimed mainly at adults, and things to keep kids entertained on a wet afternoon are few and far between. But the **attitude** to children here is as understanding as you'd expect: if museums don't allow prams they do provide snuggles to carry small children in; most restaurants have high chairs and children's menus (though they're not always that wonderful); and bars don't seem to mind accompanied kids, as long as they're reasonably under control. In short, in very few places will having a small child in your care close doors. Teenagers, while less welcome in bars, have enough to gawk at in the city streets to keep them amused.

Babysitting Services and Equipment Hire

It's worth noting that not all hotels welcome young children (they'll make this clear when you book), but many of those that do offer **babysitting services**. Otherwise there are a couple of agencies worth contacting, and even one place which hires out babycare equipment.

Baby-Rent, Hoptille 180 (☎96 30 47). Somebody had to think of it. You can hire anything you might possibly need for your baby here, from buggies to bottle warmers. A bit far out, in the southeast of the city, but handy if you're travelling light.

Babysit Centrale Kriterion, 2e Rozendwarsstraat 24 (☎24 58 48). Long-established agency with a high reputation, using students at least 18 years old. Inexpensive 24-hour service: f5–10 per hour, plus an administrative charge depending on the time of day. Book sitters between 5.30–7pm.

Babyzitcentrale Babyhome, Chassestraat 87 (☎16 11 19). Small, friendly babysitting service, using only women, aged 16 and up. Slightly cheaper than the Kriterion, but you can only book on Mondays and Thursdays from 3 to 5pm.

International Baby Nanny Sit Centrale, Asingabourg 34 (☎46 29 44). Reliable babysitting service.

Parks, Playgrounds and Trips

The city's most central green spot, the **Vondelpark**, has an excellent playground with sandpits, paddling pools, and ducks to feed. During the summer there's always some (free) entertainment for kids, either in the afternoon programme or in the park's open-air theatre. Most city parks have things to keep the kids entertained, but the best, the **Gaasperpark**, is outside of the centre (metro stop Gaasperplas, buses #60, #61, #154, #157), with terrific play facilities and paddling pools. The **Amsterdamse Bos** (p.68) has playgrounds, lakes, and wild animals, and you can hire canoes to explore the waterways for f7 per hour in a one-person boat, f10 for two, from 8am to sunset.

A good introduction for older children are the **canal trips** from Centraal Station or Damrak (see p.27) or, less historical but much more fun, a ride on a **canal bike**. This can get tiring, but jetties where boats can be picked up and dropped off are numerous, and it's quite safe; addresses on p.27. For a great view of the city, try a trek up the **towers** of the Oude Kerk, Zuiderkerk and Westerkerk (open summer only; see p.39, 60, and 54).

Museums

Aviodome Aeroplane Museum, Schipol Airport. Train from Centraal Station (☎60 41 521). April–Oct Mon–Fri 10am–5pm, Sat & Sun noon–5pm; Nov–April closed Mon; f6, f4.50 for under 12s. If you find yourself with time to kill, and the kids have tired of watching the planes take off, this offers a few ancient aircraft plus a flight simulator. Buy an all-in ticket at Centraal Station, which includes the return rail fare, museum entrance, a cup of coffee and *appelgebak* at the Schipol station bar.

Madame Tussaud's, Kalverstraat 156. Tram #1, #2, #4, #5, #9, #14, #16, #24, #25 (☎22 99 49). Daily 10am–6pm; July–Aug 9am–7pm; adults f9.25, children f6.75. Waxwork collection/workshop similar to the one in London. Among the few unique features: an attempt to recreate Hieronymus Bosch's *Garden of Earthly Delights* and a room devoted to Rembrandt. Hardly the high point of anyone's trip to the city, though the gory parts might excite the kids.

NINT Technological Museum, Tolstraat 129. Tram #3, #4 (☎66 46 021). Mon–Fri 10am–4pm, Sat–Sun 1–5pm. Adults f6, children (5–12) f4. A fairly dull collection of mostly mechanical exhibits designed to fire Dutch youth's enthusiasm for a career in industry. Hardly any info in English.

Spaarpotten Museum, Raadhuistraat 20. Tram #13, #14, #17 (☎55 67 400). Mon–Fri 1–4pm, adults f1, children under 13 f0.50. Small but marvellously entertaining collection of piggybanks with fun and ingenious devices, from African clay pots to the mechanical toys of the nineteenth century (look out for the American ones, which today seem offensively racist), and some truly horrendous plastic souvenir boxes. Lovers of kitsch should have a field day.

TM Junior Museum, Linnaeusstraat 2a. Tram #3, #6, #9, #10 (☎568 8300). Open afternoons during the school year, plus weekends; phone for complete hours. Admission f3–6. Conceived especially for children between the ages of 6 and 12, its aim is to promote international understanding by holding exhibitions about other cultures. Not as dry as it might sound, with lively exhibits and lots of things to get your hands on, it's best on Sunday, when school groups aren't visiting. For those especially interested, the Tropenmuseum, of which the TM is an adjunct, is also worth exploring.

Tramline Museum, Haarlemmermeerstation, Amstelveenseweg 264. Tram #6, #16 (☎73 75 38). End March–end Oct Sun and public holidays 11am–6pm; July–early Sept Sun, Tues, Wed, Thurs, Sat 1–6pm. Phone for exact dates; f3.50, children under 11 f3. Not so much a museum as a set of working antique trams that run along adapted railway tracks down to the Amsterdamse Bos and, beyond, into Amstelveen. Can be fun for kids, and it's a good way of getting to the Bos.

Zoological Museum, Plantage Middenlaan 53. Tram #6, #7, #9, #10, #14. Daily 9am–5pm; admission thrown with entry to the zoo – f15 for adults, kids f8, no museumcards. Essentially a natural history museum with a static collection of insects, birds, bats, and whales, as well as the usual skeletal remains. Only regularly changing exhibitions lighten an otherwise dull load.

Theatres

A number of theatres have inexpensive (around f5) entertainment for children in the afternoon, a fair proportion of which gets around the language problem by being mime- or puppet-based: check the children's section (*Jeugdagenda*) of *Uitkrant*, and look for the words *mimegroep* (mime group) and *poppentheater* (puppet theatre). For general information on children's theatre in Amsterdam, call ☎22 29 99.

De Krakeling, Nieuwe Passeerdersstraat 1 (☎24 51 23). Full-time children's theatre, and a good place to begin. The emphasis is often on full-scale audience participation. Phone for a schedule.

Melkweg, Lijnbaansgracht 234a (☎24 17 77). Sun afternoon activities for children from mid-Oct–early April.

Poppentheater Diridas, Hobbemakade 68 (☎66 21 588). Kids' puppet theatre.

Other theatres which regularly have good kids' programmes are *De Brakke Grond*, Nes 45 (☎26 68 66); *Cleyntheater*, H. Cleynderweg 63a (☎37 18 15); *De Meevaart*, Osdorpplein 205 (☎10 73 93); *Ostadetheater*, Van Ostadestraat 233 (☎79 50 96); Polantheater, Polanstraat 174 (☎82 13 11).

Circuses, Fairs – and the Zoo

Public holidays and the summer bring touring circuses and the occasional mobile funfair (*kermis*) to the city, the latter usually setting up on Dam Square and thus hard to miss. Check, too, the **festivals** listings on p.12: many, such as the Queen's birthday celebrations, can be enjoyed by kids.

Carré Theatre, Amstel 115–125 (☎225 225). Occasionally books internationally famous circuses.

Elleboog Circus, Passeerdersgracht 32 (☎26 93 70). Circus performed by and for children. Sounds deadly, but we haven't seen it. Phone bookings required.

Artis Zoo, Plantage Kerklaan 38–40. Tram #6, #7, #9, #10, #14. (☎52 33 400). Mon–Sat 9am–5pm, planetarium opens at 12.30pm on Mon; adults f15, children f12.50. Open year round and, on top of the usual creatures and creepy-crawlies, has a children's farm where kids can torment sheep, calves, goats, etc. If it's raining visit the aquarium – one of the best-stocked in Europe. There's also the **Zeiss Planetarium**, covered on the same ticket, which organises special events for kids – a useful attraction on which to centre a visit.

Shops

Bell Tree, Spiegelgracht 10 (☎25 88 30). A beautiful shop full of old-fashioned toys, mobiles, models, simple toys and kids' books.

De Bijenkorf, Damrak 90 (☎21 80 80). A department store, but with one of the best (and most reasonable) toy sections in town.

Boon Speelgoed, Heilweg 26–28 (☎22 11 22) and branches throughout the city. Amsterdam's largest toy shop.

Flying Objects, 2e Tuindwarsstraat 8 (☎26 84 25). Beautiful handmade kites at sky-high prices. A place to avoid if your kids are in an "I want" mood.

Joe's Vlieger en Frisbeehandel, Nieuwe Hoogstraat 19 (☎25 01 39). Kites, frisbees, etc. More down-to-earth than its Jordaan rival.

De Kinderboekwinkel, 1e Bloemdwarsstraat 23 (☎22 47 61); N.Z. Voorburgwal 344 (☎22 7741). Children's books, some of which are in English.

De Kinder Shoen Winkel, Bloemgracht 76. Shoes, boots, and galoshes.

De Kleine Bloem, Bloemstraat 44 (☎22 77 40). Children's clothes at reasonable prices.

Little Nemo, Elandsgracht 80 (☎25 65 04). Toys and clothes in continental cuts at continentally high prices.

Merkelbach & Co., Kalverstraat 30 (☎24 95 72). An old-fashioned kids' toy shop, with models, train sets and chess boards – and not a video game in sight.

Poppendoktor, Reestraat 20 (☎26 52 74). Candles on one side, soft toys, dolls and puppets on the other. Both exhaustive collections.

Portbobello Giftshop, Rokin 107 (☎22 69 03). A good source of educational wooden toys that salve the conscience and please the eye.

Posthumus, St. Luciensteeg 25 (☎25 58 12). Great collection of rubber stamps, all within pocket-money range.

Speel-Goed, P.C. Hooftstraat 95 (☎66 29 304). Specialises in toys for under-fives.

Wampie, 2e Anjelierdwarsstraat 19 (☎27 16 75). Children's clothes. Lots of bright colours, even for babies.

> See also Miscellaneous and ethnic shops, p.101.

MORE FOR ADULTS

Most visitors to laid-back Amsterdam tend to confine their exercise to walking around the major sights, but if you get the urge to stretch your muscles, there's a range of **participatory sports** available. In winter, skating is the most popular and enjoyable: other activities are based in private health or sports clubs, to which you can usually get a day pass, though almost all are away from the immediate centre of town.

As a **spectator**, you're limited mainly to cheering on the talented local football team *Ajax* – though their Rotterdam rivals *Feyenoord* are just a train ride away. For up-to-the-minute details on all the sports listed here, or on where to find your own favourite, obscure sporting activity, phone the city council's Sport Information Service (☎85 08 51, open daily 8.30am–5pm).

Doing

Skating

When it's **really cold**, skaters can get spoiled in Amsterdam: almost every drop of available water is utilised, and the canals provide an exhilarating way to whizz around the city – much more fun than going around a rink. But before you venture out, a few **safety points**:

❖ Wait till you see others on the ice – locals have a better idea of its thickness.

❖ If in doubt, start off on the smaller ponds in the Vondelpark.

❖ Be careful under bridges, where the ice takes longest to freeze.

❖ If the ice does give way and you find yourself in the water, head for the *darkest* spot you can see in the ice above – that's the hole.

It's also possible to skate out of Amsterdam and into surrounding towns – through the Waterland or to Muiderslot and Naarden, for example. One of the great events in Holland's sporting calendar is the annual *Elfstedentocht*, a race across eleven towns and 200km of frozen waterways in Friesland. Though the race couldn't be held for twenty years, a recent spate of cold winters has meant two competitions in a row and an increasing number of participants – over 16,000 when it was last held in 1986. If you're around in January and the ice is good, you'll hear talk of little else.

Most Amsterdammers have their own skates, and there are suprisingly few places where you can **hire** a pair. If Dutch friends can't help, you can hire at one of the rinks below (only Jaap Eden Baan officially allows them to be taken from the rink). **Buying** a pair from a department store or sport shop will cost upwards of f70, and the best place to look for a second-hand pair is from one of the noticeboards listed on p.20.

Jaap Eden Baan, Radioweg 64 (☎94 98 94), bus #8 from Amstel Station as far as the last stop on Kruislaan. Large indoor rink with all facilities, open Oct–March

Leidseplein rink, Leidseplein. Small free outdoor rink, good for a trial run before hitting the canals. Open Nov–Feb.

For more info on rinks, phone the Sports Information Office (see above).

Jogging

The main circuits are the **Vondelpark** and **Amsterdamse Bos**, the latter having special routes of varying distances signposted throughout. The Amsterdam Marathon, should you be up for it (a little over 46km), takes place in May.

Canoeing and Horseriding

Amsterdamse Manage, Nieuwe Kalfjeslaan 25 (☎43 13 42). The place for a ride – but only on dressage horses.

Roell Watersport, jetties at Prinsengracht/Leidsestraat and Lijnbaansgracht/Spiegelgracht (☎91 91 24). Canoes and kayaks for hire for use on Amsterdam's canals from f40 a day – a very fit-making way to sightsee. Take your passport along as security. You can also hire canoes in the Amsterdamse Bos (see p.68).

Tennis , Squash and Table Tennis

Most outdoor tennis courts are for members only, and those that aren't need to be booked well in advance. Your best bets for getting a game at short notice are among the following:

Frans Otten Stadion, Stadionstraat 10 (☎66 28 767). Six indoor tennis courts and ten squash courts. Tennis around f30 per hour, squash f30 per half-hour, with higher prices in the evening. Racket hire f5. Open 9am–9pm (tennis), 9am–11pm (squash).

Gold Star Tennis, K. Lotsylaan 20 near Vrij University, Buitenveldert (☎44 54 83). Bus #22, #26, #66, #173. Ten indoor tennis courts, rates from f32.50 per hour for non-members, racket hire f3.50 per hour. Summer hours 7am–11pm.

Squash City, Ketelmakerstraat 6 (☎26 78 83). f25 per court for 45 minutes between 9am and 4pm, after 4pm f30; all prices include sauna. Racket hire f3. Open Mon–Sat 9am–midnight, with early opening (7am) Tues. Phone ahead to book courts.

Table Tennis Centre Amsterdam, Keizersgracht 209 (☎24 57 80). Very central table tennis hall – an increasingly popular sport in Amsterdam. Open daily 1pm–1am, f5 per table per hour. Phone to book.

Tafeltennishuis, Overtoom 505 (☎85 13 24). Slightly further out but cheaper. f5 per table per hour. Open daily noon–1am. Again, you need to phone in advance.

Swimming

Flevoparkbad, Zeeburgerdijk 630 (☎92 50 30). Tram #3, #10. Best outdoor pool in the city; gets very busy on sunny days. f3.25, kids f2.80. Mid-May to late Sept, daily 10am–5pm.

Mirandabad, de Mirandalaan 9 (☎25 48 43). Superbly equipped swimming centre with wave machine, whirlpools, and slides. Adults f5.25, kids f4.25. Outdoor pool mid-May to mid-Sept 10am–5.30pm. Indoor pool roughly Mon–Fri 7.30am–10.15pm, weekends 10am–5.30pm; women only Wed 9am–11am, small children Sun 10–11am .

Other pools centrally located include:

Heiligewegbad, Heiligeweg 19 (☎23 69 35).

Jan van Galenbad (outdoor), Jan van Gelenstraat 315 (☎12 80 01).

Marnixbad, Marnixplein 9 (☎25 48 43).

Zuiderbad, Hobbemastraat 26 (☎79 22 17).

Saunas and Gyms

Deco, Herengracht 115 (☎23 82 15). In the running for Amsterdam's most stylish sauna and steam bath, with a magnificent art deco interior. Day tickets up to 2pm f13.50, after 2pm f21.50. Mon–Sat 11am–1pm, Sun 1–6pm.

Garden Gym, Jodenbreestraat 158 (☎26 87 72). Weight-training and dance-workout studio with saunas, solarium, massage and self-defence classes. Mainly, though not exclusively, for women. Day pass f12.50 with shower, f20 including use of sauna. Mon, Wed, Fri 9am–11pm; Tues, Thurs noon-11pm; Sat, Sun 11am–7pm.

Gym 86, Tweede Van der Helstraat 2 (☎75 05 03). Multigym with sauna; f10 for a day pass but you pay extra for some facilities.

Splash, Looiersgracht 26–30 (☎24 84 04); Kattengat 1 (in the Sonesta Hotel; ☎27 10 44). Hi-tech fitness centre with sauna, tanning salon and Turkish bath. Daily aerobic classes, gender-separated training rooms. Day pass f25. Mon–Fri 10am–10pm, Sat–Sun 11am–6pm.

De Stokerij, 1e Rozendwarsstraat 8 (☎25 94 17). Council fitness centre with facilities for football, tennis, volleyball, etc, and a gym. Price f21 an hour no matter what you do. Tram #13, #17.

Bowling, Carambole, Chess and Draughts

Knijn Bowling Centre, Scheldeplein 3, opposite RAI complex (☎66 42 211). The closest to the city centre, with 22 bowling lanes. Between f22 and f35 per hour per alley, maximum of six persons. 10am–1am.

Bavaria Snooker Club, Van Ostadestraat 97 (☎76 40 59). Six tables. f7.50–12.50 per hour. Carambole too (see below).

Keizers' Snooker Club, Keizersgracht 256 (☎23 15 86). Seven high quality tables in a seventeenth-century canal house. f10–15 an hour.

Carambole. This, a form of billiards, is a major sport in Holland: played on a table without pockets, you score by making cannons. The skill of some of the locals, often spinning the ball through impossible angles, is unbelievable. It's considered unfashionable, but you'll find tables in many cafés, and get plenty of advice on how to play if you so much as look at a ball.

Gambit, Bloemgracht 20, and **Het Hok**, Lange Leidsedwarsstraat 134, are cafés where both chess and draughts are played to the exclusion of (almost) everything else; there's a small charge for a board. See *Bars* for more details.

Watching

Football

Ajax Amsterdam, Middenweg 401 (☎94 65 15). A talented and entertaining young team still near the top of the Dutch league, though presently banished from European football due to crowd trouble. Indeed Ajax's "F-side" mob are every bit as bad as anything Britain's fans can come up with. The Ajax stadium is at the eastern end of the #9 tram line, and the cheapest (standing) tickets start at f9. For a full list of all league matches, consult the *VVV*.

Feyenoord Rotterdam, Feyenoord Stadium, Rotterdam. The country's other top-league team, with a handy train stop near the grounds. Ticket prices similar to Ajax's.

Hockey and Basketball

The RAI Centre, Europaplein (☎541 1411). Most major matches take place here, along with an unusual form of basketball called *Korfball*, in which teams are mixed and the basket is much higher.

Gambling

If you're itching to strike it rich with your last few guilders, Amsterdam is a disappointment. There's no horse racing to speak of (though you can get bets on British races at the *Ladbroke's Totalisator* offices which have recently opened across town), and legal casinos are few and far between. The **Amsterdam Casino**, Hilton Hotel, Apollolaan 138 (☎66 49 911) is open from noon to 3am. The cover is f12.50; some form of identification is required. No jeans allowed, and men must wear jackets.

Pole Sitting

Every year in late July/early August, there's the chance to witness the offbeat spectator sport of pole sitting. In Noorderwijkerhout, just north of Scheveningen, there's a **pole sitting marathon** which lasts about five days. Although not exactly a dyanmic sport, it generates a fair amount of excite-ment, as some fifteen braves sit it out on poles perched in the North Sea. The last one left is the winner.

CHAPTER FIVE

DRINKING AND EATING

A msterdam is better known for **drinking** than eating, and with good reason: its selection of bars is one of the real pleasures of the city. As for **eating**, this may not be the culinary capital of Europe, but there's a good supply of ethnic restaurants, especially Indonesian and Chinese, and the prices (by big-city standards) are hard to beat. And there are any number of *eetcafés* and bars which serve increasingly adventurous food, quite cheaply, in a relaxed and unpretentious setting. An overview of the types of food you can expect to find, as well as some basic food terms, is followed by specific recommendations for bars and restaurants.

Bars are listed geographically, divided between those in inner central Amsterdam (ie, on and within the area bordered by the Singel canal); those on and around the other major canals and in the Jordaan – the outer centre; and a handful of others outside the Singelgracht. The **map** on p.118 should make it possible to coordinate your eating or sightseeing with an evening's drinking.

Coffee shops are listed alphabetically, and divided between those that sell dope (both grass and hash) and those that don't; **restaurants** are categorised by type of cuisine, starting with a section on the city's cheapest eating alternatives – *mensas*. There are short sections, too, on **all women's** and **gay men's** bars and coffee shops, as well as a checklist of **late-night and 24-hour** eating and drinking places.

All bars, coffee shops, and restaurants are also **cross-referenced** at the end of each area section in the *City* chapter.

Food: An Overview

In all but the very cheapest hostels or most expensive hotels **breakfast** (*ontbijt*) will be included in the price of the room. Though usually nothing fancy, it's always very filling: rolls, cheese, ham, hard-boiled eggs, jam and honey or peanut butter are the principal ingredients. If you don't have a hotel breakfast, the best place to start the day in Amsterdam is *De Bijenkorf* department store, where a good value breakfast buffet in their second floor restaurant costs less than f9 a head. Many bars and cafés also serve breakfast, and those that don't invariably offer at least rolls and sandwiches.

The **coffee** that washes all this down is espresso, black and strong, and often served with *koffiemelk* (evaporated milk); ordinary milk is rarely used. If you want white coffee, ask for a *koffie verkeerd*. Most bars also serve capuccino, although bear in mind that many stop serving coffee altogether around 11pm. **Tea** generally comes with lemon if anything – if you want milk you have to ask for it. **Chocolate** is also popular, served hot or cold: for a real treat drink it hot with a layer of fresh whipped cream on top.

For the rest of the day eating cheaply and well, particularly on your feet, is no real problem, although those on the tightest of budgets may find themselves dependent on the dubious delights of **Dutch fast food**. This has its own peculiarities. Chips – *frites* – are the most common standby (*vlaamse* or "Flemish" *frites* are the best), either sprinkled with salt or smothered with huge gobs of mayonnaise (*fritesaus*); some alternative toppings are curry, goulash, or tomato sauce. Often chips are complemented with *kroketten* – spiced minced meat covered with breadcrumbs and deep fried – or *fricandel*, a frankfurter-like sausage. All these are available over the counter at evil-smelling fast food places (*Febo* is the most common chain), or, for a guilder or so, from heated glass compartments outside. As an alternative there are also a number of **Indonesian fast food** places, serving sate and noodle dishes in a McDonald's type atmosphere.

Tastier, and good both as a snack and a full lunch, are the **fish specialities** sold in street kiosks: salted raw herrings (roll-mop), smoked eel, mackerel in a roll, mussels, and various kinds of deep-fried fish; tip your head back and dangle the fish into your mouth, Dutch-style. Other street foods include **pancakes**, sweet or spicy, also widely available at sit-down restaurants; **waffles** (*stoopwafels*), doused with maple syrup; and **poffertjes**, shell-shaped dough balls served with masses of melted butter and icing sugar – an extremely filling snack. Try also **oliebollen**, greasy doughnuts filled with fruit (often apple) and traditionally served at Christmas and Easter. Dutch **cakes and biscuits** are always good, and filling, best eaten in a *banketbakkerij* with a small serving area; or buy a bag and eat them on the hoof. Apart from the ubiquitous *appelgebak* – wedges of apple and cinnamon tart – things to try include *spekulaas*, a cinammon biscuit with gingerbread texture; *stroopwafels*, butter wafers sandwiched together with runny syrup; *amandelkoek*, cakes with a biscuity outside and melt-in-the-mouth almond paste inside.

As for the kind of food you can expect to encounter in bars, there are **sandwiches and rolls** (*boterham* and *broodjes*) – often open-faced, and varying from a slice of tired cheese on old bread to something so embellished it's almost a complete meal – as well as more substantial fare. In the winter, *erwtensoep* (aka *snert*) is available in most bars, and at about f5.50 a shot makes a great buy for lunch: thick pea soup filled with smoked sausage and served with a portion of smoked bacon on *pumpernickel*. Or there's an *uitsmijter* (literally, "bouncer"): one, two, or three fried eggs on buttered bread, topped with a choice of ham, cheese, or roast beef – at about f8, another good budget lunch.

Holland's **cheeses** have an unjustified reputation abroad for being bland and rubbery. This is because they only export the nastier products and keep the best for themselves. In fact, Dutch cheese can be delicious, although

A LIST OF FOODS AND DISHES

Basics

Boter	Butter	*Nagerechten*	Desserts
Brood	Bread	*Peper*	Pepper
Broodje	Sandwich/roll	*Pindakaas*	Peanut butter
Dranken	Drinks	*Sla/salade*	Salad
Eicrcn	Eggs	*Smeerkaas*	Cheese spread
Groenten	Vegetables	*Stokbrood*	French bread
Gurst	Semolina; the type of	*Suiker*	Sugar
	grain used in Algerian	*Vis*	Fish
	couscous, popular in	*Vlees*	Meat
	vegetarian restaurants	*Voorgerechten*	Starters,
Honig	Honey		hors d'oeuvres
Hoofdgerechten	Main courses	*Vruchten*	Fruit
Kaas	Cheese	*Warm*	Warm
Koud	Cold	*Zout*	Salt

Starters and Snacks

Erwtensoep/snert	Pea soup with bacon or	*Uitsmijter*	Ham or cheese with eggs
	sausage		on bread
Huzarensalade	Egg salad	*Koffietafel*	A light midday meal of
Patates/Frites	Chips		cold meats, cheese,
Soep	Soup		bread, and perhaps soup

Meat and Poultry

Biefstuk (hollandse)	Steak	*Kalfsvlees*	Veal
Biefstuk (duitse)	Hamburger	*Karbonade*	Chop
Eend	Duck	*Kip*	Chicken
Fricandeau	Roast pork	*Kroket*	Spiced, minced meat in
Fricandel	A frankfurter-like		breadcrumbs
	sausage	*Lamsvlees*	Lamb
Gehakt	Minced meat	*Lever*	Liver
Ham	Ham	*Rookvlees*	Smoked beef
Hutspot	Beef stew	*Spek*	Bacon
Kalkoen	Turkey	*Worst*	Sausage

Fish

Garnalen	Prawns	*Mosselen*	Mackerel	*Schelvis*	Haddock
Haring	Herring	*Haringsalade*	Mussels	*Spiering*	Whitebait
Kabeljauw	Herring salad	*Paling*	Eel	*Tong*	Sole
Makreel	Cod	*Schol*	Plaice	*Zalm*	Salmon

Terms

Doorbakken	Well-done	*Gerookt*	Smoked
Gebakken	Fried/baked	*Gestoofd*	Stewed
Gebraden	Roast	*Half doorbakken*	Medium
Gekookt	Boiled	*Hollandse saus*	Hollandaise (a milk and
Gegrild	Grilled		egg sauce)
Geraspt	Grated	*Rood*	Rare

Vegetables

Aardappelen	Potatoes	*Knoflook*	Garlic	*Sla*	Salad, lettuce
Bloemkool	Cauliflower	*Komkommer*	Cucumber	*Uien*	Onions
Bonen	Beans	*Prei*	Leek	*Wortelen*	Carrots
Champignons	Mushrooms	*Rijst*	Rice	*Zuurkool*	Sauerkraut
Erwten	Peas				

Indonesian Dishes and Terms

Ajam	Chicken	*Nasi Goreng*	Fried rice with meat/chicken and vegetables
Bami	Noodles with meat/ chicken and vegetables	*Nasi Rames*	Rijsttafel on a single plate
Daging	Beef	*Pedis*	Hot and spicy
Gado gado	Vegetables in peanut sauce	*Pisang*	Banana
		Rijsttafel	Collection of different spicy dishes served with plain rice
Goreng	Fried		
Ikan	Fish	*Sambal*	Hot, chilli-based sauce
Katjang	Peanut	*Satesaus*	Peanut sauce to accompany meat grilled on skewers
Kroepoek	Shrimp chips		
Loempia	Spring rolls	*Seroendeng*	Spicy fried, shredded coconut
Nasi	Rice	*Tauge*	Bean sprouts

Sweets and Desserts

Appelgebak	Apple tart or cake	*Oliebollen*	Doughnuts
Drop	Dutch licorice, available in zoet (sweet) or zout (salted) varieties -- the latter an acquired taste	*Pannekoeken*	Pancakes
		Pepernoten	Dutch ginger nuts
		Poffertjes	Small pancakes, fritters
		(Slag) room	(Whipped) cream
		Speculaas	Spice and honey-flavoured biscuit
Gebak	Pastry	*Stroopwafels*	Waffles
IJs	Ice cream	*Taai-taai*	Dutch honey cake, often cut into shapes
Koekjes	Biscuits		

Fruits and Nuts

Vla	Custard	*Citroen*	Lemon	*Kokosnoot*	Coconut
Aardbei	Strawberry	*Druiven*	Grape	*Peer*	Pear
Amandel	Almond	*Hazelnoot*	Hazelnut	*Perzik*	Peach
Appel	Apple	*Framboos*	Raspberry	*Pinda*	Peanut
Appelmoes	Apple purée	*Kers*	Cherry	*Pruim*	Plum/prune

Drinks

Bessenjenever	Blackcurrant gin	*Melk*	Milk
Citroenjenever	Lemon gin	*Met ijs*	With ice
Droog	Dry	*Pils*	Dutch beer
Frisdranken	Soft drinks	*Proost !*	Cheers!
Jenever	Dutch gin	*Thee*	Tea
Karnemelk	Buttermilk	*Vruchtensap*	Fruit juice
Koffie	Coffee	*Wijn*	Wine
Kopstoot	Beer with a jenever chaser	*(wit/rood/rose)*	(white/red/rosé)
		Zoet	Sweet

there isn't the variety you get in, say, France or Britain. Most are based on the same soft creamy *Goudas*, and differences in taste come with the varying stages of maturity – *jong, belegen,* or *oud. Jong* cheese has a mild flavour, *belegen* is much tastier, while *oud* can be pungent and strong, with a flaky texture not unlike parmesan. Among the other cheeses you'll find, the best known is the round red *Edam*, made principally for export and (quite sensibly) not eaten much by the Dutch; *Leidse*, simply *Gouda* with cumin seeds; *Maasdammer*, strong, creamy, and full of holes; and Dutch-made *Emmentals* and *Gruyères*. The best way to eat cheese here is the way the Dutch do it, in thin slices (*kaasschaaf*) rather than large hunks.

Dutch food tends to be higher in protein content than on imagination: steak, chicken and fish, along with filling soups and stews, are staple fare. Where possible stick to *dagschotels* (dish of the day), a meat and two vegetable combination for which you pay around f15, bottom-line, for what tend to be enormous portions. The fish is generally high-quality but not especially cheap (f20 and up, on the average), while the three-course *tourist menu,* which the authorities push at several of the city's more mainstream restaurants, is – at f19–20 or so – no great bargain, and usually extremely dull.

A wide selection of **vegetarian** restaurants offer full-course set meals for around f10 to f12. Bear in mind that they often close early. Another cheap standby is **Italian** food: pizzas and pasta dishes start at a fairly uniform f10–11 in all but the ritziest places. **Chinese** restaurants are also common, as are (increasingly) **Spanish**, and there are a handful of **Tex-Mex** eateries, all of which serve well-priced, filling food.

But Amsterdam's real speciality is its **Indonesian** restaurants, a consequence of the country's imperial adventures and well worth checking out. You can eat à la carte – *Nasi Goreng* and *Bami Goreng* (rice or noodles with meat) are ubiquitous dishes, chicken or beef in peanut sauce (*sate*) available everywhere too. Or order a *rijstaffel*: boiled rice and/or noodles served with a number of spicy side dishes and hot *sambal* sauce on the side. Eaten with the spoon in the right hand, fork in the left, and with dry white or rosé wine or beer, this doesn't come cheap, but it's delicious and is normally more than enough for two. (See below for restaurant listings.)

Drinking: An Overview

Most drinking is done in the cosy environs of a *brown café* (see below for a definition), and the beverage most often drunk is **beer**. This is usually served in small (around half-pint) measures (ask for "een pils"), much of which will be frothing head – requests to have it poured English-style meet with various responses, but it's worth trying. **Jenever**, or Dutch gin, is not unlike British gin, but a bit weaker and a little oilier, made from molasses and flavoured with juniper berries: it's served in small glasses and is traditionally drunk straight, often knocked back in one gulp with much hearty back-slapping. There are a number of varieties: *Oud* (old) is smooth and mellow, *Jong* (young) packs more of a punch – though neither are terribly alcoholic. Ask for a *borreltje* (straight jenever), a *bittertje* (with angostura), or, if you've a sweeter tooth, try a *bessenjenever* – blackcurrant-flavoured gin; for a glass of beer with a jenever chaser, ask for a *kopstoot*. Other drinks you'll see include numerous Dutch **liqueurs**, notably *advocaat* or eggnog and the sweet, blue *curacao* – and an assortment of lurid-coloured **fruit brandies** which are best left for experimentation at the end of an evening. There's also the Dutch-produced brandy, *Vieux*, which tastes as if it's made from prunes but is in fact grape-based.

Beer and jenever are both dirt cheap if bought by the bottle from a supermarket: the commonest beers, *Amstel*, *Grolsch* and *Heineken*, all cost a little over fl for a half-litre (about a pint), and a bottle of Jenever sells for around f14. Imported spirits are considerably more expensive. **Wine**, too, is very reasonable – expect to pay around f6 or so for a bottle of decent French white or red.

Bars

There are two kinds of Amsterdam bars. The traditional, old-style bar is the **brown café** (*bruin kroeg*), cosy places thus named because of the dingy colour of their walls, stained by years of tobacco smoke. A more recent backlash is the slick, self-consciously modern **designer bar**, as un-brown as possible and geared to a largely young crowd. Most bars open until around 1am during the week, 2am at weekends, though some don't open until lunchtime, or even about 4pm; reckon on paying roughly f2.25 for a small beer (note that some bars serve larger, approximately pint-size measures, which work out proportionately cheaper). Other drinking spots are the **tasting houses** (*proeflokalen*), originally sampling rooms of small private distillers, now tiny places that sell only spirits and close around 8pm.

Prices are fairly standard, and the only time you'll pay through the nose is when there's music (*Le Maxim*, *De Kroeg*) or if you're foolish (or desperate) enough to step into the obvious tourist traps around Leidseplein and along Damrak. You can also use bars as a source for **budget eating**: many (often designated *eetcafes*) offer a complete menu, and most will make you a sandwich or bowl of soup; at the very least you can snack on hard-boiled eggs from the counter for a guilder or so each.

There are around 1,400 bars and cafés in Amsterdam – roughly one for every 700 people – and what follows is inevitably very selective. We've listed a broad cross-section of places across the city, so wherever you are, and whatever your tastes, you should be able to find something to suit you nearby.

Inner Centre

The American Bar, Nieuwe Nieuwstraat 18. On a shady side street off N. Z. Voorburgwal, a watering hole for dealers, prostitutes and sundry colourful characters. Exciting, if you like that sort of thing.

Anna Dodo, Kloveniersburgwal 6–8. Typical post-modern café, decorated in pastel colours and with an arty clientele. The walls are plastered with dodos. Reasonable food from around f25.

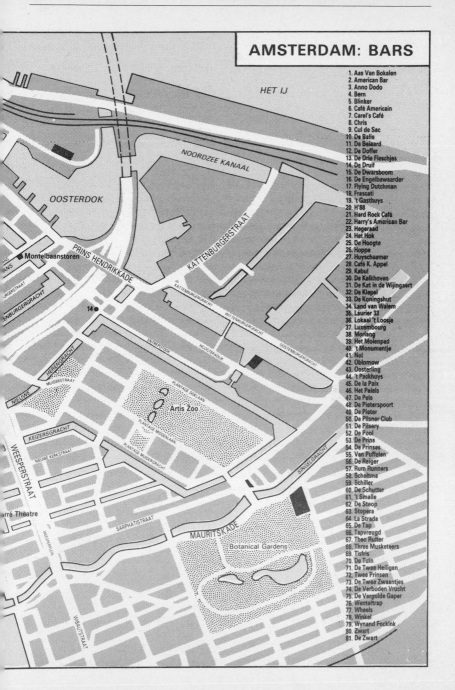

AMSTERDAM: BARS

HET IJ

NOORDZEE KANAAL

OOSTERDOK

PRINS HENDRIKKADE

KATTENBURGERSTRAAT

Montelbaanstoren

KATTENBURGERGRACHT

WITTENBURGERGRACHT

OOSTENBURGERGRACHT

ENTREPOTDOK

HOOGTEKADIJK

SINGELGRACHT

PLANTAGE DOKLAAN

Artis Zoo

PLANTAGE MIDDENLAAN

PLANTAGE MUIDERGRACHT

HERENGRACHT

MUIDERSTRAAT

NIEUWE

KEIZERSGRACHT

NIEUWE KERKSTRAAT

WEESPERSTRAAT

SARPHATISTRAAT

MAURITSKADE

Botanical Gardens

arré Theatre

WIBAUTSTRAAT

1. Aas Van Bokalen
2. American Bar
3. Anno Dodo
4. Bern
5. Blinker
6. Café Americain
7. Carel's Café
8. Chris
9. Cul de Sac
10. De Balie
11. De Beiaard
12. De Doffer
13. De Drie Fleschjes
14. De Druif
15. De Dwarsboom
16. De Engelbewaarder
17. Flying Dutchman
18. Frascati
19. 't Gasthuys
20. H'88
21. Hard Rock Café
22. Harry's American Bar
23. Hegeraad
24. Het Hok
25. De Hoogte
26. Hoppe
27. Huyschaemer
28. Café K. Appel
29. Kabul
30. De Kalkhoven
31. De Kat in de Wijngaert
32. De Klepel
33. De Koningshut
34. Land van Walem
35. Laurier 33
36. Lokaal 't Loosje
37. Luxembourg
38. Morlang
39. Het Molenpad
40. 't Monumentje
41. Nol
42. Oblomow
43. Oosterling
44. 't Packhuys
45. De la Paix
46. Het Paleis
47. De Pels
48. De Pieterspoort
49. De Pieter
50. De Pilsner Club
51. De Pilsery
52. De Pool
53. De Prins
54. De Prinses
55. Van Puffelen
56. De Reiger
57. Rum Runners
58. Scheltma
59. Schiller
60. De Schutter
61. 't Smalle
62. De Steep
63. Stopera
64. La Strada
65. De Tap
66. Tapvreugd
67. Theo Ruiter
68. Three Musketeers
69. Tisfris
70. De Tuin
71. De Twee Heiligen
72. Twee Prinsen
73. De Twee Zwaantjes
74. De Verboden Vrucht
75. De Vergulde Gaper
76. Wenteltrap
77. Wheels
78. Winkel
79. Wynand Fockink
80. Zwart
81. De Zwart

Bern, Nieuwmarkt 9. Casual and inexpensive brown café patronised by a predominantly arty clientele. Run by a native of Switzerland, its speciality is, not surprisingly, fondue.

Blincker, St. Barberenstraat 7–9. Squeezed between the top end of Nes and O. Z. Voorburgwal, this hi-tech bar, all exposed steel and hanging plants, is more comfortable than it looks. Arrive early if you want a seat – there's a direct entrance from the Frascati Theatre next door, and performances let out around 10pm.

Carel's Café, Voetboogstraat 6. Large, youth-oriented bar serving slightly overpriced food – though the *dagschotels* are a good buy. Also at Frans Halsstraat 78 and Saenredamstraat 32.

Cul de Sac, O. Z. Voorburgwal 99. Down a long alley in what used to be a seventeenth-century spice warehouse, this is a handy retreat from the Red Light district. Small, quiet and friendly.

De Drie Fleschjes, Gravenstraat 18. Tasting-house for spirits and liqueurs, which would originally have been made on the premises. No beer, and no seats either; its clients tend to be well-heeled or well-soused (often both).

De Engelbewaarder, Kloveniersburgwal 59. Once the meeting place of Amsterdam's bookish types, this is still known as the "literary café". Relaxed and informal, it has live jazz on Sunday evenings.

Flying Dutchman, Martelaarsgracht 13. Principal watering-hole of Amsterdam's British expatriate community and not a word of Dutch is to be heard. Usually packed with stoned regulars crowding in to use the pool table or darts boards, or simply to cash in on the Dutchman's reasonably priced large-size beers.

Frascati, Nes 59. Theatre bar, elegantly brown with mirrors and a pink marble bar, popular with a young media-type crowd. Good, too, for both lunchtime and informal evening eating, with a full meal for around f15, snacks and soups for much less. Recommended.

't Gasthuys, Grimburgwal 7. Convivial brown café packed during the school year with students from the university across the canal. Features include good food and summer seating outside by the water.

Gollum, Raamsteeg 4. Small, noisy bar with a huge array of different beers. A genial barman dispenses lists to help you choose.

Hard Rock Café, O. Z. Voorburgwal 246. Not the overblown burger joint found in London, but a small crowded ("smoking") bar serving 1970s-style videos to 1970s-style customers. Patronised mainly by those in Amsterdam for the weed. There's another, smaller branch, not a whole lot more appealing, at Korte Leidsedwarsstraat 28.

Harry's American Bar, Spuistraat 285. One of a number of would-be sophisticated hangouts at the top end of Spuistraat, Harry's is primarily a haunt for Amsterdam's more elderly *bon vivants*, with easy listening jazz and an unhealthily wide selection of cocktails.

De Hoogte, Nieuwe Hoogstraat 2a. "Smoking" café on the edge of the Red Light district. Good music, engaging atmosphere, and beers a little cheaper.

Hoppe, Spui 18. Quite possibly Amsterdam's best-known bar – and one of its most likeable – frequented by the city's dark-suited office crowd on their wayward way home. Summer is especially good, when the throngs spill out on to the street ten deep.

Café K. Appel, Oude Hoogstraat 27. Once known as the "Café of the Dead", this place lives up to its old name in its clientele at least. The loud (music is amplified to the pain threshold) and squalid haunt of Amsterdam's studiously wasted youth.

Kabul, Warmoesstraat 38. Bar of the adjacent budget hotel, and consequently open late.

De Koningshut, Spuistraat 269. In the early evening, at least, it's standing room only in this small, spit-and-sawdust bar, popular with office people on their way home or to dinner. Middle-aged swingers only.

Lokaal 't Loosje, Nieuwmarkt 32–34. Quiet old-style brown café that's been here for 200 years and looks its age.

Luxembourg, Spui 22–24. The latest watering-hole of Amsterdam's advertising and media brigade – striped shirts and bow ties abound. It's crowded too. If you can get in, it's actually a very elegant bar with a good (though pricey) selection of snacks. Overlooks the Singel at the back.

't Packhuys, Voetboogstraat 10. One of a clutch of bars that line this tiny street, an inviting place serving food at f12–18.

Het Paleis, Paleisstraat 16. Bar currently in vogue with students from the adjoining university buildings. Laid-back and likeable.

De Pieter, St. Pieterspoortsteeg 29. Opens at 10pm, and plays host to bands on Wed nights, a disco on Sat, and blaring music the rest of the week. Dark, very noisy, with a wildly eclectic crowd.

De Pieterspoort, St. Pieterspoortsteeg 3. A gentle prelude to *De Pieter*, just down the street.

De Pilsener Club, Begijnensteeg 4. More like someone's front room than a bar – indeed all drinks mysteriously appear from a back room. Photographs on the wall record generations of sociable drinking.

De Pilsery, Gravenstraat 10. Roomy bar behind the Nieuwe Kerk that has a comfortable back room and plays good jazz. Above all, though, you drink here for the bar's authentic nineteenth-century surroundings – little changed, right down to the cash register.

De Pool, Oude Hoogstraat 8. Pleasant bar, somewhat quieter than most of the others along this stretch.

Scheltema, N. Z. Voorburgwal 242. Journalists' bar, now only frequented by more senior newshounds and their occasionally famous interviewees, since all the newspapers that had their headquarters along here moved to the suburbs. Faded turn-of-the-century feel, with a reading table and meals for under f20.

De Schutter, Voetboogstraat 13–15. Former folk-music hangout, now simply a spacious upstairs bar, full of people munching on the cheap and basic food.

De Stoep, Singel 415. Peaceful bar in a part of town where few such places exist.

Stopera, Nieuwe Hoogstraat 41. So dubbed after the campaign to prevent the building of the new Muziektheater, this place is still well named, standing as it does directly opposite a metro station (another project over which there was much protest) and on top of much of the controversial rebuilding of the Jewish quarter. It's interesting in name only though; the bars back towards the hubbub of O. Z. Voorburgwal are much more exciting.

La Strada, N.Z. Voorburgwal 93–95. Exceptionally trendy bar whose interior changes monthly as aspiring – and not always inspiring – local artists are given free reign with the decor. Occasional fully-fledged exhibitions, poetry readings, live music on Saturdays. Good food too – pasta dishes start at f15.

Tapvreugd, Oude Hoogstraat 11. Far and away the most amicable of the loud, crowded music bars on this and surrounding streets. Like most of these places, though, its music and its regulars are strictly mid-1970s.

Three Musketeers, Martelaarsgracht 9. An alternative for the British expatriate community to the *Flying Dutchman*, a few doors down. Earthier, slightly straighter clientele than the dope-smokers of the Dutchman.

Tisfris, St. Antoniesbreestraat 142. Split-level café bar near the Rembrandt House. Youthful and popular.

De Verboden Vrucht, N. Z. Voorburgwal 256. Cosy, and a livelier choice than *Scheltma* nearby.

Wenteltrap, Gravenstraat 2. Minute bar near the Nieuwe Kerk – a handy central meeting place.

Wynand Fockink, Pijlsteeg 31. Ancient tasting-house about the size of a large cupboard. Closes 8pm.

Zwart, Dam Square. Nothing special, but arguably the city's most central bar.

De Zwart, Spuistraat 334. Less businesslike neighbour of the more famous *Hoppe* across the alley, but similarly crowded.

Outer Central

Aas van Bokalen, Keizersgracht 335. Unpretentious local bar, with good food from f17. Great collection of Motown tapes. Very small, so go either early or late.

Café Americain, American Hotel, Leidseplein 2E–30. The terrace bar here has been a gathering-point for Amsterdam media people for years, and it's worth coming here at least once for the decor: art nouveau frills coordinated down to the doorknobs. A place to be seen, with prices not surprisingly above average. Good fast lunches, too.

De Balie, Kleine Gartmanplantsoen 10. Big high-ceilinged haunt of the city's trendy lefties. Not especially inspiring, but if you're stuck on Leidseplein on a Saturday night, De Balie provides a welcome change of atmosphere.

De Beiaard, Herengracht 90. Light and airy Fifties-style bar for genuine beer aficionados. A wide selection of bottled and draught beers selected with true dedication by the owner, who delights in filling you in on the relative properties of each.

Belhamel, Brouwersgracht 60. Kitschy bar/restaurant with an art nouveau style interior and excellent, though costly, French food. The main attraction in summer is one of the most picturesque views in Amsterdam.

Chris, Bloemstraat 42. Very proud of itself for being the Jordaan's (and Amsterdam's) oldest bar, dating from the early seventeenth century. Comfortable, homely atmosphere.

De Doffer, Runstraat 12. Small, affable bar with food and a billiards table.

De Druif, Rapenburgerplein 83. One of the city's most beguiling bars, and one that hardly anyone knows about. Its popularity with the locals lends it a village pub feel.

De Dwarsboom, Boomstraat 41a. Jordaan neighbourhood bar with food from f15 upwards.

't Entrée Pôtje, Entrepot Dok 64. Just about the only bar in this up-and-coming area. The clientele hail from the surrounding hi-tech offices.

Gambit, 20 Bloemgracht. Chess bar, with boards laid out all day until midnight.

H'88, Herengracht 88. Part of a student complex, this place stays open until 6am, by which time it's strictly diehard drinkers' territory.

Hegeraad, Noordermarkt 34. Old-fashioned, lovingly-maintained brown café with a fiercely local clientele.

Het Hok, Lange Leidsedwarsstraat 134. Games bar, where you can play backgammon, chess or draughts or just drink against a backdrop of clicking counters. Pleasingly unpretentious after the plastic restaurants of the rest of the street, though women may find the overwhelmingly male presence off-putting.

Huyschkaemer, Utrechtsestraat 137. Recently reopened in rag-rolled, interior-designed glory, and already established as the favourite watering-hole of arty students.

De Kalkhoven, Prinsengracht 283. One of the city's most characteristic brown cafés. Nothing special, but warm and welcoming.

De Kat in de Wijngaert, Lindengracht 160. Hefty *bessenjenevers* and an enticing name.

De Klepel, Prinsenstraat 22. Quiet bar whose speciality is chess playing. English newspapers.

L & B, Korte Leidsedwarsstraat 82. A cosy bar, rather misplaced among the touristy restaurants and clubs of this part of town. Has a selection of 200 different whiskies and bourbons from around the world. Open until 3am.

Land van Walem, Keizersgracht 449. Walem is one of Amsterdam's nouveau-chic cafés: cool, light, and vehemently non-brown. Clientele are stylish in taste and dress, food a kind of hybrid French-Dutch with full meals going for around f20; there's a wide selection of newspapers and magazines that includes some in English. Usually packed.

Laurier 33, 1e Laurierdwarsstraat 33. Small, fashionable bar/coffee shop, good for its food, pool table, and perhaps most reputedly, its dope.

Morlang, Keizersgracht 451. Bar/restaurant of the new wave yuppie variety (much like *Walem* next door), serving good food for around f15. Live music Tues.

Het Molenpad, Prinsengracht 653. Thinking persons' bar and art gallery filled with academic types from the public library just along the canal.

't Monumentje, Westerstraat 120. Unspectacular Jordaan local haunt that plays good music. Likeable and cheap.

Mulliners Wijnlokaal, Lijnsbaansgracht 267. Upmarket wine bar (prices around f5 a glass, f25 a bottle) with food from f15. Good atmosphere.

Nol, Westerstraat 109. Probably the epitome of the jolly Jordaan singing bar, a luridly lit dive popular with Jordaan gangsters and ordinary Amsterdammers alike. Opens and closes late, especially on weekends, when the back-slapping joviality and drunken sing-alongs keep you here until closing time at least.

Oblomow, Reguliersdwarsstraat 40. On what is possibly Amsterdam's chicest street (though by day you'd never know it), Oblomow is very much the drinking spot of the city's filofax bunch, though it's a nice spot to eat and drink nevertheless, with a garden out the back and prices only slightly above average. At time of writing Oblomow had closed down and was rumoured to have gone bankrupt. Watch this space . . .

Oerwoud, Haarlemmerdijk 165. Ultra-modern café with an overpoweringly white interior. Next to The Movies arthouse cinema and populated by the same breed of beautiful people.

Oosterling, Utrechtsestraat 140. Stone-floored local bar-cum-off licence that's been in the same family since the middle of the last century. Very quiet, home to some serious drinkers.

De la Paix, Wolvenstraat 22–24. More of a restaurant than a bar, really, but a friendly place whose drinks are much more reasonably-priced than the food. Modern music and a youthful crowd.

Paris Brest, Prinsengracht 375. Next door to Van Puffelen (see below) and owned by the same man, Paris Brest is the designer alternative: all chrome and glass and black leather filofaxes. A very reasonable set menu at f29.

De Pels, Huidenstraat 25. Few surprises in this, one of Amsterdam's quieter but more pleasant bars.

De Prins, Prinsengracht 124. Boisterous student bar, with a wide range of drinks and a well-priced menu that includes fondues. A good place to drink in a great part of town.

De Prinses, Prinsengracht 96. A little way down the canal from *De Prins*, this bar is open late and, should you feel like a game, sports a dartboard.

Van Puffelen, Prinsengracht 377. More a restaurant than a café, and consequently only open from 4pm. But an appealing place to drink, with a huge choice of international beers and a peaceful reading room out the back. Food is French in style and, though not cheap (f20+), well worth it.

De Reiger, Nieuwe Leliestraat 34. The Jordaan's main meeting place, an old-style café filled with modish Amsterdammers. Affordable food.

Rum Runners, Prinsengracht 277. Tropical-type bar/restaurant converted with neo-colonial chic from the old Westerkerk hall. A broad range of cocktails, but the food – and service – can be dire.

Schiller, Rembrandtsplein 26. Art deco bar of the upstairs hotel, authentic in both feel and decor, and offering a genteel escape from the tackiness of most of the rest of Rembrandtsplein. Meals – French-Dutch – go for around f20.

't Smackzeyl, Brouwersgracht 101. Boisterous drinking-hole on the fringes of the Jordaan frequented by well-doused tourists in various stages of inebriation. Guinness on tap and a light, inexpensive menu.

't Smalle, Eglantiersgracht 12, corner of Prinsengracht. Candle-lit and comfortable, with bench seating around the wall.

De Tap, Prinsengracht 478. Roomy bar with a balcony and more individuality than you'd expect two minutes from the Leidseplein.

Theo Ruiter, Rozengracht 160. Small edge-of-Jordaan bar largely patronised by middle-aged regulars. Pleasant enough, but a stop-off rather than an all-nighter.

De Tuin, 2e Tuindwarsstraat 13. The Jordaan has some marvellously unpretentious bars, and this is one of the best: agreeably unkempt and always filled with locals.

De Twee Heiligen, Prinsengracht 178. Small bar with a pool table and some fine Mexican food. Good in summer when the church tower's lit.

Twee Prinsen, Prinsenstraat 27. Cornerside people-watching bar that's a useful starting place for touring the area. Its (heated) terrace makes it possible to sit outside, even in winter.

De Twee Zwaantjes, Prinsengracht 114. Tiny Jordaan bar whose live accordion music and raucous singing you'll either love or hate. Fun, in an oompah-pah sort of way.

De Vergulde Gaper, Prinsenstraat 30. Opposite the *Twee Prinsen*, this offers much the same kind of low-key attraction – though it's somewhat larger and there's a wider choice of food. Has a heated terrace if you fancy sitting outside.

Wheels, Wolvenstraat 2–4. Deceptively like any other brown café to look at, but actually the firmly British haunt of a number of ex-pats. Expect to be served by a friendly north London soul boy.

Winkel, Noordermarkt 43. A popular, though not particularly brown, café, where the main language seems to be English and the food – well-priced – largely Italian-oriented.

Outside the Singelgracht

Keysers, Van Baerlestraat 96. In operation since 1905, and right next door to the Concertgebouw, this café-restaurant exudes fin-de-siècle charm, with ferns, gliding, bow-tied waiters, and a dark, wood-carved interior. Slightly higher prices, especially for the food, but a great place to idle away an hour over coffee. You'll need to make bookings for the restaurant and dress accordingly.

't Orkestje, Van Baerlestraat 51. Pleasant *eetcafé* with musical-theme decor – the Concertgebouw is just across the street. Not cheap.

Welling, J. W. Brouwerstraat 32. Supposedly the traditional haunt of the gloomy Amsterdam intellectual, *Welling* is usually packed solid with performers and visitors from the Concertgebouw next door.

Wildschut, Roelof Hartplein 1. Large and congenial bar whose art deco trimmings attract the New South's trendies. The best bet for this area.

Coffee Shops and Tea Rooms

As with bars, there are two types of Amsterdam **coffee shops**: those whose principle business is the buying, selling and consuming of dope, and the more traditional places that sell neither dope nor alcohol but do serve sandwiches or a light menu for lower prices than you'd pay in a fully-fledged restaurant; some offer pastries or chocolates.

The so-called **"smoking" coffee shops** are easy to identify: brightly lit, with starkly modern furniture and an accent on healthy food, they're about as far from the cosy Dutch *brown café* as it's possible to get. Smoking dope is the primary pastime (all sell a range of hash and grass), and most also have video screens, (loud) music, and a selection of games from baccarat to pool; they're open roughly from late morning/midday until around midnight. There are a number of chains – *The Bulldog, Prix d'Ami, Fancy Free* – each of which has several branches all over the city, but the boom-time of the smoking bar seems to have come and gone: the police raided the main Bulldog branch recently and there's been a clampdown on the degree to which the coffee shops may advertise their products. Time was when cannabis-leaf symbols and customer-grabbing slogans were part of the fabric of an Amsterdam street; nowadays coffee shops just leave their doors wide open so you can sniff their wares. For real dopeheads there's the **Hash Info Museum** (p.89), which also survives despite crackdowns. For more on dope see p.11.

The growth of "smoking" coffee shops has made "straight" places increasingly defensive, and all of the coffee shops listed as **"non-smoking"** go to great lengths to emphasise that they don't sell dope, and that its consumption on the premises is strictly forbidden; some are even considering calling themselves "tea rooms" to avoid confusion. Again, if you're not sure, ask.

"Smoking"

Biba, Hazenstraat 15. In a street of coffee shops, this is one of the best.

Bon Ami, Brouwersgracht 137. Very loud music.

The Bulldog, Leidseplein 13–17; O. Z. Voorburgwal 90; O. Z. Voorburgwal 132; Hekelveld 7. The biggest and most famous of the coffee-shop chains, and a long way from its pokey Red Light district-dive origins. The police raid on its Leidseplein branch a year or so ago dented its reputation slightly, but its commercial viability not at all, and it has recently opened a branch in The

Hague. Amsterdam's main Leidseplein branch (the "Palace"), housed in a former police station, has a large cocktail bar, coffee shop, juice bar, souvenir shop. It's large and brash, not at all the place for a quiet smoke, though the dope they sell (packaged up in neat little brand-labelled bags) is reliably good.

Extase, Oude Hoogstraat 2. Part of a chain run by the initiator of the *Hash Info Museum*. Considerably less chi-chi than the big cheeses.

Fairy Nuff, 2e Laurierdwarsstraat 1b. Small and quiet, with a low-key atmosphere.

Fancy Free, Martelaarsgracht 4; Haarlemmerstraat 64. Slick, plush and commercial, very much in *The Bulldog* mould.

Goa, Kloveniersburgwal 42. A member of the *Extase* chain (see above).

Grasshopper, N. Z. Voorburgwal 59. One of the city's more welcoming "smoking" coffee shops, though at times overwhelmed by tourists.

Haussmann, Singel 458; Zieseniskade 2. White, modernistic coffee shop with more than a hint of soullessness.

Just a Puff, 2e Tuindwarsstraat 1, Instantly recognisable friendly Jordaan smoking-hole. Open irregularly, though.

Pie in the Sky, 2e Laurierdwarsstraat 64. Beautiful canal-corner setting, great for outside summer lounging.

Prix d'Ami, Haringpakkersteeg 3; Nieuwendijk 239. Super-entrepreneurial Amsterdam chain, but with little of the character of its rivals.

Roma, O. Z. Achterburgwal 162. Red Light district smoker, part of the *Exstase/Goa* concern.

Rusland, Rusland 16. One of the first Amsterdam coffee shops, and a cramped and vibrant place that's a favourite with both dope fans and tea addicts (43 different kinds). A little worse for a recent extension, but still a cut above the rest.

Siberië, Brouwersgracht 11. Set up by the former staff of *Rusland* and notable for the way it has avoided the over-commercialisation of the large chains. Very relaxed, very friendly, and worth a visit whether you want to smoke or not.

So Fine, Prinsengracht 30. Long-established coffee shop, big on atmosphere at night with good food and music, a pool table, and a video room.

"Non-smoking"

Arnold Cornelis, Elandsgracht 78. Confectioner with a snug tea room.

Back Stage Boutique/Coffee Shop, Utrechtsedwarsstraat 67. Run by former cabaret stars, the Christmas Twins, this off-beat place also sells knitwear and African jewellery.

Bâton, Herengracht 82. Convivial coffee shop with a huge array of sandwiches. Handy for cheap lunches in a central location.

Berkhoff, Leidsestraat 46. *The* place for pastries and chocolates, with a small tea room at the back.

J. G. Beune, Haarlemmerdijk 156. Age-old chocolatier with a tea room attached.

Café Panini, Vijzelgracht 3–5. Coffee shop-cum-restaurant that features good sandwiches and, in the evening, pasta dishes.

Cocky's Coffeeshop en Sandwich Bar, Raadhuisstraat 8. Good no-nonsense coffee shop with a wide variety of sandwiches.

De Eenhorn, Warmoesstraat 16. Raw brick walls, oak beams, paintings and classical music. A stark contrast to the surrounding Red Light district.

Garbo, N.Z. Voorburgwal 163. Good salads and *dagschotels*. A rarity among the rip-off places that spill out from the Dam.

Granny, 1e van der Helststraat 45. Just off the Albert Cuyp market, with terrific *appelgebak* and *koffie verkeerd*.

Karbeel, Warmoesstraat 58. Once run by the present owner of *De Eenhorn* (see above), and similar in style and set up.

Lindsay's Teashop, Kalverstraat 185. An attempt to recreate a little piece of England in the unlikely location of the basement of the American Discount Book Centre. The food, though, is fine: real English cream teas, with home-made pies and trifles. And it's a refreshing escape from the Kalverstraat shopping mafia.

Museum Coffee Shop Dialoog, Prinsengracht 261a. A few doors down from the Anne Frank House, one long room filled with paintings, restrained classical music and, downstairs, a gallery of Latin American art. A good choice of sandwiches and salads, too.

Pompadour Patisserie, Huidenstraat 12. Another Amsterdam patisserie specialising in handmade chocolates.

The Sandwich Shop, P. C. Hooftstraat 86. Plain but worthy alternative to the chic eateries on this affluent street.

Studio 2, Singel 504. Pleasantly situated, airy coffee shop that sells a delicious selection of rolls and sandwiches. Recommended.

De Utrechtsepoort, Utrechtsestraat 113. Small and homely and serving delicious pancakes.

Women-Only Bars and Coffee Shops

Many of Amsterdam's women-only bars have a strong lesbian following, though straight women are welcome everywhere.

Het Bruine Paard, Prinsengracht 44. Quiet local café, handy for a relaxing evening.

Floor, Lindengracht 95. Likeable local café with billiard table. Mainly lesbian.

Françoise's Coffeeshop and Gallery, Kerkstraat 176. Lively and elegant atmosphere, good breakfasts and lunches.

Groep 7152. A non-political group of lesbian and bisexual women that organises open meetings in a different bar each month.

Saarein, Elandstraat 119. Though some of the former glory of this café is gone, still a useful starting point for contacts and info, even for joining a women's football team. Mon 8pm–1am, Tues–Thurs 3pm–1am, Sat 3pm–2am, Sun 3pm–1am.

VivelaVie, Amstelstraat 7. Small, stylish but non-exclusive bar that runs a monthly women-only night at a nearby disco.

Gay Men's Bars and Coffee Shops

Amstel Taveerne, Amstel 54. Always packed, and at its most vivacious in summer when the crowds spill out on to the street. Probably the best-established gay hangout in town.

April, Reguliersdwarsstraat 27. Arguably the most enjoyable of Reguliersdwarsstraat's line up of gay bars, with a good selection of foreign newspapers, cakes, and coffee as well as booze.

Argos Club, Warmoesstraat 95. Amsterdam's oldest leather bar. Tame enough in its front bar; the back bar, on the other hand, is not for those with inhibitions.

't Balkje Coffeeshop, Kerkstraat 46–48. Pleasant ambience makes this a popular meeting place for the Kerkstraat gay scene; 8am–2pm.

Café Amstel 102, Amstel 102. Mixed bar in the centre of the Amstel gay area. Good range of beers.

Chez Manfred, Halvemaansteeg 10. Between Rembrandtsplein and the Amstel, this tiny bar is the Amsterdam gay scene at its gregarious best. Can be outrageous at party times.

Club Jaecques, Warmoesstraat 93. Backroom bar for leather and denim types. A meeting place for locals, but appropriate visitors are made welcome.

Coffeeshop Downtown, Reguliersdwarsstraat 31. Excellent and inexpensive meals in a youthful venue.

Company, Amstel 106. Western-style leather bar with pool table. Fills up later in the evening. Back-room available.

Cosmo Bar, Kerkstraat 42. Part of the *West End Hotel* (for which see p.34), this late-night bar/club launches into action as Kerkstraat's other nightspots fade. Open till 3am.

Cuckoo's Nest, N. Z. Kolk 6. Leather bar sporting "the world's largest play-room". Other attractions include films, monthly parties, and a free buffet Sun.

Eagle, Warmoesstraat 86. Air-conditioned leather bar with large back room. Popular with men of all ages, gets very busy late at night. Open until 5am.

The Eighties, Brouwersgracht 139: High-class ambience, but an extremely small menu and out-of-place black plastic furnishings. Open until 8pm, 10pm in summer.

Eldorado Bar, Amstel 50. Local bar catering for a good mixture of natives and visitors. Fairly quiet, and a nice place for a relaxing drink.

Gaiety, Amstel 14. Small gay bar with welcoming staff and inexpensive drinks.

De Komedie, Amstel 100. Friendly bar in traditional brown café setting.

Madame Arthur, Warmoesstraat 131. Transvestite show bar open Wed–Sun, no admission charge but beers f5 a throw. Fun if you like drag.

Open, Amstelstraat 5. Trendy but non-cruising atmosphere, regular exhibitions. Best late-night, with an intimate atmosphere more suitable for dates than pick-ups.

Monopole Taveerne, Amstel 60. A place to mix and mingle, especially on hot afternoons.

Route 66, Kerkstraat 66. Convivial place and the city's only gay bar with a juke box.

De Spijker, Kerkstraat 4. Amiable bar under the American Repertory Theatre office. Can be crowded Tues.

Taveerne De Pul, Kerkstraat 45. Favourite meeting place for the city's gay expatriates, and worth a visit for the ceiling alone.

Traffic, Reguliersdwarsstraat 11. Late-night hi-tech bar with hi-profile customers. Trendy.

Restaurants

Apart from a short section on budget eating at the city's *mensas*, the restaurants and *eetcafés* that follow are grouped by cuisine and listed alphabetically: you'll find some indication of what each place is likely to **cost** within its listing, but as a broad guide, very few will cost more than f25 for a main course, and there are many that charge less than this; Dutch restaurants and *eetcafés* in particular serve plenty of smaller dishes for much less. For good-value eating, the **bar listings** on p.117 are also worth checking: many serve food, and at lunchtime it's possible to fill up extremely cheaply with a bowl of soup or a french bread sandwich.

Bars, of course, are **open** all day; most restaurants open around 5pm. The Dutch eat out early – rarely later than 9pm – and in both restaurants and bars, kitchens are normally closed by 11pm at the latest; vegetarian restaurants tend to shut their doors even earlier.

Mensas
These are Amsterdam's student caféterias, and as such are not frequented so much for the quality of the food as for the prices which at around f7.50 for a full meal can hardly be beaten. The food itself isn't bad, filling enough if not especially tasty.

Atrium, O. Z. Voorburgwal 237. Open Mon–Fri noon–2pm and 5–7pm, all year round.

De Weesper, Weesperstraat 5 (☎22 40 36). Open Mon–Fri 5–7.25pm, year-round.

Dutch

De Bak, Prinsengracht 193 (☎25 79 72). Good portions for moderate prices, though lately somewhat of a tourist hangout and with a menu that seems to have shrunk down to spare ribs and not much else. See also *De Bak's* sister restaurant, *Sing Singel*, below.

De Bijenkorf, Damrak 90 (☎21 80 80). Restaurant of the top-notch department store, and one of the best places for a full Dutch breakfast – around f6 – and good value, if unexciting, lunches for f10 upwards.

De Blauwe Hollander, Leidsekruisstraat 28 (☎23 30 14). Dutch food in generous quantities – something of a boon in an otherwise touristy, unappealing part of town. Most meals f15–f20.

Claes Claesz, Egelantiersstraat 24–26 (☎25 53 06). Exceptionally friendly Jordaan restaurant that attracts a good mixed crowd and serves excellent Dutch food, though not at all cheaply. Reckon on f25 and up for a main course. Live music most nights. Often has (pricey) special menus to celebrate specific occasions – carnival, Easter, the Queen's Birthday, etc; best check first.

Dorrius, N. Z. Voorburgwal 336–342 (☎23 58 75). An institution as far as traditional Dutch food is concerned. Hearty helpings served by seasoned, white-aproned waiters. Pricey.

De Eenhorn, 2e Egelantiersdwarsstraat 6 (☎23 83 52). A less attractive alternative to *De Eetuin* (see below), but handy if it's full.

De Eettuin, 2e Tuindwarsstraat 10 (☎23 77 06). Hefty portions of Dutch food, all with a salad from a serve-yourself bar for f15–18. Non-meat eaters can content themselves with the large, if dull, vegetarian plate, or the delicious fish casserole.

Haesje Claes, N. Z. Voorburgwal 320 (☎24 99 98). Dutch cuisine at its best – and cheaper than the more famous *Dorrius*, along the street. extremely popular; go as early as you can manage.

Keuken van 1870, Spuistraat 4 (☎24 89 65). Basic, traditional Dutch cooking – a good deal if money's short.

Leto, Haarlemerdijk 114 (☎26 56 95). Unexciting food but colourful management.

Moeder's Pot, Vinkenstraat 119 (☎23 76 43). Ultra-cheap Dutch food. Recommended.

Rosereijn, Haarlemerdijk 52 (☎23 44 25). Open all day every day, and a good option for lunch or dinner, with dishes from around f18, snacks and soups for much less.

Sassafras, Leidsegracht 68 (☎24 32 21). Inexpensive Dutch meals, though not very friendly.

Simon's Real Dutch Restaurant, Spuistraat 299 (☎23 11 41). Supremely uninteresting food, but lots of it and inexpensive.

Sing Singel, Singel 101 (☎25 25 81). Sister restaurant to *De Bak*, above.

Fish

Albatros, Westerstraat 264 (☎27 99 32). Family-run restaurant serving some mouth-wateringly imaginative fish dishes – though, at f30 up, for no mean cost. A place to splash out and linger over a meal.

De Gouden Leeuw, Prinsengracht 274 ☎(23 94 20). Overpriced and over-rated. Go only if someone else is paying.

Lucius, Spuistraat 247 (☎24 18 31). Pricey, but one of the best fish restaurants in town, though the service they give – particularly to credit card-paying customers – leaves something to be desired.

Noordzee, Kalverstraat 122 (☎23 73 37). Central Amsterdam branch of a chain that specialises in cheap fish lunches and sandwiches. Meals for under f10, sandwiches f3–f5.

De Oesterbar, Leidseplein 10 (☎26 34 63). Pricey veteran overlooking the Leidseplein action, popular with a largely older crowd. Main courses f35 up, and not really worth it.

Sluizer, Utrechtsestraat 45 (☎26 35 57). Next door to its trendy meat-based partner, main courses here average out at about f20–25 – which, for the quality of the food, service and decor, is fine value.

Pancakes

Bredero, O. Z. Voorburgwal 244 (☎22 94 61). On the edge of the Red Light district, one of the city's best pancake deals.

The Pancake Bakery, Prinsengracht 191 (☎25 13 33). Open all day; has a large selection of pancakes from f8.

Welcome, Prinsengracht 332 (☎22 36 28). Homely restaurant serving pancakes for around f10.

Vegetarian and Health Food

Baldur, Weteringschans 76 (☎24 46 72). Standard vegetarian food. Dishes of the day f12–15, other dishes – though a limited selection – f10 upwards.

De Bast, Huidenstraat 19 (☎24 97 47). Pleasant and tasty food, though the ambience is a bit clinical and service can be slow. Good lunch specials.

Beit-Hamazon, Anjelierstraat 57 (☎27 42 55). Buried in the back end of the Jordaan, but worth seeking out for a fresh-tasting, macrobiotic-ish menu, generously portioned, and some almost cringingly friendly – if slow – service. Reasonable prices, open until 10pm.

Bolhoed, Prinsengracht 60 (☎26 18 03). Health food place with set lunches for f10, dinner for f17. The food is healthy with a vengeance; try the natural beer to wash it down. Open until 10pm.

Egg Cream, St. Jacobstraat 19 (☎23 05 75). Amsterdam's most famous vegetarian restaurant, cheap and atmospheric, though the food isn't always exclusively veggie. Set meals f8–f12. Bear in mind the early closing time of 8pm.

Golden Temple, Utrechtsestraat 126 (☎26 85 60). Laid-back place with a little more soul than the average Amsterdam veggie joint. Gentle live music. Open until 9pm.

Klaver Koning, Koningstraat 29 (☎26 10 85). Excellent upmarket vegetarian restaurant, with decent wine and a refreshingly un-ascetic atmosphere. But not cheap.

Manou Macrobiotic Restaurant, Kerkstraat 148 (☎24 13 94). A central place for those who take their vegetarianism seriously.

Sisters, Nes 102 (☎26 39 70). A busy vegetarian restaurant serving *dagschotels* and other main courses for around f16, as well as plenty of snack-type items. Open until 10pm.

De Vliegende Schotel, Nieuwe Leliestraat 162 (☎25 20 41). Very basic, very cheap, with a good noticeboard.

Ethnic

Chinese, Japanese, Thai and Filipino

Dynasty, Reguliersdwarsstraat 30 (☎26 84 00). Festive choice of Indo-Chinese food, but not for the shoestring traveller. A rather middle-aged crowd.

De Klaas Compaen, Raamgracht 9 (☎33 87 08). Good Thai food at affordable prices.

Lana Thai, Warmoesstraat 10 (☎24 21 79). The best Thai restaurant in town, with seating overlooking the water of Damrak. Quality food, chic surroundings and fair prices. Closed Tues.

Mango Bay, Westerstraat 91 (☎38 10 39). Slow service and high prices for the Filipino food, but the cocktails are terminal.

New San Kong, Amstelveenseweg 338–344 (☎66 29 370). Don't be put off by the ranch-style decor: the food is excellent and inexpensive (try the *dim sum*). Take tram #24 to the end of the line.

Nieuwe Lange Muur, Berenstraat 28 (☎25 89 53). Friendly, cheap takeaway with a couple of tables. Chinese, Vietnamese, Indonesian dishes.

TAKEAWAY FOOD

As well as the usual *Febo* snack bars and *frites* stalls, many pizzerias, Indian, Chinese and Indonesian restaurants have takeaway services. There are also **pizza-lines**, which deliver pizza for free in response to a telephone call. The pizzas generally start at around f12; phone numbers include ☎75 07 36 and ☎23 55 39.

For **more upmarket takeaway meals**, *De Traiterie*, Scheldestraat 100 (☎79 66 56), will deliver; *Delicious*, at Heisteeg 8 (☎22 48 50), will too, though it's central enough to pop into yourself. *Julius Traiteurs*, Utrechtsestraat 55 (☎23 15 64), is the last word to date on the yuppification of Amsterdam.

Oshima, Prinsengracht 411 (☎25 09 96). Amsterdam's first centrally-located and reasonably-priced Japanese restaurant. Sushi a speciality, from f12.50; main courses f25 plus. In summer the restaurant can get a bit sticky; book early if you don't want to sit on Tatami.

Roeng Warie, Rokin 85 (☎26 79 13); Amstel 32 (☎20 02 52). Thai food, well priced and centrally located among the costlier reaches of Rokin.

Umeno, Agamemnonstraat 27 (☎76 60 89). Reasonably priced Japanese restaurants are hard to find, but this one, though down in the residential New South, has cooking and prices that are well worth the journey. Closed Wed; tram #24.

Yoichi, Weteringschans 128 (☎22 68 29). High-class Japanese cuisine in an improbable dark-brown, old Dutch atmosphere. Closed Mon.

French

Beddington's, Roelof Hartstraat (☎76 52 01). Refined French blended with Japanese delicacy, within walking distance of Museumplein. Not cheap, but never disappointing. Splash-outs and celebrations only.

Bistro de Vlier, Prinsengracht 422 (☎23 22 81). Fairly basic cooking in an affable atmosphere; main meals from f22. Open Sundays, which is a boon.

Cafecox, Marnixstraat 429 (☎20 72 22). Stylish but amicable bar and restaurant underneath the Stadsschouwburg which serves a wide range of dishes, most for around f25. *Dagschotels* from f16.50.

't Fornuis, Utrechtsestraat 33 (☎26 91 39). A slightly cheaper alternative to *Orient Express* (see below), though it's usually very busy. Delicious f29 three-course menu.

De Gouden Reael, Zandhoek 14 (☎23 38 83). Fine French food at reasonable prices. Closed Sun.

Grand Café Restaurant First Class, Centraal Station, Stationsplein 15 (☎25 01 31). Gourmet French cuisine with well-balanced menu in the railway station's restored late-nineteenth-century restaurant. Good value, and has a wide array of snacks.

Intermezzo, Herenstraat 28 (☎26 01 67). Wonderful French-Dutch cooking at above-average prices, but worth every penny. Among the best in this section.

De Kikker, Egelantiersstraat 130 (☎27 91 98). Two-tier, top quality restaurant that has a downstairs eetcafé with dagschotels for around f23. Upstairs is only really accessible for the well-dressed, wealthy, committed gourmet.

L.P. Jardin Parisien, Utrechtsestraat 30a (☎26 80 93). Cheap and plain, with around thirty different menus on offer, most of which seem to start with prawn cocktail. Two-courses f17.

Orient Express, Utrechtsestraat 29 (☎20 51 29). Not cheap, but very good French food; you can also choose from a menu which changes every month including French-flavoured items from each of the countries the Orient Express passes through.

Petra van Niftrik, Reestraat 7 (☎26 01 37). Small French-European restaurant with prices only slightly inflated. Closed Sun–Mon.

Robert & Abraham Kef, Marnixstraat 192 (☎26 22 10). Not a restaurant or bar but a cheese shop with a few tables for sampling the (mainly French) cheeses with a bottle of wine. Ideal for lunch or a snack. Open Tues–Sat until 6pm.

Schransen Bij Jansen, Voetboogstraat 12 (27 75 74). Inexpensive nouvelle cuisine. Trendy but nice.

Sluizer, Utrechtsestraat 41–43 (☎22 63 76). French-oriented food, in one of Amsterdam's most atmospheric and up-and-coming restaurants. There's a fish restaurant of the same name next door, see above.

De Smoeshaan, Leidsekade 90 (☎27 69 66). First-floor theatre restaurant, or downstairs bar, with inexpensive French cuisine.

Het Tuinhuysch, Wolvenstraat 16 (☎ 23 91 56). Delicate cooking at fairly gentle prices; set menu f29.

Greek and Turkish

Aphrodite, Lange Leidsedwarsstraat 91 (☎22 73 82). Refined Greek cooking in a street where you certainly wouldn't expect it. Fair prices too.

Filoxenia, Berenstraat 8 (☎24 42 92). Small, friendly, reasonably-priced – and filling.

Knossos, Herenstraat 3 (☎26 33 32). Good standby Greek restaurant.

Plaka, Egelantiersstraat 124 (☎27 93 38). Enormous platefuls of Greek grub for under f20; vegetarian dishes too. Popular (either book ahead or turn up early) and friendly.

Sultan Ahmet, Haarlemmerdijk 176 (☎24 83 58). Low-key – and cheap – Turkish restaurant.

Indian

Koh-I-Noor, Westermarkt 29 (☎23 31 33). One of the city's better Indian restaurants, and not overpriced.

Mughal, Rokin 107 (☎24 24 16). Above-average and centrally located.

New Delhi, Overtoom 350 (☎16 78 58). On the far side of the Vondelpark but well worth the journey. Northern-style, very filling dishes from f8.

Purna, Hartenstraat 29 (☎23 67 72). The speciality here is spicy tandoori; they also sell Indian silk paintings.

Rishi Roti Room, 1e Oosterparkstraat 91 (☎92 86 28). Cheap and cheerful place.

The Tandoor, Leidseplein 19 (☎23 44 15). Doesn't live up to its excellent reputation, but the tandoori dishes are very tasty, if nothing like as cheap as the *New Delhi* (see above).

Indonesian

Bojo, Lange Leidsedwarsstraat 51 (☎22 74 34). Possibly the best-value – if not the best – Indonesian place in town, and open until 6am. Expect to wait for a table, though – we weren't the first to discover it. Highly recommended.

Jaya, 1e Anjeliersdwarsstraat 18 (☎24 01 22). One of the smallest and finest of the city's Indonesian restaurants, with classical music as an accompaniment to your food. Bookings advised.

Mr Moto, Oude Doelenstraat 1 (☎24 51 99). Fast food Indo-Chinese, similar to *Yu & Mie* (below) but not as good.

Sama Sebo, P. C. Hooftstraat 27 (☎66 28 146). Amsterdam's best-known Indonesian restaurant, especially for *rijstaffel* – though the prices may put you off. However, it's easy to eat quite reasonably by choosing your dishes à la carte And the food is usually great. Make bookings.

Speciaal, Nieuwe Leliestraat 142 (☎24 97 06). Moderately priced and one of the best in town.

Tempo Doeloe, Utrechtsestraat 75 (☎25 67 18). Reliable place close by Rembrandtsplein. As with all Indonesian restaurants, be guided by the waiter when choosing a *rijstaffel* – some of the dishes are very hot indeed.

Yu and Mie, Reguliersbreestraat 15–17 (☎27 67 68); Damrak 47 (☎20 43 67). Cheap, though plastic, fast food Indonesian style: good, surprisingly fresh-tasting fodder. More a lunch stopover than an evening eating joint.

Italian

Burger's Patio, 2e Tuindwarsstraat 12 (☎23 68 54). Moderately priced, young and convivial Italian restaurant. Despite the name, not a burger in sight.

La Botta, Lijnbaansgracht 120 (☎23 55 39). Best pizzeria in this part of town. Also a takeaway that delivers.

Caprese, Nieuwendijk 9 (☎20 00 59). Centrally located and inexpensive Italian restaurant.

Casa di David, Singel 426 (☎24 50 93). Solid-value place with a sister self-service restaurant at Kalverstraat 180.

Mamma Mia, 2e Leliedwarsstraat 13 (☎25 82 38). Good selection of pizzas, from f12, in a pleasant family atmosphere.

Pizzeria Collina, Rozenstraat 145 (☎25 67 15). Cheap, reliable pizzeria.

Pizzeria Mimo, Lange Leidsedwarsstraat 37 (☎22 79 35). Perhaps the best of the dozens of Italian restaurants along this street.

Pizzeria Pastorale, Haarlemmerdijk 139 (☎25 99 28). Good-value pizzas.

Tartufo, Singel 449 (☎27 71 75). Two-tiered, two-menu place with a good choice of fair-priced pasta dishes downstairs.

Toscana, Haarlemmerdijk 178 (☎22 03 53). Fairly average food, but the pizzas and pasta dishes are all half-price from Monday to Thursday. At other times, prices start at f11.

North, Latin and South American

Alfonso's, Korte Leidsedwarsstraat 69 (☎27 05 80); Utrechtsestraat 32 (☎ 25 94 26). Substantial helpings of relatively bland Mexican food at well under f20 per person for the main course. Good value for Leidseplein, and not too touristy, but avoid the *margaritas*, which are watery and overpriced.

Café Pacifico, Warmoesstraat 31 (☎24 29 11). If you like Mexican food, or its California adaptation (or both), this is the place – only minutes from Centraal Station.

Cajun Louisiana Kitchen, Ceintuurbaan 256–260 (☎66 24 369). Not cheap, but it offers authentic Cajun flavours.

Canecao Rio, Reguliersdwarsstraat 8 (☎25 05 92). Brazilian food with live music.

Caramba, Lindengracht 342 (☎27 11 88). Steamy, busy Mexican restaurant in the heart of the Jordaan. The margaritas almost on a par with Rose's.

Curly's, N. Z. Voorburgwal 22 (☎24 60 92). The food, plentifully supplied, is only average Tex-Mex fare. But relaxed atmosphere, music and service.

Mexico, Prinsengracht 188 (☎24 65 28). A cheaper and more amiable alternative to the glossier, more central eateries.

Rose's Cantina, Reguliersdwarsstraat 38 (☎25 97 97). In the heart of trendy Amsterdam, this qualifies as possibly the city's most crowded restaurant. No bookings, and you'll almost definitely have to wait, but it's no hardship to sit at the bar nursing a cocktail and watching the would-be cool bunch – the margaritas should carry a public health warning. The Tex-Mex food is good too, from around f16.

Sarita's Cantina, Lange Leidsedwarsstraat 29 (☎27 78 40). Nothing like as nice as Rose's (above), but serving good food at similar prices.

Spanish

La Cacerola, Weteringstraat 41 (☎26 53 97). Small and secluded, with very eccentric service.

Casa Tobio, Lindengracht 31 (☎24 89 87). Small Jordaan restaurant which doles out vast servings of Spanish food for around f20 a head, less if you risk annoying the management by sharing a paella for two between three – a good general rule for all Spanish places. Recents reports have been of unfriendliness though.

Centra, Lange Niezel 29 (☎22 30 50). Sister restaurant to *Rias Altas*, below.

Iberia, Kadijksplein 16 (☎23 63 13). A little more expensive than some of the others listed here, but good service and great food.

Rias Altas, Westermarkt 25 (☎24 25 10). Food in abundance, masterfully cooked and genially served. Good starters, fine house wine, full meals f19–20. Arguably the city's best Spanish restaurant.

Surinamese and Caribbean

Rum Runners, Prinsengracht 277 (☎27 40 79). Caribbean-style bar/restaurant situated in the old Westerkerk hall. Expensive cocktails but well-priced if not always devastatingly tasty food. Summer terrace and live South American music Wed–Sun evening.

Riaz, Bilderdijkstraat 193 (☎83 64 53). Out in the Old West, an excellent, inexpensive Surinamese restaurant.

Sin Doe, 1e van der Helstraat 62 (☎66 24 690). Very cheap Surinam take-away with a couple of bare tables.

Warung Span Macaranda, Gerard Doustraat 39 (☎73 01 29). Surinamese/Javanese *eetcafé*. Cheap and cheerful; closed on Wednesdays.

LATE-CLOSERS

Most bars are open until around 2am at the latest; restaurants are normally closed by midnight or 1am. The following listings cover the few places that stay open later.

● **BARS OPEN LATE**

H'88, Herengracht 88 (open until 6am).

Eetablissementje, 1e Anjeliersdwarsstraat 46 (open until 4am).

● **RESTAURANTS OPEN LATE**

Bojo, Lange Leidsedwarsstraat 51 (open until 6am).

Chacaro, Lijnbaansgracht (☎23 02 49).

Homolulu, Kerkstraat 23 (gay men's disco with restaurant open until 3am).

Kiekboe, Vondelpark 3 (☎12 00 21).

Nachtrestaurant, Reguliersgracht 66 (☎24 09 47).

't Oxshoofd, Herengracht 114 (☎22 76 85).

For late-night food shops see p.98.

CHAPTER SIX

NIGHTLIFE

A msterdam is not a major cultural centre, by any standards. Its performance spaces are small for the most part, and the city is not a regular stop on the touring circuits of major companies. Rather, it's a gathering spot for fringe performances, and buzzes with places offering a wide – and often inventive – range of affordable entertainment.

The city has a great many **multi-media centres**; these are listed first, and, along with smaller places, are **cross-referenced** at the end of each relevant section. Programmes everywhere can be varied and unpredictable, so always check "what's on" listings carefully.

As far as live music goes, Amsterdam is a regular tour stop, and testing-ground, for current **rock** bands – especially British acts – while **jazz**, including **salsa and Latin American**, is well represented in a number of small bars and clubs. The Concertgebouw assures Amsterdam a high ranking in the **classical music** stakes, and the city has recently pulled itself up into the big leagues for **dance and opera** with the building of the new Muziektheatre on the Amstel. As for **theatre**, a number of companies perform regularly in English, and at **cinemas**, foreign-language films are rarely shown without English subtitles.

Information and Tickets

Your first stop should be the *Uitburo*, in the Stadsschouwburg on the corner of Marnixstraat and Leidseplein (Mon–Sat 10am–6pm, Thurs until 9pm; ☎21 12 11), which offers advice on anything remotely cultural, sells tickets, and is the best source of the major **listings magazines**. Of these, the free monthly *Uitkrant* is the most comprehensive. *What's On In Amsterdam* (f1.50) carries less information but is in English, and *Het Parool*'s Wednesday entertainment supplement, *Uit en Thuis*, is inevitably the most up-to-date reference. The Uitburo's *Uitlijst* noticeboards include a weekly update on pop music performances, and *Agenda* magazine, free in bars and cafés, has listings (in Dutch). Or there's the *Sleep-in*'s *Use It* magazine – a guide to the city in English for young visitors on a budget, free at hostels, hotels, and cafés.

Tickets for most performances can be bought at the Uitburo and *VVV* offices (fees f2 and f2.50 respectively), or can be reserved by phone from the *VVV*. Some major entertainment venues – the Carré, Muziektheatre, Stadsschouwburg, and others – sell tickets for each other's productions at no extra cost through the *Kassadienst* plan. You can also book seats, again free of charge, through the *National Bookings Centre* (☎070 20 25 00); and the *Netherlands Board of Tourism* has a service whereby you can make bookings at the really large venues (the Concertgebouw and Muziektheatre, for example) from other European countries – though fees are, not surprisingly, high.

Festival and Annual Events

Aside from the first two weeks of August, when many places are closed, summer sees a citywide expansion on the entertainment scene; walk the streets and you'll often be entertained whether you like it or not. There are free concerts and theatre performances in the **Vondelpark** from the beginning of June to the end of August up to five days a week. The once very popular summer Sunday afternoon live bands, organised by the *Melkweg*, have been stopped due to pressure form local residents, but the *VVV* claims that there will be some form of live music by local bands on a smaller (and quieter) scale. The end of August **Uitmarkt** is a three-day jamboree during which hundreds of cultural groups and organisations from all over Holland arrive with their new season's programmes, providing hours of free indoor and outdoor entertainment.

The largest of the festivals is the annual **Holland Festival**, a prestigious and international, if slightly highbrow, series of opera, music, theatre, and dance performances held throughout the city (programmes, in English, from the Uitburo). The **Summer Festival** (*Zomerfestijn*), based at the Shaffy Theatre during the first two weeks of July, is quite different, presenting the latest in non-mainstream developments in the arts (theatre, dance, music, video) at smaller outlets all over town – and with events that are deliberately accessible to non-Dutch–speakers. There's also the annual gay **Festival van Verleiding** at the *Melkweg*, coinciding with Gay Pride Week at the end of June, which consists of exhibitions and performances of everything from erotic art to camp comedy.

Watch, too, for the **Boulevard of Broken Dreams**, a travelling cultural circus that pitches its tents on Museumplein and stages performances of music, theatre, dance and poetry from the 1930s to the 1960s; the **Amsterdam Roots Meeting**, from mid-May to the first week of June, which – again in a number of different theatres – concentrates on the culture of ethnic minorities; and, during the first two weeks of November, the **Stagedoor Theatre Festival**, which is held at the Balie, Engelenbak, and Soeterijn theatres.

For easily accessible **jazz and pop festivals outside Amsterdam**, see the relevant sections on p.143 and p.142.

Concert Halls and Multi-Media Centres

Amstelveen Cultureel Centrum, Plein 1960, Amstelveen (☎45 84 44). Down in the southern suburbs of the city and a long way from the centre (bus #64, #66), it offers a varied, if middle-of-the-road, programme of pop, classical music and dance. Worth keeping an eye on for the occasional gem.

Carré Theatre, Amstel 115–125 (☎22 52 25). A splendid 100-year-old structure (originally built as a circus) that now hosts all kinds of top international acts: anything from the Peking Circus to rap and Russian folk dance, with Elvis Costello and Alison Moyet squeezed in between. Tickets range from f20 to f50 depending on who's performing.

Jaap Eden Hall, Radioweg 64 (☎94 98 94). Large concert hall in the east of the city which occasionally stages big-name gigs. Heavy metal bands a favourite. Prices f15–f40; tram #9.

Meervaart, Osdorpplein 205 (☎10 73 93). A modern multi-media centre on the outskirts of town (tram 1, bus #19, #23) with a varied programme of international music, film, theatre, and dance. Rock performances irregularly (there's a blues festival in March), classical music/opera Sunday at midday and the occasional Monday, as well as a good, varied selection of films, with lots of re-runs. Film tickets f8, other events f5–f20.

Melkweg, Lijnbaansgracht 234a (☎24 17 77). Probably Amsterdam's most famous entertainment venue, and these days one of the city's prime arts centres, with a young, hip clientele at odds with Melkweg's erstwhile hippy image. Its theatre space serves as an outlet for small, inventive international groups, virtually all of which perform in English, and the concert hall plays host to a broad range of bands, with the emphasis on African music and lesser-knowns. Later, on Friday and Saturday nights, excellent, offbeat disco sessions go on well into the small hours – admission f4 plus f3 membership (valid one month) after 1am. Other features include a fine monthly film programme, a tea room selling dope and space cake (hash brownies), and a bar and restaurant (Marnixstraat entrance) open weekdays 11am–midnight, 2pm–midnight on weekends. Otherwise, concerts begin around 10.30pm and admission ranges from f7.50–f25. Those visiting more than once should buy a *reductiekaart* (f5) – valid for three months and giving a worthwhile discount on admission. The *Melkweg* is closed on Mondays.

Stadsschouwburg, Leidseplein 26 (☎25 04 35). These days somewhat overshadowed by the Muziektheatre but still a significant stager of opera and dance (it's a favourite of the Netherlands Dance Theatre) – as well as, in its small hall, performances by *ESTA* and *ART* (see p.150). Tickets f10–f25.

Live Music

Although concerts are occasionally held at the Carré Theatre, Meervaart or Jaap Eden hall (see above), Amsterdam doesn't have a really major **rock music** venue, and the superstars usually go to Rotterdam (the *Ahoy* sports hall or *Feyenoord* stadium) or Utrecht (the *Music Centre Vredenburg*). However, the multi-media centres provide a constant and varied supply of music, as do *Paradiso* and a number of other smaller places. Look out, too, for the city's clubs and discos which sporadically host performances by live bands.

For **classical music**, there's the perennial *Concertgebouw*, and the latest, biggest, and most prestigious outlet for **opera** is the *Muziektheatre* by the Amstel on Waterlooplein – home of the national opera and ballet companies and part of a f306-million complex that includes the new town hall. It's not one of the city's more successful modern buildings, and caused considerable controversy when it went up. But it's now firmly part of the Amsterdam skyline – and its cultural scene.

Pop and Rock

Until recently, **Dutch rock** was almost uniformly dire, dividing up fairly evenly between the traditional songs, accompanied by a loud accordion, being belted out of cafés in the Jordaan – a brash and sentimental adaptation of French *chansons* – and, with a few notable exceptions, the anaemic copies of English and American groups by bands lacking identity and singing (unconvincingly) in English. The best place to hear the former – if you must – is still the Jordaan, at cafés such as *Nol* and the *Twee Zwaantjes*, detailed on pp.124 and 125. As for modern pop and rock, times have mercifully changed, and Dutch groups nowadays have both quality and originality. Current names worth watching out for include the jazz/pop singer Mathilde Santing and new-wave group Eton Crop, who have both toured Europe; folksy singer-songwriter Fay Lovsky; Ramones sound-alikes Fatal Flowers; the raw, post-punk Claw Boys Claw; and Richenel, whom one critic described as Kate Bush on acid. Look out, too, for the bands I've Got The Bullets (soul-rock and bluesy ballads); 5 Slag; 1 Wijd (swing jazz and improvised rock); and the much praised Urban Dance Squad and Amsterdam favourites The Nits – all talented and a sure bet live. There's also a new and vibrant scene based on House music, with acts like Cannibal Island Experience, Frank Wijdenbosch, and Mike Red and Dub Duba turning out electro-pop mixed with rapping and African beats. Bear in mind, too, that Amsterdam is often on the circuit of up-and-coming British bands, and keep a sharp eye on the listings.

As far as **prices** go, for big names you'll pay anything between f30 and f50 a ticket; ordinary gigs go for f10 to f15. If no price is listed, entrance is usually free.

Aside from summer Sundays in the Vondelpark, Amsterdam doesn't have any **outdoor festivals**. Of those outside the city, the most famous is the *Pink Pop Festival* on June 8, down in the south at the Sport Park de Bercht, Baarlo (phone ☎04494 52500). Others include *Goffert Pop*, May 28, in Nijmegen, and *Park Pop*, June 28, in The Hague. Dates change, so check with the *VVV* before heading out.

Where to Go

Akhnaton, Nieuwe Zijds Kolk 25 (☎24 33 96). Three-storey youth centre with live music at the weekends. Unknown but lively bands – hip-hop's a recent speciality. Names you might catch include Alkmaar's The Mystery Crew and M.C. Alldream from Rotterdam. Starts around 10pm, admission around f5. Currently under renovation and due to reopen in September 1990.

Bamboo Bar, Lange Leidsedwarsstraat 66 (☎24 39 93). Unpretentious, friendly bar which hosts a variety of different sounds every night. Everything from be-bop to Country & Western. Open 10pm–2 or 3am and a great refuge from the disco-kids of nearby Leidseplein.

De Kikker, Egelantiersstraat 130 (☎27 91 98). Easy-listening music accompanies pricey French cuisine in a chic art deco interior in the middle of the Jordaan. Smooth trios playing bossanova and French chansons. Normally open Fri–Sun f10 if you don't eat. From 10.30pm.

Korsakov. Performances by some of the better-known local bands in a lively setting with cheap drinks and a very post-punk clientele. Free admission. Next door to *Maloe Melo*.

Maloe Melo, Lijnbaansgracht 160 (☎25 33 00). Describes itself as a blues club, though its tiny stage just as often reverberates to rockabilly and rock 'n' roll. Groups usually raw and enthusiastic, surroundings dark, smoky and filled with a fast-turnover crowd moving on to the clubs next door. Nightly from around 10.30pm.

Mazzo, Rozengracht 114 (☎26 75 00). Live bands – mainly British new wave – every Tues/Wed. Admission f5 (includes free drink).

Morlang, Keizersgracht 451 (☎25 26 81). Super-trendy café with live music every Tues. Soul, jazz and classical.

Paradiso, Weteringschans 6–8 (☎26 45 21). A converted church that features bands ranging from the up-and-coming to well-known names on the brink of stardom. Also hosts classical concerts, lectures and debates. Entrance f10–f25, plus f3 for a month's membership. The bands usually get started at 10.30pm.

PH 31, Prins Hendriklaan 31 (☎73 68 50). Amply amplified hardcore punk and new wave bands from 11pm every night in a bare, whitewashed room smack in the middle of the posh Vondelpark neighbourhood. Sun night jazz and blues sessions from 8.30pm. Tram #2.

De Pieter, St. Pieterspoortsteeg 29 (☎23 60 07). Once a chaotic punk stronghold, now a bar with a much wider selection of music. Live music Wed; DJ Sat.

See also **Amstelveen Cultureel Centrum**, p.140; **Carré Theatre**, p.140; **Jaap Eden Hall**, p.141; **Kleine Komedie**, p.150; **Meervaart**, p.141; **Melkweg**, p.141; **Shaffy**, p.150.

Jazz and Latin

For **jazz** fans, Amsterdam can be a treat. There's an excellent range of jazz outlets for such a small city, varying from tiny bars staging everything from traditional to avant-garde, to the *Bimhuis* – the city's major jazz venue – which plays host to both big international names and homegrown talent. Saxophonists Hans Dulfer, William Breuker and Theo Loevendie, and percussionist Martin van Duyhhoven, are among the Dutch names you might come across – and they're well worth listening to if you do.

It's worth remembering, too, that The Netherlands has one of the best jazz **festivals** in the world, the *North Sea Jazz Festival*, held in the *Congresgebouw* in The Hague during July: three days and nights of continuous jazz on twelve stages, involving over 700 musicians and costing about f70 a day – a bargain if you've got the time to travel down. October – jazz month – is also a special time for jazz, with extra concerts and small festivals all over the country. For information on this and (if your Dutch is up to it) jazz all over Holland at any time of year, phone *Jazzline* ☎26 77 64.

Latin American music is less in evidence, but far from nonexistent. *De Kroeg* is a wonderful place for salsa (and more besides), *Canecao Rio* for Brazilian music, while *Rum Runners* specialises in Latin-American music in a neo-colonial Latin atmosphere.

Where to Go

Café Alto, Korte Leidsedwarsstraat 115 (☎26 32 49). Legendary little jazz bar just off Leidseplein. Quality modern jazz every night from 10pm until about 2.30am (though often much later). Big on atmosphere, though slightly cramped. Drink prices hiked up, so fill up before you go.

Bimhuis, Oude Schans 73–77 (☎23 33 73). Recently rebuilt, with an excellent auditorium and ultra-modern bar. Concerts Thurs–Sat at 9pm (f7.50–f15), free jazz sessions Mon–Tues at 10.30pm. Live music in the bar, Sun afternoons at 4pm, also free.

Cab Kaye's, Beulingstraat 9 (☎23 35 94). Jazz pianist Cab Kaye's bar offers piano music weekend nights 10pm–2am. Slightly middle-aged, though with an intimate atmosphere that attracts after-hours musicians.

De Engelbewaarder, Kloveniersburgwal 59 (☎25 37 72). Jazz Sun night 10pm–1am.

Café Gypsy, Westerstraat 200 (☎27 34 48). During the day an ordinary Jordaan café, after dark a venue for "Gypsy" music, which means anything from Django Reinhardt-style jazz to Spanish flamenco. Official closing time is 1am, though if the joint is jumping things can go on much later. Starts at 9pm; inexpensive restaurant on first floor.

Joseph Lamm Jazz Club, Van Diemenstraat 8 (☎22 80 86). Traditional jazz centre which encourages dancing. Live music Fri–Sat 9pm–3am, f5; jam sessions Sun 8pm–2am, free.

Latin Club, O. Z. Voorburgwal 254 (☎24 22 70). Salsa/cocktail bar with occasional live bands and a selection of tapes imported from South America. 2pm–2am (weekends until 3am).

Le Maxim, Leidsekruisstraat 35 (☎24 19 20). Intimate piano bar with mainstream and undemanding live music nightly.

Café Quelle, J. P. Heijestraat 133 (☎16 22 26). A curious small and cluttered bar, with regular live jazz and classical performances by conservatory students on Thurs & Sun evening (sometimes Fri–Sat too). Starts at either 5pm or 9pm. An interesting spot in what is an otherwise dull area. Tram #7, #17.

Rum Runners, Prinsengracht 277 (☎27 40 79). Trendy Caribbean restaurant and cocktail bar in the former hall of the Westerkerk. Live (mainly laid-back Latin American) bands Sun at 2pm and 7.30pm, Wed at 7.30pm. Very busy, very noisy, but in spite of the early closing time (12.30am), should not be missed.

See also **Concertgebouw**, p.145; **Morlang**, p.143.

Folk and Ethnic

The Dutch **folk music** tradition is virtually extinct. But there is a small and thriving scene in Amsterdam, due mainly to a handful of American and British expatriates and a few sympathetic cafés – as well as a good outlet for **ethnic music** in the *Soeterijn*. For more information, call the Amsterdam folk organisation *Mokum Folk* (☎62 04 26).

Café Corrupt, Ceintuurbaan 9 (☎76 09 41). Folk every Mon.

Dubliner, Dusartstraat 51 (☎79 97 43). Live folk, irregularly.

Soeterijn, Linnaeusstraat (☎56 88 00). Part of the Tropenmuseum, this theatre specialises in the drama, dance, film, and music of developing countries. A great place for ethnic music and to pick up on acts that wouldn't normally come to Amsterdam. Admission f5–f15; political and ethnic films, f7.50; ethnic dance and theatre, much of it in English, f15. Tram #9, #10, #14.

The String, Nes 98 (☎25 90 15). Folk every evening.

Contemporary and Classical

Under its new conductor, Ricardo Schailly, the *Concertgebouw* is one of the most dynamic orchestras in the world. The *Rotterdam Philharmonic* and *Utrecht Symphony* orchestras also have worldwide reputations, while Ton Koopman's *Amsterdam Baroque Orchestra* and Frans Bruggen's *Orchestra of the 18th Century* are two internationally renowned period instruments orchestras.

In addition, the **opera scene** has been drastically improved with the opening of the *Muziektheater*, now home of the *Netherlands Opera Company*, which has a reputation for incisive, modern and sometimes controversial productions.

The *Concertgebouw* is Amsterdam's principal outlet for **classical music**, while **contemporary** and **chamber music** have an excellent home in the *Ijsbreker* – and many notable Dutch exponents of contemporary music in the *ASKO Ensemble*, *Circle Ensemble* and *Volharding Orchestra*. Note, also, that a number of Amsterdam's churches (and former churches) host regular performances of classical and chamber music.

Where to Go

Concertgebouw, Van Baerlestraat 98 (☎71 83 45). After a recent facelift and renewal of its crumbling foundations, the Concertgebouw is now looking – and sounding – better than ever. Two halls, the smaller one used for chamber concerts; regular performances by the resident Concertgebouw Orchestra and Netherlands Philharmonic as well as a star-studded international programme. Also free lunchtime concerts Sept–May (doors open 12.15pm, arrive early), and swing/jazz nights from time to time. f15–f50.

Engelse Kerk, Begijnhof 48 (☎24 96 65). Of the churches, this has the biggest programme – three to four performances a week, lunchtime, afternoon and evening. f5–17.

Ijsbreker, Weesperzijde 23 (☎68 18 05). Large, varied programme of international modern, chamber and experimental music. Out of the town centre by the Amstel, a great place for summer afternoons. f12.50. Tram #3, #6, #7, #10.

Lutherse Kerk, Kattengat 1. Part of the Sonesta Hotel complex, this domed former Lutheran church has lunchtime/afternoon concerts every Sun f5–f20.

Muziektheater, Amstel 3 (☎25 54 55). Via the Netherlands Opera, which is resident here, the fullest programme of opera in Amsterdam. Tickets f15–f50 and, except for weekends, go very quickly.

Stedelijk Museum, Paulus Potterstraat 13 (☎57 32 37). Musical performances from string quartets to experimental percussionists on weekend afternoons at 3pm – all for the price of admission to the museum, f5.

Villa Baranka, Prins Hendrikkade 140 (☎27 64 80). New arts forum which aims to create a "salon" in a six-storey building and which stages (mainly classical) theatre and music, poetry readings, and art workshops. Performances both afternoons and evenings, but mainly confined to the weekends. f10–f20.

Waalse Kerk, O. Z. Achterburgwal 157. Weekend afternoon and evening concerts. f5–f20.

See also **Amstelveen Cultureel Centrum**, p.140; **Paradiso**. p.143; **Café Quelle**, p.144; **Morlang**, p.143; **Meervaart**, p.141; **Stadsschouwburg**, p.141.

Discos and Clubs

Nightclubbing in Amsterdam is not the exclusive, posing, style-conscious business it is in many other capitals. There is no one really extravagant nightspot, and other than those in hotel chains such as the Hilton or Sonesta, or the tacky pick-up joints around Leidseplein, most Amsterdam clubs – even trendy ones – are not expensive or difficult to get into, and you go more to dance than to people-watch. Which is good news if funds are low, bad if the city's reputation had led you to expect more. The Dutch fashion magazine, *Avenue*, has even reported of late that Amsterdam trendsetters have given up clubbing for drinking tea in chic cafés such as *Morlang* and *Walem*, favouring an early night and a clear head over life in the fast lane.

That said, there is a growing hip-hop scene, based around the *Akhnaton* club, and Acid House has taken off in a big way, in the form of special nights at the *Roxy*, and far-out events in the city's dock areas. Also, in addition to the following listings, it's worth checking out some of the city's **gay nightspots**, which are – the non-exclusive ones at least – often among the city's best clubs.

Technically, you have to be a member to **get in** some clubs (those that call themselves "societies"), though in practice this can either be waived or inexpensively arranged at the door. Most open around 10pm and close up around 4am or slightly later, but there's no point in arriving before midnight. On the whole – and unless we state otherwise – music is basic Top 40 fodder, drink prices normally 50 percent or so more than what you pay in a bar.

Clubs

Akhnaton, N. Z. Kolk 25 (☎24 33 96). Currently closed for renovation (due to reopen in Sept 1990), but once known for its Fri–Sat night basement discos.

Bebop, Amstelstraat 24 (☎25 01 11). A massive and spectacular disco celebrating the USA, with a New York skyline mural, effigies of Marilyn Monroe and a 30-foot replica of the Statue of Liberty – all set off by a laser and light system that descends and tilts above the dance floor. Open 11am–4pm Thurs (free), Fri (f5), & Sat (f10), and with occasional live music.

The Box, Westermarkt 11. Small disco opposite the Westerkerk, playing a broad selection of music and featuring theme evenings every two weeks; subjects range from African to rock'n'roll. Open throughout the week 10pm–5am; free entry before midnight, f2.50 (weekends f5) admission afterwards.

Bios, Leidseplein 24 (☎27 65 44). Former theatre, and one of the flashiest of the loud, tasteless and unappealing Leidseplein discos. Plush black decor, business-oriented clientele and dress leaning towards the formal. On the whole best avoided. 10pm–4am all week, admission f10, and expensive drinks.

Dansen bij Jansen, Handboogstraat 11 (☎22 88 22). Founded by – and for – students, and now a firmly functional disco for a predominantly young set. Open every night 11pm–4am, admission f3.50.

Escape, Rembrandtsplein 10–15 (☎22 35 42). Though by no means its best, Amsterdam's largest disco, with a dance floor that can accommodate 2000 people, half a million watts of computerised light show, and a superb sound system. All of which have made it the showcase for weekly TV pop programmes and, on occasion, for big-name live bands. Open Wed 8pm–2am, Thurs 10pm–4am, Fri–Sat 10pm–5am. Admission free during the week, f10 at weekends.

Fizz, N. Z. Voorburgwal 165 (☎27 19 97). Where the less fastidious but still fashion-conscious crowd dance rather than size each other up. Interesting mix of music and people, two bars, video room, and large hall for live music (sometimes Fri). Open every night except Mon 11pm–4/5am, admission f3 weekdays, f5 weekends.

Havana Club, Reguliersdwarsstraat 17–19 (☎20 67 88). Recently opened and already very popular with a mixed clientele (gay, yuppie, art crowd). Also perhaps the only place in town to cater for people who want to dance but still get up for work the next day. Early disco weekdays, 8pm–1am (Fri, Sat 2am), Sun 5pm–1am.

Kosmos, Prins Hendrikkade 142 (☎76 74 77). Famous meditation and learning centre in a beautiful seventeenth-century building on the edge of the harbour. Discos Fri night only, admission a hefty f12.

Mazzo, Rozengracht 114 (☎26 75 00). One of the city's hippest discos. Originally set up as a club for media people, now more or less anyone can get in. Angular bar, video screens and a sharp, image-obsessed crowd. Live music Tues/Wed. Open every night 11pm–4/5am, admission f5 (includes free drink).

Nijlpaardenhuis, Warmoesstraat 170 (☎27 15 45). Roller-disco open every night 8pm–1am. Fri–Sat f5, rest of the week free; skate hire f5.

Odeon, Singel 460 (☎24 97 11). Converted seventeenth-century building with two dance floors (the upstairs one only open weekends) and a stylishly elegant interior playing host to an invariably yuppie gang. Open throughout the week, 10pm–5/6am, admission f7.50 on weekends, other times f5.

Oxshoofd, Herengracht 114 (☎22 76 85). One of the longest established discos in Amsterdam, a large and brimming place that's been going for nearly two decades. Broad selection of music, plus late-closing restaurant. Open all week midnight–6/7am, admission f5 (including f2.50 drink voucher).

(Op de schaal van) Richter 36, Reguliersdwarsstraat 36 (☎26 15 75). Open again after a shutdown due to drug violations, this is a small, split-level club supposed to resemble a building after an earthquake, with shattered mirrors, broken-down walls and cracked ceilings mocked up to draw in one of the city's most conspicuously chic crowds. Fairly flexible door policy, and host to a TV chat show. Open throughout the week 11pm–5am, admission f5.

The Roxy, Singel 465 (☎20 03 54). Latest home of Amsterdam–based Belgian DJ, Eddy de Clercq – well-known on the city's club scene, both for his outrageous disco parties and his notorious new-wave club *De Koer* (now *Fizz*). Housed in an old cinema with varied music – wildest night right now is Friday, Acid House night. Good place to get invited to parties. Wed-Sun 11pm–5am. Admission f10, though the door policy is highly selective, and members only are admitted when it's crowded.

Zorba the Buddha, O. Z. Voorburgwal 216 (☎25 96 42). A by-product of the Bhagwan Rajneesh movement, and a slick, sophisticated place with a sunken marble dance floor and excellent sound system. Three bars, no drugs except alcohol and cigarettes, and a very young clientele. The only signs of the Bhagwan are in the over-zealous cleaning-up by the staff. Every night except Mon, 9pm–2/3am, admission f5 (weekends f10).

See also **Melkweg**, p.141; **De Pieter**, p.143.

Lesbian and Gay Clubs

De Club, Amstel 178 (☎23 44 80). Private lesbian and gay club with dance floor. Visitors welcome. Nightly 10.30pm–4am, weekends until 5am.

COC Disco, Rozenstraat 14 (☎26 30 87). Women's night every Sat until 3am, popular with younger lesbians.

C'Ring (Cockring), Warmoesstraat 96 (☎23 96 04). Currently Amsterdam's most popular gay men's disco. Light show and bars on two levels. Get there early at the weekend to avoid queuing. 11pm–5am.

DOK, Singel 460 (☎23 75 03). Amsterdam's biggest and best-known gay disco, established in 1953 and still going strong. Occasional transvestite floorshows. Nightly 11pm–5/6am, admission f2.50.

Exit, Reguliersdwarsstraat 42 (☎25 87 88). Along with *C'Ring* (above), the city's most popular gay club. Sister to the April café on the same street, with a similiar crowd. Nightly 11pm–5am; very popular at weekends. Admission f5.

Gay Life Disco, Amstelstraat 32 (☎22 94 18). Good dance floor, discreetly lit movie room, and a separate bar for those who prefer a quieter atmosphere. 11pm–5am. There's a special women's night on the last Sunday of each month.

Homolulu, Kerkstraat 23 (☎24 63 87). Well-established gay/lesbian disco with restaurant. Door policy in force, but many straights on Sat 10pm–4am, 5am on weekends.

IT, Amstelstraat 24 (☎25 01 11). Brand new large disco with a superb sound system. Often features well-known live acts. Admission f10. Open 11pm–4am.

La Louvre, Singel 447 (☎23 39 84). Bar, night restaurant, and disco with two good dance floors. Mon–Thurs 10pm–4am, Fri & Sat 10pm–5am; admission f5.

De Trut, Bilderdijkstraat 165. Housed in a former factory building, *De Trut* has a large dance floor, cheap drinks, and plays non-commercial music. Sunday nights are exclusively gay: for more details, call in (there's no phone).

Film

Most of Amsterdam's thirty or so commercial cinemas are huge, multiplex picture palaces showing a selection of **general releases** – and are interesting for just that. However, there is one – the extravagantly art deco *Tuschinski*, Reguliersbreestraat 26 (☎26 26 33) – which is worth visiting no matter what's showing; screen one tends to be especially interesting. If you're more into film than architecture, the multi-media centres and film houses (*filmhuizen*) show **revival and art films** and often hold retrospectives – as does, though less regularly, the Netherlands Film Museum (p.88).

Language is no problem, since the Dutch use subtitles for foreign films, most of which are in English. If you want to be sure, look out for the words *Nederlands Gesproken* printed next to the title in the listings; this indicates it's been dubbed into Dutch. Most major cinemas have four showings a day, two in the afternoon, two in the evening and, sometimes, a late-night showing, beginning just after midnight on Friday and Saturday. Tickets go for about f13, though *Alfa*, *Bellevue*, *Cinerama* and *De Uitkijk* have considerably reduced prices Monday to Thursday. Prices for the *filmhuizen* are always substantially cheaper.

Programmes change Thursday: most bars and cafés have a weekly film schedule pinned up; otherwise check the usual listings sources, principally the what's-on supplement of Wednesday's *Het Parool* and *Uitkrant*'s *Filmagenda* section.

Filmhuizen and Revival Cinemas.

Amsterdams Filmhuis, Ceintuurbaan 338 (☎66 23 488). The main forum for retrospectives or film series with a theme. Two screens, the Rialto (for retros) and the Rivoli (for premieres), with prices around f10 (f7.50 with ISIC card). Tram #3, #12, #24, #25.

De Boomspijker, Recht Boomsloot 52 (☎26 40 02). An inexpensive alternative film showcase within walking distance of Centraal Station. f7.50 evenings, matinees f5.

Desmet, Plantage Middenlaan 4a (☎27 34 34). Often used by the Dutch company Film International to promote independent films. Tram #9, #14.

Filmmuseum Cinematheek, Vondelpark 3 (☎83 16 46). Dutch films showing every Tues evening; international films (with English and Dutch subtitles) every Wed at 2pm and 6pm. Admission f8.50 evenings, matinees f6.

Kriterion, Roeterstraat 170 (☎23 17 08). Stylish duplex cinema around the corner from the *Desmet* showing arthouse and quality commercial films. Weesperplein metro.

The Movies, Haarlemmerdijk 161 (☎24 57 90). Another beautiful art deco cinema, and with its own distribution company, this triplex is the place for intellectual, arty or independent films. Also, a café with live music every Fri/Sat from 9pm; admission f10. Tram #3.

See also **Meervaart**, p.141; **Melkweg**, p.141; **Netherlands Film Museum**, p.88; **Shaffy**, below; **Soeterijn**, p.145.

Theatre

Surprisingly, for a city that functions so much in English, there are only two English-language theatre groups: the *American Repertory Theater (ART)*, which has an office at Kerkstraat 4 (☎25 94 95) and concentrates on contemporary work; and the *English Speaking Theatre of Amsterdam (ESTA)*, Leidsestraat 106 (☎22 97 42), which stages more varied productions and emphasises modern British drama. Neither has its own theatre, but you can catch both at venues all over town. There are also regular English-language productions and performances by touring groups at the theatres listed below and at multi-media centres. For details of annual festivals, see p.140.

English-language

Bellevue, Leidsekade 90 (☎24 72 48). Regular venue of *ESTA*.

Kleine Komedie, Amstel 56 (☎24 05 34). One of the oldest theatres in Amsterdam, established in 1786, with occasional English-language shows, f15–f25, and performances by the odd pop mega-star – around f20.

Mickery, Rozengracht 117 (☎24 41 32). Experimental, often hi-tech productions, mainly in English. Avant-garde groups from America a favourite. f15.

Shaffy, Keizersgracht 324 (☎23 13 11). Avant-garde dance and drama – sometimes both combined – and base for the experimental group *Maatschappij Discordia*. Admission f12.50. Also live music in the bar every Thurs evening from 11.30pm (anything currently "in") and a small cinema at the top of the building featuring mainly art-house films (f8, shows 10pm). Rumour has it they are about to lose the lease.

Stadhouderij, 1e Bloemdwarsstraat 4 (☎26 22 82). Amsterdam's only non-subsidised English language theatre company, mounting new productions every six weeks or so in one of the city's smallest, most intimate theatre spaces. Contemporary and modern works, Shakespeare, readings, classes and workshops.

Otherwise, most of the larger companies in the city concentrate either on foreign works in translation or Dutch-language theatre, neither of which, for the nonspeaker, are likely to be terribly interesting. If, however, your Dutch is strong enough, **other theatres** include . . .

Balie, Kleine Gartmanplantsoen 10 (☎23 29 04).

De Engelenbak, Nes 71 (☎26 36 44).

Frascati, Nes 63 (☎23 57 23).

Nieuwe De La Mar, Marnixstraat 404 (☎23 34 62).

Polanen Theatre, Polanenstraat 174 (☎88 05 18).

See also **Meervaart**, p.141; **Melkweg**, p.141; **Soeterijn**, p.145; **Stadsschouwburg**, p.141.

Dance

Of the three **major Dutch dance companies**, the most innovative is the *Netherlands Dance Theatre*, with a repertoire of ballet and modern dance and inspired choreography by director Jiri Kylian. In comparison, the Muziektheatre-based *Dutch National Ballet* under Hans van Manen, although very accomplished, can seem lacking in verve and imagination – as can the third company, the largely traditional *Scapino Ballet*. Two other notable Dutch choreographers, Toer van Schayk and Rudi van Dantzig, work regularly in Amsterdam and are worth catching; and for folk dance fans, there's the excellent *Folklore Dance Theateristisch* – also frequent visitors to the city.

On a smaller scale, Amsterdam is particularly receptive to the latest trends in **modern dance**, and has many experimental dance groups, often incorporating other media into their productions; small productions staged by dance students also abound. Modern Dutch companies include *Dansproduktie*, one of the most original; *IntroDans*, similar in style to the Netherlands Dance Theatre, and *Danskern* who have humour, imagination and vitality.

The listings which follow are theatres for dance only; dance also takes place on occasion at a number of other places city-wide, so check the usual sources carefully, in particular for those places detailed at the end.

Where to Go
Captain Fiddle, Kloveniersburgwal 86 (☎26 03 63). Small theatre specialising in modern dance performances. Tickets f7.50.

Liefde, Da Costakade 102 (☎83 31 14). A dance school studio where students put on their own productions.

Muziektheater, Amstel 3 (☎25 54 55). Home of the National Ballet, but with a third of its dance schedule given over to international companies. Tickets f15–f50.

Shaffy, Keizersgracht 324 (☎23 13 11). Centre for modern, often experimental, dance. Two frequent visitors – *Dansgroep Krisztina de Chatel* and *Danstheatre Vals Bloed* – are particularly worth catching. Tickets f10–f15.

Het Veem, Van Diemenstraat 10–12 (☎26 01 12). Old warehouse converted into dance studios and a small theatre. Good modern dance. Tickets f7.50.

See also **Amstelveen Cultureel Centrum**, p140; **Bellevue**, p150; **Carré**, p140; **Meervaart**, p.141; **Soeterijn**, p.145; **Stadsschouwburg**, p.141.

CHAPTER SEVEN

OUT FROM THE CITY

A lthough Amsterdammers may try to persuade you there's nothing remotely worth seeing outside their own city, The Netherlands is a compact country, its rail services fast and frequent, and a number of extremely worthwhile destinations are within easy day-trip reach of the capital.

If you're interested in visiting a town, **Haarlem** is the best choice – just a short distance from Amsterdam by train but with a character of its own, and with enticing attractions like the Frans Hals Museum. Further down the line, **Leiden** has a highly reputed university and a number of fine museums, while to the east, **Utrecht** exudes a pleasant provincialism that offers a refreshing change from the capital. As for smaller places, **Muiden** and **Naarden** each have highly individual – and enjoyable – historical centres, easily combined for a day out; while **Alkmaar** and **Gouda** are renowned for their cheese markets – and their consequent popularity with visitors. And don't forget the **bulbfields**, which in spring explode in a blaze of colour between Haarlem and Leiden – essential viewing even if you're not an enthusiast. A few warnings too: much of the country around Amsterdam, especially the villages to the north, such as **Marken** and **Volendam**, has a packaged prettiness that can be unbearable with the thick summer crowds.

Practicalities

The quickest and most convenient method of getting anywhere is by *Nederlandse Spoorwegen* or *NS*, the Dutch **rail network**. It offers day-return tickets (*dagretour*) that give substantial savings on the normal return fare. Also, if you're heading for one specific attraction – say the Keukenhof Gardens – or taking kids along, it might be worth using one of their Day Excursion fares (*dagtoerisme*), which combine travel and admission on a reduced ticket – though bear in mind that your **museumcard** is valid for free entry to most state- and municipally-run museums. Those intending to take a longer tour of the country should consider Rail Rover tickets (currently f108 for seven days), which allow travel throughout the Dutch rail network. The *NS* literature outlines all these offers, and is available from most Dutch train stations and, in Great Britain, from the *NS* office at 25-28 Buckingham Gate, London SW1E 6LD (☎01-630 1735). It's possible to cut costs further by travelling on a one-day bus pass (f17.70), though this will necessarily lengthen travel time and shorten tour time.

If you're not pressed for time, **cycling** is an ideal way of seeing the countryside: distances are small, the landscape gentle and there's an extensive

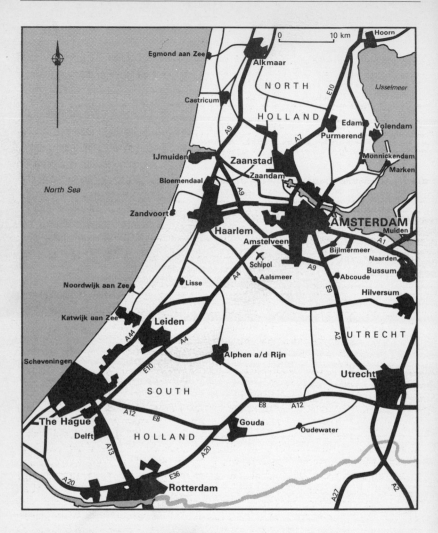

system of bike paths, often diverted from the main roads. Bikes can be hired from almost all train stations (see p.26 for details of Amsterdam bike rental), or from companies like *Ena's Bike Tours* (☎015 14 37 97), which offer leisurely tours in the city environs.

A good starting point wherever you go is the local *VVV* office, which can help with detailed maps, restaurant listings and, should you need to stop over, accommodations – usually at around f30 per person per night in a lower grade hotel. The open times listed are for summer months (April–Sept); expect hours to be slightly reduced at other times of the year.

Haarlem

A little over ten minutes from Amsterdam by train, **HAARLEM** has quite a different pace and feel from the capital. It sees itself, perhaps, as a cut above its neighbours, but it's an easily absorbed small town, and a historically significant one too. The Frans Hals Museum, in the almshouse where the artist spent his last – and for some his most brilliant – years, is worth an afternoon in itself; there are numerous beaches within easy reach (as well as bulbfields); and the city's young and vigorous nightlife may well keep you until the last train back – which is, conveniently, after midnight.

For a long time the residence of the counts of Holland, the town was sacked by the Spanish under Frederick of Toledo in 1572. There are reminders of this all over Haarlem, since, after a seven-month siege, the revenge exacted by the inconvenienced Frederick was terrible: very nearly the whole population was massacred, including the entire Protestant clergy. Recaptured in 1577 by William the Silent, Haarlem went on to enjoy its greatest prosperity in the seventeenth century, becoming a centre for the arts and home for a flourishing school of painters.

Nowadays, the place retains an air of quiet affluence, with all the picturesque qualities of Amsterdam but little of the sleaze. The core of the city is **Grote Markt**, an open space flanked by perhaps a greater concentration of Gothic and Renaissance architecture than any other Dutch square. Much of the gabled and balconied **Stadhuis**, at one end, dates from the fourteenth century, while at the other end there's a statue of one Laurens Coster, who, Haarlemmers insist, is the true inventor of printing. Legend tells of him cutting a letter "A" from the bark of a tree and dropping it into the sand by accident. Plausible enough, but most authorities seem to agree these days that Gutenburg was the more likely source of the printed word.

If you've been to the Rijksmuseum, the **Grote Kerk of St. Bavo** (Mon–Sat 10am–4pm, f1.50), in whose shadow Coster stands, may seem familiar, since it was the principal focus of the seventeenth-century painter Berckheyde's many views of this square; only the black-coated burghers are missing. Finished in the early sixteenth century, the church dwarfs the surrounding cluttered maze of streets and houses, and serves as a landmark from almost anywhere in the city. Inside, it has a beauty that is more breathtaking than serene: sheer height, enhanced by the bare, white-painted power of the Gothic lines. The mighty Christian Muller organ is said to have been played by Handel and Mozart and is one of the biggest in the world, with 5000 pipes and razzmatazz baroque embellishment to match. Beneath, Xaverij's lovely group of draped marble figures represents Poetry and Music, offering thanks to the town patron for her generosity, while in the choir there's a late fifteenth-century painting that the church traditionally (though dubiously) attributed to Geertgen tot Sint Jans, along with memorials to painters Pieter Saenredam and Frans Hals – both of whom are buried here. Outside, at the western end of the church, the **Vishal** and, opposite that, Lieven de Key's profusely decorated **Vleeshal** (the former fish and meat markets, respectively), hold regular art exhibitions.

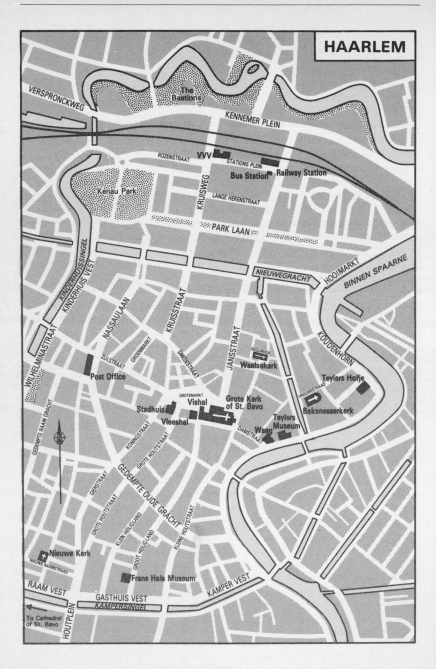

HAARLEM

VERSPRONCKWEG

The Bastions

KENNEMER PLEIN

ROZENSTRAAT VVV STATIONS PLEIN
Bus Station Railway Station

Kenau Park

KRUISWEG LANGE HERENSTRAAT

PARK LAAN

KINDERHUISSINGEL
KINDERHUIS VEST

NIEUWEGRACHT HOOIMARKT BINNEN SPAARNE

NASSAULAAN
KRUISSTRAAT
GROENMARKT
SMEDESTRAAT
JANSSTRAAT

KOUDENHORN

ZULSTRAAT

WILHELMINASTRAAT

Post Office

BEGIJNHOF
Waalsekerk

Teylers Hofje

GROTEMARKT
Vishal
Stadhuis
Vleeshal

Grote Kerk of St. Bavo

VROUWESTRAAT
Bakenesserkerk

Teylers Museum
Waag
DAMSTRAAT

GEDEMPTE RAAM GRACHT

KONINGSTRAAT
GIERSTRAAT
GROTE HOUTSTRAAT

GEDEMPTE OUDE GRACHT

KLEIN HEILIGLAND
GROOT HEILIGLAND
KLEINE HOUTSTRAAT

Nieuwe Kerk
NIEUWE RAAMSTRAAT

Frans Hals Museum

RAAM VEST GASTHUIS VEST KAMPER VEST
KAMPERSINGEL

HOUTPLEIN

To Cathedral of St. Bavo

The Frans Hals Museum

But Haarlem's chief attraction, the **Frans Hals Museum**, is just a five-minute stroll away at Groot Heiligland 62 (Mon–Sat 10am–5pm, Sun 1–5pm; f4, children f2); it's housed in the **Oudemannhuis** almshouse where the aged Hals is supposed to have lived out his last destitute years on public funds. Little is known about Frans Hals. Born in Antwerp, the son of Flemish refugees who settled in Haarlem in the late 1580s, his extant oeuvre is relatively small: some 200 paintings and nothing like the number of sketches and studies left behind by Rembrandt – probably because Hals wasn't fashionable until the nineteenth century, and a lot of his work was lost before it became collectable. His outstanding gift was as a portraitist, showing a sympathy with his subjects and an ability that some say even Rembrandt lacked to capture fleeting expressions. Seemingly quick and careless flashes of colour form a coherent whole, leaving us a set of seventeenth-century figures that are curiously alive.

The museum begins, however, with the work of other artists: first a small group of **sixteenth-century works**, the most prominent a triptych by Gerard David and what could be the first anti-imperialist painting – *West Indian Scene* by Jan Mostaert, in which the naked natives try fruitlessly to defend themselves against the cannon and sword of their invaders. Van Scorel's *Baptism of Christ* and *Knights of Jerusalem* follow, along with works by van Goyen, Brouwer and van Ostade, and a good group of paintings by the **Haarlem mannerists**, including works by Carel van Mander (see p.187), leading light of the Haarlem School, and mentor of many of the other painters represented here. Cornelis Cornelisz van Haarlem best follows van Mander's guidelines: *The Marriage of Peleus and Thetis* was a popular subject at the time, probably because it was interpreted as a warning against discord, appropriate during the long war with Spain – though Cornelisz gives as much attention to the arrangement of elegant nudes as to his subject. The same is true of the *Massacre of the Innocents*, which could refer to the siege of Haarlem just twenty years earlier.

Frans Hals was a pupil of van Mander too, though he seems to have learned little more than the barest rudiments from him. His paintings in the west wing – a set of "Civic Guard" portraits of the companies initially formed to defend the country from the Spanish – established his reputation as a portraitist, and earned him a regular income. There was a special skill involved in painting these: for the first time Hals made the group portrait a unified whole instead of a static collection of individual portraits; his figures are carefully arranged, but so cleverly as not to appear contrived. For a time, Hals himself was a member of the Company of Saint George, and in the *Officers of the Militia Company of Saint George* the artist appears in the top left-hand corner – one of his few self-portraits.

After this, there are numberless scenes of Haarlem by Berckheyde and Saenredam, among others; landscapes by the Ruisdaels and Berchem; and some group portraits by Veerspronck and the elderly Frans Hals. Hals' later paintings are darker, more contemplative works, closer to Rembrandt in their lighting. The *Governors of the Saint Elizabeth Gasthuis*, painted in 1641, is a good example, as are the portraits of the *Regents* and *Regentesses of the Oudemannhuis* itself – possibly the museum's finest treasures. These were commissioned when Hals was in his eighties: poor despite a successful painting career, hounded for money by the town's tradesmen and by the mothers of his illegitimate children, and dependent for charity on the people depicted here. Their cold, hard faces stare out of the gloom, the women reproachful, the men only slightly more affable – except for the character just right of centre who has been labelled (and indeed looks) completely drunk. There are those who claim Hals had lost his firm touch by the time he painted these, yet the sinister, almost ghostly power of these paintings, facing each other across the room, suggests quite the opposite. Van Gogh's remark that "Frans Hals had no less than twenty-seven blacks" suddenly makes perfect sense.

Other galleries hold lesser works by lesser artists. There's a new wing, which houses temporary exhibitions, usually of modern and contemporary artists, and permanent paintings by Israëls, Appel & Jan Sluyters – though lamentably few of the latter. But more interesting is the Oudemannhuis itself, a fairly typical *hofje* whose style of low buildings and peaceful courtyards you'll see repeated with slight variations all over town – and indeed the country (Amsterdam's are detailed on pp.45 and 56). There are regular classical concerts held here throughout the year, usually in the afternoon on the third Sunday of each month; prices are around f3; phone ☎31 91 80 for details.

The Hofjes ... and Haarlem's other sites

As for the rest of town, Haarlem has a greater number of *hofjes* than most Dutch cities – proof of its prosperity in the seventeenth century. The VVV can give information on where to find them; most are still inhabited, so you're confined to looking around the courtyard, but the women who sit outside seem used to the occasional visitor and won't throw you out.

Second in the pecking order of Haarlem museums, the **Teylers Museum**, at Spaarne 16 (Tues–Sat 10am–5pm, Sun 1–5pm, during winter until 4pm; f4, children f2), is Holland's oldest museum, founded in 1778 by wealthy local philanthropist Pieter Teyler van der Hulst who also gave his charity and name to the **Teyler's Hofje** nearby. The museum should appeal to scientific and artistic tastes alike, containing everything from fossils, bones, and crystals to weird, H.G. Wells-type technology (including an enormous eighteenth-century electrostatic generator), and sketches and line drawings by Michelangelo, Raphael, Rembrandt and Claude, among others. The drawings are covered for protection from the light, but don't be afraid to pull back the curtains and peek. Look in, too, on the rooms beyond, filled with work by eighteenth- and nineteenth-century Dutch painters, principally Breitner, Israëls, Weissenbruch, and, not least, Hendriks, who was the keeper of the art collection here.

Two other sights which may help structure your wanderings are on the opposite side of town. Van Campen's **Nieuwe Kerk** was built and – rather unsuccessfully – added on to Lieven de Key's bulbed, typically Dutch tower in 1649, though the interior is symmetrical with a soberness that is quite chilling after the soaring heights of the Grote Kerk. Just beyond, and much less self-effacing, the Roman Catholic **Cathedral of St. Bavo** (March–Oct 9.30am–noon/2–4pm) is one of the largest ecclesiastical structures in Holland, designed by Joseph Cuijpers and built between 1895 and 1906. It's broad and spacious inside, cupolas and turrets crowding around an apse reminiscent of Byzantine churches or mosques, the whole surmounted by a distinctive copper dome.

HAARLEM: PRACTICAL DETAILS

There are numerous daily trains from Amsterdam Centraal to Haarlem. Just go to the station; you shouldn't have to wait longer than ten minutes. Day return tickets (dagretours) go for about f8. At the *VVV*, outside the railway station (Mon–Sat 9am–6pm; ☎023 31 90 59), you can pick up an excellent map and copies of the monthly events guide, "Swinging Haarlem". For cheap **food** try *Café Mephisto*, Grote Markt 29, which is open all day and serves Dutch food for f12–f20 (snacks less) and has live music Tuesday and Thursday evenings. Or there's *Alfonso's* Mexican restaurant just behind the Grote Kerk; *Café 1900*, Barteljorisstraat 10, a trendy locals' hangout for drinks or light meals with an impressive turn-of-the-century interior; *H. Ferd. Kuipers*, an excellent patisserie and tearoom at Barteljonsstraat 22; or *De Ark*, around the corner from the Frans Hals Museum at Nieuw Heiligland 3, which has Dutch food at reasonable prices.

Around Haarlem: Dikes, Dunes, Sea and Bulbfields

A few miles north of Haarlem, **SPAARNDAM** is well known for its statue commemorating the boy who saved the country from disaster by sticking his finger in a hole in the dike. This tale has no basis at all in reality and few Dutch people even know it, but it had a sufficient ring of truth for a little-known American writer to weave a story around it – and create a legend. The monument to the heroic little chap was unveiled in 1950; more, it seems, as a tribute to the opportunistic Dutch tourist industry than anything else.

You'll find slightly more of interest **west and south** of Haarlem. Take bus #80 west, and the monied Haarlem suburbs quickly give way to the thick woodland and rugged dune landscape of the **Kennemerduinen National Park**, which stretches down to the sea. BLOEMENDAAL-AAN-ZEE is the rather grandiose name for a group of shacks that house a thriving ice-cream trade, while a little further south, **ZANDVOORT**, an agglomeration of modern and faceless apartment complexes that rise out of the dunes, is a major Dutch seaside resort. As resorts go it's pretty standard – packed and oppressive in summer, depressingly dead in winter. The best reason to visit is the championship motor racing circuit, which provides background noise to everyone's sunbathing. If you come for the beach, and manage to fight your way through the crush to the water, watch out – the sea here is murky and ominously close to the smoky chimneys of IJMUIDEN to the north.

Heading south from Haarlem towards Leiden you enter the heart of the Dutch **bulb-growing industry**, which in spring divides the countryside into dazzling geometric blocks of pure colour. This is the major business here, not only a tourist pull but a lucrative, growing concern for some 10,000 growers. Carolus Clusius brought the first tulip bulbs from Asia Minor to Holland in the late sixteenth century, planting them, watching them flourish on the sandy soil, and giving birth to the billion guilder industry. The view from the train, which cuts directly through the main fields, can be sufficient in itself, and if you have transport you can take in the full beauty of the flowers by way of routes marked by hexagonal signposts – local *VVV*s sell pamphlets suggesting the best vantage points. But should you want to get closer, the town of **LISSE** affords access to the **Keukenhof Gardens** (late March–end of May daily 8am–6.30pm; f12.50), the largest flower gardens in the world, and the place to look at the best of the Dutch flower industry. The Keukenhof was set up in 1949, designed by a group of prominent bulb growers to convert people to the joys of growing flowers from bulbs in their own gardens. Literally the "kitchen garden", its site is the former estate of a fifteenth-century countess, who used to grow the herbs and vegetables for her dining table here – hence the name. Some seven million flowers are on display for their full flowering period, complemented, in case of especially harsh winters, by 5000 square metres of greenhouses holding indoor displays. You could easily spend a whole day here, swooning among the sheer abundance of it all. There are three restaurants in the 70 acres of grounds, and well-marked paths take you right the way through the gardens, which hold daffodils and narcissi in April, hyacinths in April, and tulips from mid-April until the end of May.

If you can't visit in the spring, the **Bulbdistrict Museum**, Heereweg 219 (June–March Tues–Sun 1–5pm, Sun 11.30am–5pm; f2.50, children f1.50), offers the history of the bulb business, dating from the time the first tulip was brought over from Turkey – but it's a poor substitute for the real thing.

To see the industry in action, the **AALSMEER** flower auction, also the largest in the world and held in a building approximately the size of 75 football pitches, is a bus ride away, held weekdays 7.30–11.30am. The dealing is fast and furious here, and the turnover staggering. In an average year around f1.5 billion (about £500 million) worth of plants and flowers are traded here, many of which arrive in high street florists in Britain the very same day.

Leiden

The home of Holland's most prestigious university and a dozen or so good museums, **LEIDEN** has an academic air, and gives one the sense that, like Haarlem to the north, it regards itself as separate from – and independent of – the capital. Which is fair enough. There's more than enough to justify a day trip, and the town's energy, derived largely from its students, strongly counters the myth that there's nothing worth experiencing outside Amsterdam.

The **University** was a present from William the Silent, a reward for this town which, like Haarlem and Alkmaar before it, had endured a year-long siege by the Spanish, emerging victorious on October 3, 1574, when William cut through the dikes around the city and sailed in with his fleet for a dramatic eleventh-hour rescue. This event is still commemorated with an annual fair and fireworks and the consumption of two traditional foods: herring and white bread, which the fleet was supposed to have brought with them, and *hutspot,* or stew – a cauldron of which was apparently found simmering in the abandoned Spanish garrison.

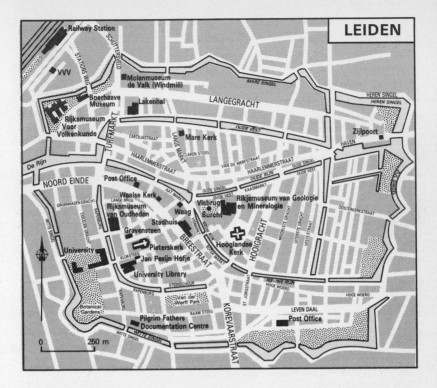

After the Reformation, Leiden's university quickly became a major centre of Protestant scholarship. Its original home at Rapenburg 73 still stands (visiting hours are Wed–Fri 1–5pm; free) on the edge of Leiden's most appealing area, bordered by Steenschur and Breestraat. Cross Rapenburg and you're in the network of narrow streets that constituted the medieval town, converging on a central square and the **Pieterskerk** (1.30–4pm; free), the town's principal church. It's deconsecrated now, and used for exhibitions, concerts and a Saturday antique market. It has an empty warehouse-like feel, but among the fixtures that remain are a simple and beautiful Renaissance rood screen in the choir, and a host of memorials to the sundry notables buried here – among them John Robinson, leader of the Pilgrim Fathers.

Robinson lived in a house on the site of what is now the **Jan Pesijn Hofje**, next door to the church. A curate in England at the turn of the seventeenth century, he was suspended from preaching in 1604, later fleeing with his congregation to pursue his Puritan form of worship in the more tolerant atmosphere of Holland. Settling in Leiden, Robinson acted as pastor to growing numbers but still found himself at odds with the establishment. In 1620, a hundred of his followers ("The Pilgrim Fathers") sailed via Plymouth for the freedom and abundance of America – though Robinson died before he could join them. If you want to find out more, take a look at the **Pilgrim Fathers**

Documentation Centre, Boisotkade 2a (Mon–Fri 9.30am–4.30pm; free), part of the city archives and a mine of information on Robinson's group during their stay in Leiden.

Breestraat marks the border of Leiden's centre proper, flanked by the long, ornate Renaissance front of the late-sixteenth-century **Stadhuis**, the only part of the building to survive a fire in 1929. Behind, the rivers which cut Leiden into islands converge at the busiest point in town, the site of a vigorous Wednesday and Saturday general **market** which sprawls right over the sequence of bridges into the pedestrian Haarlemmerstraat. On the island formed by the split between Oud and Nieuwe Rijn, the **Hooglandsekerk** (May–Sept Mon 1–3.30pm, Tues–Sat 11am–3.30pm) is a light, lofty church that is plain without being spartan, and doesn't have the secularised atmosphere of the Pieterskerk. A central pillar features an epitaph to the heroic burgomaster, van der Werff, who led the citizens of Leiden during the siege of 1574. When the situation became so desperate that most people were all for giving up, the burgomaster, no doubt remembering the massacre of Haarlem, offered his own body to them as food. His invitation was rejected, but – the story goes – it succeeded in instilling new determination in the flagging citizens.

Leiden's Museums

Leiden's museums are varied and comprehensive enough to merit a visit in themselves, and it's possible to spend several days here, trudging from one to the other and rarely seeing daylight – not a course we'd recommend. The following rundown should make it easier to be selective.

The **Rijksmuseum Van Oudheden**, Rapenburg 28 (Tues–Sat 10am–5pm, Sun 1–5pm; f3.50, children f2) is Leiden's star attraction – The Netherlands' principal archaeological museum, with a huge holding. The first thing you'll see as you enter is the *Temple of Taffeh*: a present from the Egyptian government in gratitude for the Dutch part in the 1960s UNESCO excavations in Abyssinia (Ethiopia), which succeeded in uncovering submerged Nubian monuments. Dating back to the first century AD, the temple was adapted in the fourth century to the worship of Isis, eventually being sanctified as a Christian church 400 years later. The Egyptians placed firm conditions on their gift: no one should have to pay to see it, and the temperature and humidity must be carefully regulated, with the lights overhead simulating the passage – and shadow – of the sun.

Past the entrance hall, the first exhibit is the remains of the Temple to Nehellania – a goddess of seamen – which was uncovered in Zeeland; next come classical Greek and Roman sculpture, leading chronologically through Hellenistic works to busts, statues and friezes of Imperial Rome. The best collection, though, is the Egyptian, beginning with wall reliefs, statues and sarcophagi from tombs and temples and continuing in the rooms immediately above with a set of mummies and sarcophagi as complete as you're likely to see outside Egypt. The *Three Figures of Maya*, to name just one exhibit, are exceptionally well preserved. The second floor is specifically Dutch: an archaeological history of the country, from prehistoric, Roman and medieval times – perhaps inevitably, less interesting than the rest.

A short walk away, on Hooglandsekerkgracht, there's another national museum, the **Rijksmuseum van Geologie en Mineralogie** (Mon–Fri 10am–5pm, Sun 2–5pm; f3, children f1.50), which has a predictable display of minerals, fossils, bones and skeletons. If you walk back up Rapenburg toward the railway station, you'll find more to grab your interest in Leiden's municipal museum, housed in the old **Lakenhal**, or cloth-hall, at Oude Singel 28–32 (Tues–Sat 10am–5pm, Sun 1–5pm; f2.50, children f1.25). This museum includes a picture gallery devoted to natives of the town as well as mixed rooms of furniture, tiles, glass, and ceramics. Upstairs, the rooms are grouped around the *Grote Pers* (Grand Press), and look much as they would have when Leiden's cloth trade was at its height – though most have since been decorated with paintings or now house temporary exhibitions. Downstairs are sixteenth-century paintings centring around Lucas van Leyden's *Last Judgement* triptych, plus canvases by Jacob van Swanenburgh, the first teacher of the young Rembrandt, and by Rembrandt himself and associated Leiden painters – among them Jan Lievens (with whom he shared a studio), Gerrit Dou, who initiated the Leiden tradition of small, minutely finished pictures, and the van Mieris brothers.

Nearer to the station, the **Museum Boerhaave** (Tues–Sat 10am–5pm, Sun 1–5pm; f3.50), named after a seventeenth-century Leiden surgeon, is a brief but surprisingly interesting guide to scientific developments over the last three centuries, with particular reference to Dutch achievements. Next door, the **Rijksmuseum Voor Volkenkunde** (open hours same as the Boerhaave), the national ethnological museum, has complete sections on Indonesia and the Dutch colonies and middling ones on the South Pacific and Far East, but gives most other parts of the world a less-than-thorough showing – and is a lot less enterprising than the Tropenmuseum in Amsterdam.

Lastly, and most prominently, there's the **Molenmuseum de Valk**, 2e Binnenvestgracht 1 (Tues–Sat 10am–5pm, Sun 1–5pm; f3, children f1.50): a restored grain mill, one of twenty that used to surround Leiden. Downstairs rooms are furnished in simple, period style; upstairs a slide show recounts the history of windmills in The Netherlands, while displays detail their development and showcase tools and grinding apparatus, all immaculately preserved. An absorbing way to spend an hour, and only five minutes' stroll from the station.

LEIDEN: PRACTICAL DETAILS

Leiden is easily reached from Amsterdam by train: departures from Centraal Station – via either Haarlem or Schipol —— are frequent (at least 3 trains per hr.), tickets cost around f18 for a day return, and the journey takes just over half an hour. The *VVV* in Leiden is opposite the railway station at Stationsplein 210 (Mon.–Sat. 9am–6pm; ☎071 14 68 46). It's easy to **eat and drink cheaply**: the streets around the Hooglandsekerk and the thirteenth-century Burcht castle hold a concentration of lively bars and restaurants; and, more specifically, there's *Eethuis de Trommelaar*, a pleasant and reasonably-priced vegetarian restaurant; *Menuet*, offering cheap Indonesian meals from f7.50 (7.30pm closing); and *Eethuisje de Engelenbak*, Lange Mare 38, which has Dutch food for f10 upwards.

Katwijk and Noordwijk
Like all of the towns in this part of The Netherlands, Leiden has easy access
to some fine beaches, though the coastal resorts themselves – accessible by
bus from the railway station – aren't much to write home about. **KATWIJK-
AAN-ZEE** is the stock Dutch seaside town, though it doesn't have the
crowds of Zandvoort or the pretentions of Scheveningen. **NOORDWIJK-
AAN-ZEE**, three miles up the coast, is smaller and equally unexciting, but
again offers some excellent stretches of beach.

Gouda

Like those of Alkmaar to the north, **GOUDA**'s tourist brochures focus on one
thing: cheese. Each Thursday morning in July and August (conveniently coinciding with the tourist season) the cheeses are sold in the traditional market
around the seventeenth-century **Waag**. As you'd expect, tourist buses roll in
to savour the sight and unless you're wildly interested in it all, it's best to
come some other day – chiefly for the superb stained glass of **St. Janskerk**
(Mon–Sat 9am–5pm; f2). Just off the Markt, the sprawling church has seventy
windows of stained glass, revealing how radically religious art changed after
the Reformation. In the mid-sixteenth century this part of South Holland was
still Catholic, and the windows executed by Dirk and Wouter Crabeth are
based firmly on biblical themes. Their last work, *Judith Slaying Holofernes*, is
perhaps the finest, the story unfolding in intricate perspective with amazing
clarity of detail and richness of colour. The Post-Reformation windows are
more secular, generally celebrating civic pride. *The Relief of Leiden* shows
William the Silent retaking the town from the Spanish, though Delft is given
prominence – no doubt because the town paid for the window.

Gouda is at its best around the church: the cheese-shaped **Markt** is the
largest in Holland, with a prominent Gothic **Stadhuis** smack in the middle –
look out for the carillon built into its wall: lively, animated figures depict Count
Floris V handing over the town's charter in 1272. Nearby, **Jeruzalemstraat**
has a variety of old houses and **St. Catherine's Hospice**, an interesting
conglomeration of sixteenth-century rooms and halls that serves as the municipal **Museum** (Tues–Sat 10am–5pm, Sun noon–5pm; f3, children f2); paintings by Pieter Pourbus the Elder and a fifteenth-century silver chalice are
highlights of a mixed collection. **De Goutse Librij** at Spieringstraat 1 (Mon–
Fri 2–4pm; free) has a collection of ancient books, that, atypically, you're
encouraged to take off the shelves and finger. Finally there's the **De Moriaan**
collection at Westhaven 29 (Mon–Sat 10am–12.30am/1.30–5pm, Sun noon–
5pm; f1.50), which displays just about every variation on the theme of pipes
possible – the town was once the country's largest producer of clay pipes.

GOUDA: PRACTICAL DETAILS

Trains from Amsterdam to Gouda take around 50 minutes: change at Leiden (every
half hour.) or Woerden (hourly). A day return costs f24. The *VVV* is at Markt 27
(Mon–Fri 9am–6pm, Sat 9am–1pm; ☎018 201 3666).

Delft

DELFT has considerable charm: gabled red-roofed houses stand beside tree-lined canals, and the pastel colours of the pavements, brickwork and bridges give the town a faded, placid tranquility – a tranquillity that from spring onwards is systematically destroyed by tourists. They arrive by air-conditioned coachloads and descend to congest the narrow streets, buy an overpriced piece of gift pottery, and photograph the spire of thc Nieuwe Kerk. And beneath all the tourists, the gift shops, and the tea rooms, old Delft itself gets increasingly difficult to find.

Why is Delft so popular? Apart from its prettiness, the obvious answer is **Delftware**, the clunky and monotonous blue-and-white ceramics to which the town gave its name in the seventeenth century. If you've already slogged through the vast collection in Amsterdam's Rijksmuseum (see p.74), it needs no introduction; and though production of the "real" Delftware is down to a trickle, cheap mass-produced copies have found a profitable niche in today's shops. For those sufficiently interested, *De Pocelyn Fles* at Rotterdamsweg 119 runs **tours** of its Delftware factory throughout the day, and the **Huis Lambert van Meerten Museum** at Oude Delft 119 (Tues–Sat 10am–5pm, Sun 1–5pm; f3.50) has a large collection of Delft (and other) tiles.

The other reason for Delft's popularity is the **Vermeer** connection. The artist was born in the town and died here too — leaving a wife, eleven children, and a huge debt to the local baker. He had given the man two pictures as security, and his wife bankrupted herself trying to retrieve them. Only traces remain of the town as depicted in Vermeer's famous *View of Delft*, now in the Mauritshuis collection in The Hague. To find them, you'll do best on foot – it's not a difficult place to explore. The **Markt** is the best place to start, a central point of reference with the Renaissance Stadhuis at one end and the Nieuwe Kerk at the other. Lined with cafés, restaurants and teenagers blaring disco music on ghetto-blasters, it really gets going with the Thursday general market – not, therefore, the ideal day to visit.

The **Nieuwe Kerk** (April–Oct Mon–Sat 9am–5pm; Oct–April Mon–Fri 10am–noon/1.30–4pm, f2; tower f3.25 extra) is new only in comparison with the Oude Kerk, as there's been a church on this site since 1381. Most of the original structure, however, was destroyed in the great fire that swept over Delft in 1536 and the remainder in a powder magazine explosion a century later — a disaster, incidentally, which claimed the life of the artist Carel Fabritius, Rembrandt's greatest pupil and (debatably) the teacher of Vermeer. The most striking part of the restoration is in fact the most recent – the 330-foot spire, replaced in 1872 and from whose summit there's a wonderful view of the town. Unless you're a Dutch monarchist, the church's interior is uninspiring: it contains the burial vaults of the Dutch royal family, the latest addition being Queen Wilhelmina in 1962. Only the Mausoleum of William the Silent grabs your attention, an odd hotchpotch of styles concocted by Hendrik de Keyser, architect, also, of the Stadhuis opposite.

South of the Stadhuis, signs direct you to the **Koornmarkt**, one of the town's most characteristic seventeenth-century streets. At number 67 is the

Museum Tétar van Elven (May–Oct Tues–Sat 1–5pm; f2.50, children f1.50), slightly drab in appearance but an authentic restoration of the eighteenth-century patrician house that was the studio and home of Paul Tétar van Elven, a provincial and somewhat forgettable artist/collector. **Wynhaven**, another old canal, leads to Hippolytusburt and the Gothic **Oude Kerk** (April–Oct Mon–Sat noon–4pm; f2), arguably the town's finest building. Simple and unbuttressed, with an unhealthily leaning tower, it's the result of a succession of churches here from the thirteenth century to the seventeenth century; the strong and unornamented vaulting proves interiors don't have to be elaborate to avoid being sombre. The pride of the church is its pulpit of 1548, intricately carved with figures emphasised in false perspective, but also notable is the modern stained glass, depicting and symbolising the history of The Netherlands – particularly the 1945 liberation – in the north transept. If you're curious about the tombs – including that of Admiral Maarten van Tromp, famed for hoisting a broom at his masthead to "sweep the seas clear of the English" as he sailed up the Medway – take a look at the *Striking Points* pamphlet available at the entrance.

Opposite the Oude Kerk is the former Convent of Saint Agatha or **Prinsenhof** as it came to be known (Tues–Sat 10am–5pm, Sun 1–5pm; f3.50). Housing Delft's municipal art collection (a good group of works including paintings by Aertsen and Honthorst), it has been restored in the style of the late sixteenth century – an era when the building served as the base of **William the Silent** in his Protestant revolt against the Spanish invaders. From here William planned sorties against the Imperial Catholic troops of Phillip II, achieving considerable success with his *Watergeuzen* or sea-beggars, a kind of commando-guerilla unit that initially operated from England. Here, too, he met his death at the hands of a French assassin: the bullets that passed through him, made by three pellets welded into one, left their mark on the Prinsenhof walls and can still be seen. Tickets for the Prinsenhof also include admission to the unremarkable **Nusantra** ethnographical museum and the Huis van Meerten tile collection.

Finally, if you have time, the **Royal Army and Weapon Museum** (Tues–Sat 10am–5pm, Sun 1–5pm; f2) near the station has a good display of weaponry, uniforms and military accoutrements – which may sound supremely dull, but isn't, even if you're not an enthusiast. The museum attempts to trace The Netherlands' military history from the Spanish wars up to the imperialist adventures of the 1950s – which are shown in surprisingly candid detail.

DELFT: PRACTICAL DETAILS

Three trains an hour link Amsterdam to Delft: the journey takes just under an hour and a day return ticket costs f27. The *VVV* (☎01512 61 00) is at Markt 85, open Monday to Saturday from 9am to 7pm, Sunday 11am to 3pm. For **eating**, the *Hotel Monopole*, centrally located on the Markt, is pretty tourist-oriented but has pancakes, *uitsmijters*, and other light meals for under f10. *Locus Publicus*, Brabantse Turfmarkt 67, is a popular local hangout, serving a staggering array of beers as well as sandwiches. Try, also, *Café de Wynhaven* on Wynhaven and *Café der Oude Jan* opposite the Oude Kerk.

Muiden and Naarden

By far the majority of day-trippers from Amsterdam head west or north; few venture east to the towns of Muiden and Naarden – something entirely to your advantage. Both places can easily be reached by bus, making for a lazy day's travel from the city that takes in Muiden in the morning, Naarden in the afternoon.

MUIDEN is squashed around the Vecht, a river usually crammed with pleasure boats and dinghies sailing out to the Ijsselmeer. Most of the sight-seeing is done by weekend sailors eyeing each other's boats, but **Muiderslot** (open daily, usually until 4pm; f4), a castle more storybook than stronghold, is the place to head for. In the thirteenth century this was the home of Count Floris V, a well-known figure in Dutch story books. A sort of aristocratic Robin Hood, he favoured the common people at the expense of the nobles; the nobles eventually retaliating by kidnapping the unfortunate Floris, imprisoning him in his own castle, and stabbing him to death.

Destroyed and rebuilt in the fourteenth century, Muiderslot's interior now reflects the period of a more recent occupant, the poet **Pieter Hooft.** He was chatelain (castle keeper) here from 1609 to 1647, a sinecure that allowed him to entertain a group of artistic friends who became known as the *Muiden Circle*, and included Grotius, Vondel, Huygens and other Amsterdam literary bigwigs. The (obligatory) guided tour focuses around this clique, and as a recreation of the seventeenth century the castle is both credible and engaging – two things period rooms generally are not.

Look at a postcard of **NAARDEN** and it seems the town was formed by a giant pastry-cutter: the double rings of ramparts and moats, unique in Europe, were engineered in the seventeenth century to defend the town and the eastern approach to Amsterdam. They were still in use in the 1920s, and one of the fortified spurs is now the wonderfully explorable **Fortress Museum** (Easter–end-Oct Mon–Fri 10am–4.30pm, Sat–Sun noon–5pm; f3), whose claustrophobic underground passages show how the garrison defended the town for 250 years. Make your visit on the third Sunday of the month and you'll be deafened by a demonstration of cannon fire and ferried around the fortifications.

Naarden's quiet centre is peaceful rather than dull. Most of the low houses date from after 1572 when the Spaniards sacked the town and massacred the inhabitants, an act designed to warn other towns and villages in the locality. Fortunately they spared the late Gothic **Grote Kerk** (May–Aug Sat–Thurs 2am–4pm; f3) and its superb early-sixteenth-century vault paintings. Based on drawings by Dürer, these twenty wooden panels show an Old Testament scene on the south side, paralleled by a New Testament story on the north. To study the paintings without breaking your neck, borrow a mirror at the museum's entrance. A haul up the Grote Kerk's **tower** (hourly tours 1–4pm; f2) gives the best view of the fortress island and, less attractively, of Hilversum's TV tower.

If you've never heard of Jan Amos Komenski or Comenius, a seventeenth-century polymath and educational theorist, it's unlikely that the **Comenius**

Museum (Tues–Sun 2–5pm; free) at Turfpoortstraat 27 will fire your enthusiasm for the man. A religious exile from Moravia (now in Czechoslovakia), Comenius lived in Amsterdam and is buried in Naarden. He's a national hero to the Czechs, and they donated most of the exhibits in the museum and also constructed his **Mausoleum** in the *Waalse Kapel* on Kloosterstraat – a building permanently on loan to the Czech people.

MUIDEN AND NAARDEN: PRACTICAL DETAILS

CN Bus #136, #137, #138 leave every half hour from the Amstel railway station, stopping first at Muiden (travel time 40 min.) then Naarden (55 min.). The Naarden *VVV* is at Adriaan Dortmansplein 1b (Mon.–Fri. 9:15am–5pm, Sat. 10am–4pm, Sun. noon–4pm; mornings only in winter; ☎021 594 2836).

Utrecht

"I groaned with the idea of living all winter in so shocking a place", wrote Boswell in 1763, and **UTRECHT** still promises little as you approach: surrounded by shopping centres and industrial developments, the town only begins to reveal itself in the old area around the Dom Kerk, roughly enclosed by the Oude and Nieuwe Grachts. These distinctive sunken canals date from the fourteenth century and their brick cellars, used as warehouses when Utrecht was a river port, have been converted to chic cafés and restaurants. Though the liveliest places in town, they don't disguise Utrecht's provincialism: just half an hour from Amsterdam, all the brashness and vitality of the capital is absent, and it's for museums and churches rather than nightlife that the town is enjoyable.

The focal point of the centre is the **Dom Tower**, at 366 feet the highest church tower in the country. It's one of the most beautiful too, soaring, unbuttressed lines rising to a delicate octagonal lantern added in 1380. A guided tour (April–Oct Sat–Sun noon–5pm, plus Mon–Fri 10am–5pm; f1.50, no museumcards) takes you unnervingly near to the top, from where the gap between the tower and Gothic **Dom Kerk** is most apparent. Only the eastern part of the great cathedral remains, the nave having collapsed (with what must have been an apocalyptic crash) during a storm in 1674. It's worth peering inside (May–Sept 10am–5pm, Oct–April 11am–4pm, Sun 2–4pm; free) to get a sense of the hangar-like space the building once had, and to wander through the **Kloostergang**, the fourteenth-century cloisters that link the cathedral to the chapter house, now part of the university.

Except for the Dom, Utrecht's churches aren't all that interesting: the oldest is the **St. Pieterskerk** (Fri–Sat 9am–noon, 2–4pm), a shabbily maintained building that's a mixture of Romanesque and Gothic styles with twelfth-century paintings and reliefs. The **Buurkerk** was the home of one sister Bertken until her death in 1514; she was so ashamed of being the illegitimate daughter of a cathedral priest that she hid away in a small cell

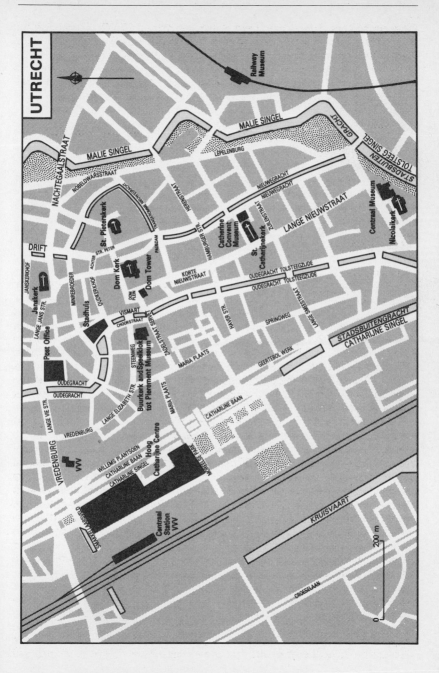

here – for 57 years. Now the church is a peculiar home to the **Speelklok tot Pierement Museum** (Tues–Sat 10am–4pm, Sun 1–4pm; f6, children f3), a collection of burping fairground organs and ingenious musical boxes worth an hour of anyone's time.

The city's other museums are a little way from the centre. The national collection of ecclesiastical art, the **Catherine Convent Museum** (Tues–Fri 10am–5pm, Sat–Sun 11am–5pm; f3.50, children f2), at Nieuwe Gracht 63, has a mass of paintings, manuscripts and church ornaments from the ninth century on, brilliantly exhibited in a complex built around the old convent. This excellent collection of paintings includes work by **Geertgen tot Sint Jans**, **Rembrandt**, **Hals** and, best of all, a luminously beautiful *Virgin and Child* by **van Cleve**. Part of the convent is the late-Gothic St. Catherine's church, its radiant white interior enhanced by floral decoration.

Keep walking down along Nieuwe Gracht and you reach Utrecht's other important museum, the **Centraal**, at Agnietenstraat 1 (Tues–Sat 10am–5pm Sun 2–5pm; f2.50). Its claim to hold "25,000 curiosities" seems a bit exaggerated, but it does have a good collection of paintings by Utrecht artists of the sixteenth and seventeenth centuries. **Van Scorel** lived in Utrecht before and after he visited Rome and he brought the influence of Italian humanism north. His paintings, like the vividly individual portraits of the *Jerusalem Brotherhood*, combine High-Renaissance style with native Dutch observation. The central figure in white is van Scorel himself: he made a trip to Jerusalem around 1520, which accounts for his unusually accurate drawing of the city in *Christ's Entry into Jerusalem*. A group of painters influenced by another Italian, Caravaggio, became known as the Utrecht School. Such paintings as Honthorst's *The Procuress* adapt his chiaroscuro technique to genre subjects, and develop an erotic content that would itself influence later genre painters like Jan Steen and Gerrit Dou. Even more skilled and realistic is Terbrugghen's *The Calling of St. Matthew*, a beautiful balance of gestures dramatising the tax collector's summoning by Christ to become one of the apostles.

Gerrit Rietveld, the de Stijl designer, was most famous for both his zig-zag and his brightly coloured geometrical chairs, displayed in the applied art section. Part of the de Stijl philosophy (see p.192) was that the approach could be used in any area of design, though Rietveld's angular furniture is probably better to look at than to sit on. Out of town, his **Schröder House**, at Prins Hendriklaan 50, is one of the most influential pieces of modern architecture in Europe, demonstrating the organic union of lines and rectangles characteristic of the movement. To join a conducted tour (Tues–Sun; f7.50, children f3.75) phone first: ☎030 51 79 26.

Two final museums that might detain you: the **Phonographic Museum** (Tues–Sat 10am–4.30pm; f3.75, children f2.50) in the Hoog Catharijne centre has a collection of sound-oriented devices from the earliest Edison up to the compact disc; and east of the centre, at Johan van Oldenbarneveldtlaan 6, the **National Railway Museum** (Tues–Sat 10am–5pm, Sun 1–5pm; f7.50, children f4.50) has trains, buses, and trams sitting in Utrecht's out-of-use railway station – not much information, but enthusiastic attendants.

UTRECHT: PRACTICAL DETAILS

Trains run roughly every fifteen minutes from Amsterdam to Utrecht: travel time is thirty minutes and a day-return costs f15. The station leads into the Hoog Catharijne shopping centre and a *VVV* kiosk: the main *VVV* office is at Vredenburg 90 (summer hours Mon–Sat 9am–8pm, Sun 10am–3pm; ☎030 31 41 32). **Restaurants** are mainly along the Oude Gracht; the best are *Oudaen* at number 99 and the mostly vegetarian *De Werftring* at number 123. The junction of Oudegracht & Wed has the town's best collection of **bars**: *Café Graf Floris*, opposite the central Vismarkt, is a good place to hear the Dom Tower's carillon concerts, and the nearby *De Witte Ballons* at Vismarkt 12 has a lively atmosphere.

Alkmaar

Cheese is as Dutch as clogs and windmills, and the **ALKMAAR cheese market** ranks as one of the best-known and most extravagant spectacles in Holland. Since the 1300s yellow blobs of cheese have been sold on the main square here, and it's an institution that continues to draw crowds – though these days they're primarily tourists. If you do want to see it (it's held every Friday, mid-April to Sept), be sure to get there early, as by the 10am opening the mob is already thick.

The ceremony starts with the buyers sniffing, crumbling and finally tasting each cheese, followed by heated bartering. Once a deal has been concluded, the cheeses – golden disks of Gouda mainly, laid out in rows and piles on the square – are borne away on ornamental carriers by four groups of porters for weighing; payment, tradition has it, takes place in the cafés around the square. The rest of the week Alkmaar is quiet, so if you don't want to see the cheese market – and frankly, you wouldn't be missing much – this is a better time to come: it's a pleasant enough place to spend a day, and offers a good insight into small-town Holland. The *VVV* and a **Cheese Museum** share the **Waag** on the main square; the structure was originally a chapel dedicated to the Holy Ghost but was converted, and given the magnificent east gable shortly after the town's famous victory against the Spanish in 1573, when its citizens withstood a long siege by Frederick of Toledo. With some justification, they've never let anyone forget this, and everywhere there are reminders of the defeat that was the beginning of the end for the Spaniards. The **Stedelijk Museum** in Doelenstraat (March–Dec Tues–Sat 10am–5pm, Sun 1–5pm; f2, children free) displays pictures and plans of the siege, as well as a *Holy Family* by Honthorst and portraits by Caesar van Everdingen, a local and very minor seventeenth-century figure who worked in the Mannerist style of the Haarlem painters. Nearby, at the far end of Langestraat, **St. Laurenskerk** is worth looking into for its huge organ, commissioned at the suggestion of Constantijn Huygens by Maria Tesselschade, local resident and friend of the Golden Age elite.

As for **practical details**, Alkmaar is linked with Amsterdam Centraal by two trains an hour, which take about thirty minutes; tickets cost around f15 for a day return. In the town itself, cheap eating places are grouped around the centre, while the cafés *De Pilaren* and *Stapper* are about the closest you'll come to any action.

Around Alkmaar – and Points North

The seaside close to Alkmaar is the area's best feature, and if the weather is warm, it's a good place to cool off after the crush of the cheese market. Bus #168 runs out to **BERGEN**, a cheerful little village that's home to a thriving community of artists, and on to **BERGEN-AAN-ZEE** – a bleak place in itself but with access to some strikingly untouched dunes and beach. About 3km south, **EGMOND-AAN-ZEE** (also directly accessible from Alkmaar) isn't much more attractive, but also has huge expanses of sand. Otherwise, if you're in no hurry to get back to Amsterdam, bear in mind that DEN HELDER, just another half an hour north, is the port for ferry links (frequent in summer) to the island of TEXEL – which, like all of the Dutch islands, offers dunes, beaches, birds and peace for the asking.

Marken, Volendam and Edam

The polders immediately north of Amsterdam and the towns that line the Ijsselmeer are a favourite for day-trippers from Amsterdam: umpteen bus companies run excursions from the capital, and the towns here (villages really) are packed to the gills throughout the summer season. Don't expect anything too pristine.

MARKEN (take bus #11 from opposite the St. Nicolaaskerk) is a popular first stop; this former island in the Zuider Zee was, until its joining to the mainland by road a few years back, largely a closed community, supported by a small fishing industry. At one time its biggest problem was the genetic defects caused by close and constant intermarrying; now it's how to contain the tourists, who have increased severalfold over recent years and show no signs of abating. Marken's distinctness has in many ways been its downfall; its character – that which remains – has been artificially preserved: the harbour is still brightly painted in the local colours, and local costumes and clogs are worn. If visitors now supply the income lost when the Zuider Zee was closed off, the tourist trade turns out to have been a desperate remedy.

The road follows the dike as far as **VOLENDAM** (accessible on bus #110), a larger village which retains some semblance of its fishing industry in conjunction with the more lucrative business of tourism – into which it, too, has thrown itself wholeheartedly. This is everyone's picture-book view of Holland: fishermen in baggy trousers sit strategically along the harbour wall, women scurry about picturesquely, and to piped music, clad in the winged lace caps that form the most significant part of the well-publicised village costume. A convincing charade on the whole, and a lucrative one.

So close to Volendam as to be virtually the same place (and connected by the same #110 bus), you would expect **EDAM** to be just as bad, especially considering its reputation for the small red balls of cheese that the Dutch produce for export. But in fact, it's a relief after the mob rule of Volendam, a pretty little town that is more a suburb of Amsterdam than a major cheese-producer, and which has only a fraction of the souvenir shops of its neighbours. Aside from the intrinsic charm of the place, the main draw is the **Grote Kerk**, an enormous building almost totally rebuilt after a fire in 1602, with some remarkable stained glass dating from that time. Otherwise there's Damplein, Edam's nominal centre, and the eighteenth-century **Raadhuis**, which, although rather plain from the outside, has a superabundance of luxuriant stucco work within. In a distinctive step-gabled building across the bridge there's a small **museum** (Easter–Sept Mon–Sat 10am–4.30pm, Sun 2–4.30pm), and the *VVV* (April–Oct Mon–Fri 10am–12.30am/1.30–5pm, Sat noon–5pm; Oct–March Mon–Sat 10.30am–noon; ☎02993 71727) which may be found in the leaning Speeltoren, on Kleine Kerkstraat.

Should you want to head out further afield, HOORN and, more to the north, ENKHUIZEN (home of the much-lauded Zuider Zee Museum) are also possibilities for day-long excursions. Both are connected with Amsterdam by twice-hourly train – 35 minutes to Hoorn, another twenty or so to the end of the line at Enkhuizen.

In the other direction, west of Edam, **PURMEREND** has a once-weekly summer cheese market, on Thursday at 11am – a slightly less crowded affair than its counterpart at Alkmaar (p.171) – and is directly accessible via bus #106 (35 min). Farther west still, **ZAANDAM** has been a popular tourist hangout since the nineteenth century, when Peter the Great came here to study shipbuilding (you can still visit his house); it became known as "La Chine d'Hollande" for the faintly oriental appearance of its windmills, canals, masts, and row upon row of brightly painted houses. Claude Monet spent some time here in the 1870s, and immortalised the place in a series of paintings – despite being suspected of spying and consequently put under constant police surveillance.

Today, if anything, the tourist traffic is somewhat sparser, since most visitors are attracted to adjacent **ZAANSE SCHANS**, where a collection of windmills, farmhouses and Dutch craftshops have been assembled from all over the country, in an energetic – but fairly bogus – attempt to recreate the past. Most of the buses head to Zaanse Schans; bus #94 to Zaandam takes about thirty minutes.

PART THREE

THE
CONTEXTS

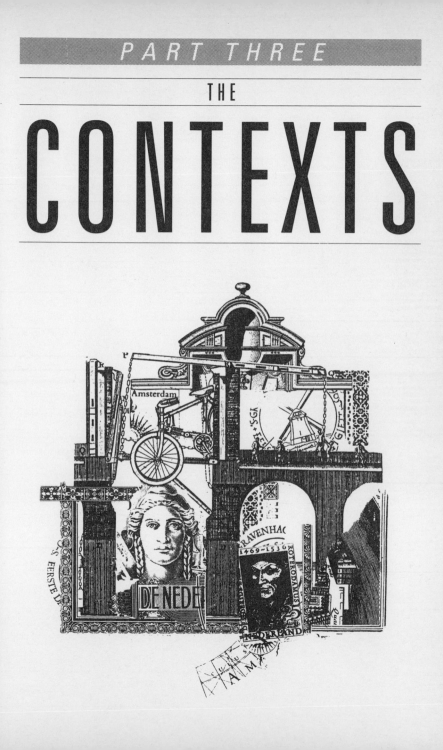

THE
HISTORICAL
FRAMEWORK

THE EARLIEST YEARS

Amsterdam's earliest history is as murky as the marshes from which it arose. A settlement appeared in the eleventh century, founded with a number of other small towns on the barely populated coast. Previously, this stretch of peat bogs and marshes had been uninhabitable, and it was only when the level of the sea fell and floods became less frequent that colonies sprung up, settling on the higher ground of river banks and dams for protection against the floods.

As the name suggests, Amsterdam was founded on a dam on the River Amstel, and the first mention of the settlement comes in a toll privilege charter granted by Count Floris V in 1275 (a document that can be seen in the city archives). By this time Haarlem, Delft and Leiden were already established; Amsterdam itself began to flourish in 1323, when the Count of Holland designated the small town as a toll port for beer imported from Hamburg. Amsterdam soon became an important transit port for grain and a trading force within the Baltic.

As the city grew, its **market** diversified. English wool was imported, made into cloth in Leiden and Haarlem and exported via Amsterdam; the cloth trade drew workers into the town to work along Warmoesstraat and the Amstel, and ships were able to sail right up to Dam Square to pick up the finished work and drop off imported wood, fish, salt and spices.

Though the city's **population** rose steadily throughout the sixteenth century to around 12,000, Amsterdam was relatively small compared to Antwerp or London: building on the water-logged soil was difficult and slow, requiring timber piles to be driven into the firmer sand below. And with the extensive use of timber and thatch, fires were a frequent occurrence. A particularly disastrous blaze in 1452 resulted in such destruction that the city council made building with slate and stone obligatory – one of the few wooden houses that survived the fire stands at the entrance to the Begijnhof. In the mid-sixteenth century the city underwent its first expansion as burgeoning trade with the Hanseatic towns of the Baltic made the city second only to Antwerp as a marketplace and warehouse to northern and western Europe. The trade in cloth, grain, gems and wine brought craftspeople to the city, and the city's merchant fleet grew: by the 1550s three-quarters of all grain cargo going out of the Baltic was carried in Amsterdam vessels. The foundations were being laid for the supreme wealth of the Golden Age.

THE RISE OF
PROTESTANTISM

At the beginning of the sixteenth century the superstition and elaborate ritual in the established **Church** was being attacked throughout northern Europe. Erasmus of Rotterdam advanced the concept of an idealised human, seeing man as the crowning of creation rather than the sinful creature of The Fall. In 1517 Martin Luther produced his 95 theses against the church practice of indulgences; his writings and Bible translations were printed in The Netherlands. But it was Calvin (who differed from Luther in his views on the role of church and state) who gained the most popularity in Amsterdam. In 1535 the Anabaptists, an early **Protestant movement**, rioted, occupying Amsterdam Town Hall and calling on passers by to repent. Previously the town had accepted the Anabaptists, but it acted swiftly when civic rule was challenged: the town hall was besieged and the surviving Anabaptists executed on Dam Square. Following this, an atmosphere of anti-Protestant repression temporarily prevailed.

Around this time, the fanatically Catholic **Philip II** succeeded to the Spanish throne. Through a series of marriages the Spanish monarchy had come to rule over the Low Countries, and Philip was determined to rid the country of the heresy of Protestantism. He came face to face with a rapidly spreading Calvinist movement, and in 1564 Amsterdam Calvinists voiced complaints about nepotism in the city administration to Margaret of Palma, Philip's sister and regent of the Low Countries. Their protests were acknowledged, thus once again reinforcing the power of the Protestant movement, which was by now gaining favour among Amsterdam nobles, too. In 1565 a winter crop failure caused a famine among mainly Calvinist workers and roused discontent against Catholic Spain and Philip's anti-Protestant edicts. Later that year, a wave of **iconoclasm** swept the country: in Amsterdam, Calvinist mobs ran riot in the churches, stripping them of their wealth and their rich decoration; only by being promised the Franciscan church for worship were they mollified. Many churches, particularly in North Holland, were never restored, leaving most with the plain whitewashed interiors seen today. The ferocity of the outbreak shocked the nobility into renewed support for Spain; most radical Protestant leaders saw what was coming and quietly slipped away abroad.

WAR WITH SPAIN

Philip's answer to the iconoclasm was to send in an army of 10,000 men led by the **Duke of Alva** to suppress the heresy absolutely; his first act was to condemn to death 12,000 of those who had taken part in the rebellion the previous year. **William the Silent**, an apostate Prince of the House of Orange-Nassau and the country's largest landowner, organised the Protestant revolt against Spanish rule, taking the cities of Delft, Haarlem and Leiden from Alva's troops. Amsterdam, however, prudently remained on the side of the stronger force until it became clear that William was winning the battle – and his forces had surrounded the town. After the fall of Amsterdam the Catholic clergy was expelled and Catholic churches and monasteries handed over for Protestant use.

In 1579 the seven Dutch provinces signed the Union of Utrecht and brought about the formation of the **United Provinces**, an alliance against Spain that was the first consolidation of the northern Low Countries into an identifiable country. The Utrecht agreement stipulated **freedom of religious belief**, ensuring that anti-Spanish sentiment wasn't translated into divisive anti-Catholicism. Though this tolerant measure didn't extend to freedom of worship, a blind eye was turned to the celebration of mass if it was done privately and inconspicuously – a move that gave rise to "clandestine" Catholic churches like that of the **Amstelkring** on O. Z. Voorburgwal.

With the Revolt against Spain concluded, Amsterdam was free to carry on with what it did best – trading and making money.

THE GOLDEN AGE

The brilliance of Amsterdam's explosion on to the European scene is as difficult to underestimate as it is to detail. The size of its **merchant fleet** had long been considerable, carrying Baltic grain into Europe. Even the determined Spaniards had been unable to undermine Dutch **maritime superiority**, and, following the effective removal of Antwerp as a competitor, Amsterdam became the emporium for the products of northern and southern Europe and the new colonies in the West Indies. The city didn't only prosper from its market; its own ships carried the produce, a cargo trade that greatly increased its wealth.

Dutch **banking and investment** brought further prosperity, and by the mid-seventeenth century Amsterdam's wealth was spectacular. The Calvinist bourgeoisie indulged themselves in fine and whimsically decorated canal houses, and commissioned images of themselves in group portraits. Civic pride knew no bounds as great monuments to self-aggrandisement such as the new **Town Hall** were hastily erected, and if some went hungry, few starved, as the poor were cared for in municipal almshouses.

The arts flourished and **religious tolerance** extended even to traditional scapegoats, the Jews (especially the Sephardis), who had been hounded from Spain by the Inquisition but who were guaranteed freedom from religious persecution under the terms of the Union of

Utrecht. They brought with them their skills in the gem trade, and by the end of the eighteenth century accounted for ten percent of the city's population. Guilds and craft associations thrived and in the first half of the century the city's population increased fourfold. Agricultural workers were drawn to the better wages offered in Dutch industry, arriving along with Huguenot refugees from France and Protestants escaping persecution in the still-Catholic south.

To accommodate its growing populace, Amsterdam **expanded** several times during the seventeenth century. The grandest and most elaborate plan to enlarge the city was begun in 1613, with the building of the western stretches of the **Herengracht**, **Keizersgracht** and **Prinsengracht**, the three great canals that epitomise the wealth and self-confidence of the Golden Age. In 1663 the sweeping crescent was extended east and north beyond the IJ, but by this time the population had begun to stabilise, and the stretch that would have completed the ring of canals around the city was left only partially developed – an area that would in time become the *Jodenhoek* or Jewish quarter.

One organisation that kept the city's coffers brimming throughout the Golden Age was the **East India Company**. Formed by the newly powerful Dutch Republic in 1602, the Amsterdam-controlled enterprise sent ships to Asia, Indonesia, and as far as China to bring back spices, woods and other assorted plunder. Given a trading monopoly in all lands east of the Cape of Good Hope, it had unlimited military powers over the lands it controlled, and was effectively the occupying government in Malaya, Ceylon and Malacca. Twenty years later the **West Indies Company** was inaugurated to protect new Dutch interests in the Americas and Africa. Expending most of its energies in waging war on Spanish and Portugese colonies from a base in Surinam, it never achieved the success of the East India company, and was dismantled in 1674, ten years after its small colony called New Amsterdam had been captured by the British – and renamed New York. Elsewhere, Amsterdam held on to its colonies for as long as possible – **Java** and **Sumatra** were still under Dutch control after World War II.

GENTLE DECLINE – 1650 TO 1800

Part of the reason Amsterdam achieved such economic pre-eminence in the first part of the seventeenth century was that its rivals were expending their energies elsewhere: England was in the turmoil of the Civil War, France was struggling with economic problems brought on by skirmishes with the Spanish, and Germany was ravaged by the Thirty Years' War. By the second half of the century all three countries were back on their feet and fighting: England's navy was attacking the Dutch fleet, Louis XIV of France attempted an invasion of the Low Countries which all but reached Amsterdam, and the troops of the Bishop of Münster occupied the east of the country. While none of these threats became a reality, they signalled the passing of Amsterdam's – and the country's – headiest days.

Though the French had been defeated, Louis retained designs on the United Provinces. When his grandson succeeded to the Spanish throne and to control of the Spanish Netherlands (Brabant, Flanders and Antwerp), Louis forced him to hand the latter over into French hands. The United Provinces, England and Austria, formed an alliance against the French and so began the **Wars of the Spanish Succession**, a haphazard conflict that dragged on until 1713. The fighting tarnished Amsterdam's dazzling riches, draining the nation's wealth. A slow decline in the city's fortunes began, furthered by a mood of conservatism growing out of a reaction against the lucrative speculation of the previous century. Towards the end of the eighteenth century, Amsterdam, and the United Provinces, saw a rising tension between Dutch loyalists and pro-French ruling families (who styled themselves "Patriots"). By the 1780s there was near-civil war, and in 1795 the French, aided by the Patriots, invaded, setting up the **Batavian Republic** and administering it from Amsterdam. Effectively under French control, the Dutch were enthusiastically at **war with England**, and in 1806 Napoleon installed his brother **Louis** as King of The Netherlands in Amsterdam's town hall (giving it, incidentally, its name, **Royal Palace**) in an attempt to create a commercial gulf between the country and England. Amsterdam merchants, with an ever-canny eye to profit, had continued trading with England while the naval battles raged. From his headquarters Louis, however, wasn't willing to allow the country to become a simple satellite of France: he ignored Napoleon's directives and after just four years of rule was forced to abdicate. Following Napoleon's disastrous retreat from Moscow, French rule weakened, and eventually the country was returned to **Dutch control** under William I.

THE NINETEENTH CENTURY

With the **unification of The Netherlands** in 1813, a process that incorporated parts of the former Spanish Netherlands and brought about the formation of Belgium, the **status of Amsterdam** changed. Previously the self-governing city, made bold by its economic independence, could (and frequently did) act in its own self-interest at the expense of the national interest; now it was integrated within the country with no more rights than any other city – it was the capital in name, but the seat of government and all decision-making was The Hague.

Though the **industrial revolution** arrived late, in the first years of the nineteenth century Amsterdam regained parts of its **colonies** in the West and East Indies. Colonial trade improved, but like other trade, it was hampered by the Zuider Zee, whose shallows and sandbanks prevented new, larger ships from entering. The North Holland Canal, completed in 1824 to bypass the Zuider Zee, made little difference, and it was Rotterdam, strategically placed on the Rhine inlets between the industries of the Ruhr and Britain, that prospered at Amsterdam's expense. Even the opening of the **North Sea Canal** in 1876 failed to push Amsterdam's trade ahead of Rotterdam's, though the capital did house the country's **shipbuilding industry**, remnants of which can still be seen at the Kromhout yard in the Eastern Islands.

Between 1850 and the turn-of-the-century the population of Amsterdam, which had remained static since the 1650s, doubled. Most of the newcomers to the city were poor and the **housing** built for them reflected this; the small homes around De Pijp in the Old South remain good examples of the low-cost housing that the more affluent working classes could afford. The Jordaan, for the early parts of the century one

of the city's most impoverished quarters, was cleared. Its polluted canals were filled in and small, inexpensive homes were built. The Jordaan project was one of many put together by philanthropic social organisations, and the council, too, had what were, for the time, forward-looking policies to **alleviate poverty** and increase education for the poor. The political climate was outstandingly liberal, influenced by cabinet leader **J. R. Thorbecke** and an increasingly socialist contingent on the Amsterdam City Council.

Before the hard years of the depression the city continued to grow. The rise in the standard of living among working people meant that they could afford better homes, usually under the auspices of housing associations or the city's own building programmes. The most interesting of these were the estates built in what came to be called the **New South**: designed by a group known as the **Amsterdam School** of architects, they combined modernism with the best of home-grown styles – and were extremely successful.

WAR

At the outbreak of **World War I** The Netherlands had remained neutral, though it suffered privations as a result of the Allied blockade of ports through which the Germans might be supplied. Similar attempts to remain neutral in **World War II** soon failed: German troops invaded on May 10, 1940, and the Dutch were quickly overwhelmed, Queen Wilhelmina fled to London, and Arthur Seyss-Inquart was installed as Berlin's puppet leader. Members of the **NSB**, the Dutch fascist party which had welcomed the invaders, found themselves rapidly promoted to positions of authority, but, in the early years of the occupation at least, life for the ordinary Amsterdammer went on much as usual. Even when the first roundups of the Jews began in 1941, most people pretended they weren't happening, the single popular demonstration against the Nazi action being the quickly-suppressed **February strike**.

The **Dutch Resistance** was instrumental in destroying German supplies and munitions and carrying out harassing attacks in the city, and as the resistance grew, underground newspapers flourished – today's *Trouw* (Loyalty) and *Het Parool* (The Password) began life as illegal newsletters. Around 13,000 Resistance fighters and sympathisers lost their lives during the war, and the city's old **Jewish quarter**, swollen by those who had fled Germany during the persecutions of the 1930s, was obliterated, leaving only the deserted Jodenhoek and the diary of a young girl as testaments to the horrors.

THE POST-WAR YEARS

The years immediately after the war were spent patching up the damage of occupation and liberation. It was a period of intense **poverty** in the capital, as food, fuel and building materials were practically nonexistent; a common sight on the streets were handcart burials of those who had died of hunger or hypothermia, black cardboard coffins being trundled to mass graves. As the liberating Canadians had moved nearer to Amsterdam, the Germans had blown up all the dikes and the sluices at Ijmuiden, and repairing these further slowed the process of rebuilding. The sea itself claimed victims in 1953, when an unusually high tide swept over Zeeland's coastal defences, flooding 40,000 acres of land and drowning more than 1800 people. The resultant **Delta Project**, which secured the area, also ensured the safety of cities to the south of Amsterdam. The opening of the **Amsterdam-Rhine canal** did much to boost the fortunes of the city, with massive cargo-handling facilities being built to accommodate the imports of grain and the supply of ore for the Ruhr furnaces. Steadily the rebuilding continued: in Amsterdam all the land projected for use by the year 2000 was used up by the "garden cities" in 1970. Giant suburbs such as **Bijlmermeer** to the southeast were the last word in 1960s large-scale residential plans, with low-cost modern housing, play areas and traffic-free foot and bicycle paths, and a new **metro line** built to link the suburb to the city centre. Today, however, Bijlmermeer is a ghetto few willingly visit.

THE CONTEMPORARY CITY

The social consciousness and radicalism of the 1960s reached Amsterdam early, and word of the psychedelic revolution was quick to catch on. Dam Square and the Vondelpark became open-air urban campsites, and the pilgrims of alternative culture descended on the easy-going, dope-happy capital. Just as quickly the revolution faded, replaced by the cynicism of the 1970s and, more recently, the resurgence of the right. The city's **housing problems** became a counter-culture focus in the 1960s and early 1970s (see below), and US deployment of **cruise missiles** in The Netherlands temporarily galvanised opposition in the early 1980s. In spite of large-scale protest (over 4 million people signed an anti-cruise petition, the *volkspetitonnment*, and there were many demonstrations in the city), the missiles were scheduled to be deployed in 1985; the nearest missile base to Amsterdam, **Woensdrecht**, was seventy miles away and the focus of popular opposition. However, arms negotiations between the US and USSR meant that the missiles never arrived – and that the buildings created to house them were all a waste of time and money.

Today, even under the socialist mayor Ed van Thijn, new housing is firmly aimed at Amsterdam's luxury hotel market rather than at its residential needs, and the city's former radicalism seems – for the moment at least – suspended.

RADICAL AMSTERDAM: SQUATTERS AND RIOTS

The 1960s were swinging, the summer of 1965 was warm, and a group of young people were making it a weekly ritual to gather round a statue in the centre of Amsterdam to watch a remarkable performer, one-time window cleaner and magician extraordinaire, Jasper Grootveld. Grootveld had won notoriety a couple of years earlier by painting K for kanker (cancer) on cigarette billboards throughout the city. Later he set up an "anti-smoking temple" and proclaimed the statue of the Lieverdje ("Lovable Rascal") on the Spui the symbol of "tomorrow's addicted consumer" since it had been donated to the city by a cigarette manufacturer.

PROVOS AND KABOUTERS

But Grootveld wasn't the only interesting character around town: Roel van Duyn, a philosophy student at Amsterdam University and initiator of a New Left movement, and the Provos (short for provocatie – provocation) started joining in Grootveld's magic happenings, sparking a chain of rebellion that would influence events in The Netherlands for the next twenty years.

The number of real Provos never exceeded about 25, but their actions and street "Happenings" appealed to a large number of young people. The group had no coherent structure: they emerged into public consciousness through one common aim – to bring points of political or social conflict to public attention by spectacular means. More than anything they were masters of publicity, and pursued their "games" with a spirit of fun rather than grim political fanaticism. They reflected the swinging sixties attitude of young people all over the western world.

In July 1965 the police intervened at the Saturday night Happening for the first time, and set a pattern for future confrontations; they had already confiscated the first two issues of the Provos' magazine in which their initiator, Roel van Duyn, published the group's manifesto and in which their policies later appeared under the title "The White Plans". These included the famous but unsuccessful **white bicycle plan**, which proposed that the Council ban all cars in the city centre and supply 20,000 bicycles (painted white) for general public use – the idea being that you picked up a bike, rode it to your destination, and then left it for someone else to use.

There were regular incidents throughout 1965 and 1966 involving a variety of Provo protests, but it was the action taken on March 10, 1966, the wedding day of Princess Beatrix and Claus von Amsberg, that provoked the most serious unrest: smoke bombs were thrown at the wedding procession and fights with the police broke out across the city. The following month Provo Hans Tuynman was arrested for handing a policeman a leaflet protesting police actions. Street demonstrations followed, along with further arrests, and when Tuynman was sentenced to three months' imprisonment on May 11, anger spread. Through all this conflict, however, the Provos were also winning increased public support; in the municipal elections of 1966 they received over 13,000 votes – two and a half percent of the total, and enough for a seat on the Council. But this achievement didn't mean the end of the Provos' street actions. Indeed, the next event in which they were involved was one of the most violent of the 1960s. It started with a demonstration by city construction workers on June 13, during which one worker suddenly died. Such was the anti-police feeling that it was assumed he had been killed by police patrolling the protest, and the following day the workers staged a strike and marched through the city with thousands of supporters, including the Provos who by now were regarded as the champions of the public versus the police. The worker actually died of a heart attack, but the mood had been set and there were clashes between police and rioters for four days. A month later The Hague government ordered the dismissal of Amsterdam's Police Chief and, a year later, that of the mayor.

But by May 1967 the Provos' inspiration was waning, and at a final gathering in the

Vondelpark they announced that they would disband, even though they still had a member on the City Council.

The next phase in the Provo phenomenon was the creation of the "Oranje Free State", a so-called alternative society set up by Van Duyn in 1970 in the form of a mock government with its own "ministers" and "policies". The new movement, whose members were named **Kabouters** after a helpful gnome in Dutch folklore, was successful if short-lived. It adopted some of the more reasonable "white policies" of the Provos and went so far as to win seats in six municipalities, including five in Amsterdam on a vaguely socialist ticket. "No longer the socialism of the clenched fist, but of the intertwined fingers, the erect penis, the escaping butterfly . . . ", their manifesto proclaimed. But by the close of 1981 the Kabouter movement, too, faded amid disputes over methodology.

As the Provo and Kabouter movements disappeared, many of their members joined **neighbourhood committees**, set up to oppose certain plans of the City Council. By far the most violently attacked scheme was that of building a **metro line** through the Nieuwmarkt to the newly constructed suburb of **Bijlmermeer**. The initial idea was conceived in 1968 and consisted of a plan to build a four-line network for an estimated f250 million. By 1973, the cost had risen to f1500 million – for just one line.

It was the Council's policy of coping with the ever-growing problem of housing by **moving residents** to these suburbs that infuriated Amsterdammers, who felt that their town was being sold off to big businesses and their homes converted to banks and offices, thereby creating a city centre that ordinary people couldn't afford to live in. The opponents of the metro plan objected to the number of houses that would have to be demolished, contending it was merely an elitist development, of no real use to the public.

Official **clearance of the Nieuwmarkt** area was scheduled for February 1975 but confrontation between police and protesters began the previous December. Many residents of the condemned houses refused to move, and further violent clashes were inevitable. The worst came on March 24, 1975, a day that became known as **Blue Monday**: the police began a clearing action early in the morning

and their tactics were heavy-handed. Tear-gas grenades were fired through windows smashed by water cannons, armoured cars ripped through front doors, and the police charged in to arrest occupants (residents and supporters), who threw paint cans and powder bombs in retaliation. The fighting went on late into the night with thousands of demonstrators joining in At the end of the day, thirty people – including nineteen policemen – had been wounded, and 47 arrested; 450 complaints were filed against the police. A couple of weeks later came another big clash, but this time the demonstrators used different tactics, forming human barricades in front of the houses to be cleared. The police charged, armed with truncheons; it was an easy eviction. But the protestors had made their point, and afterwards showed their spirit of rebellion by holding parties on the rubble-strewn sites. Despite continuing opposition, the metro eventually opened in 1980.

THE SQUATTING MOVEMENT

Meanwhile the ever-increasing problem of housing was bringing about the emergence of a new movement – the **squatters**. At first the squatters' movement was peripheral, consisting mainly of independently-operating neighbourhood committees. There was little sense of unity until joint actions to defend a handful of symbolic Amsterdam squats took place. These shaped the development of the squatters' movement, today a strong political force with clearly defined rights and the ear of the City Council.

Four events help explain how this transformation of the squatters' movement occurred: the actions at the key squats of Vondelstraat, Lucky Luyk and Wyers – and the national day of squatting on April 30, 1980.

The eviction of the **Vondelstraat** squat in Amsterdam's most prestigious neighbourhood near the Rijksmuseum is perhaps the most famous squatting event in The Netherlands. Three days after the empty office premises were occupied in March 1980, police tanks were ordered to remove the squatters. About a thousand police took part and the resulting riots spread through the streets and reached the tourist area of Leidseplein. Battles raged the whole day and fifty people were wounded.

The squatters were evicted, but it wasn't long before they reoccupied the building. The significance of the Vondelstraat squat was that the attempted eviction and ensuing riots cost the Council a considerable amount of money – a fact the squatters used tactically, making future evictions too expensive for the authorities to undertake.

The next major event involved not a specific squat but protest actions on April 30, 1980 – the **coronation day** of Queen Beatrix. Squatters in Amsterdam and throughout The Netherlands staged protests against the huge amounts of money being spent on the festivities, in addition to the reputed f84 million spent on the rebuilding of her residence in The Hague. Two hundred buildings in 27 cities were squatted. Half of these squats were cleared the same day, and it was one of these clearances that sparked off the first battle in Amsterdam. Then, in the afternoon, a protest demonstration set off to march through the city to Dam Square where the crowning ceremony was taking place. Confrontation with the police began almost immediately on Waterlooplein, and from then on the city centre turned into complete chaos. The squatters' ranks were swelled by other protesters angered by the coronation expenditure at a time when the Amsterdam City Council claimed it could not afford to build homes. Public festivities came to an abrupt halt as fighting broke out in the streets and continued until the early hours. Tear gas enveloped the city while Special Squad Police made repeated charges, and many revellers were caught up with the rebels as the police cordoned off the most militant areas.

By 1982 the squatting movement was reaching its peak. After the success of the Vondelstraat squat in 1980, hundreds of premises were being occupied every week, and an estimated 10,000 squatters took over buildings across Amsterdam. The eviction of those who had occupied **Lucky Luyk**, a villa on the Jan Luykenstraat, was the most violent and the most expensive (damage ran into millions of guilders) the city had known to date.

Lucky Luyk was originally squatted in 1980 after standing empty for a few years. In October 1980 squatters were forcibly evicted twice by the *knockploegen* – groups of heavies rented by property owners to protect their investments. Two months later the owners of the villa won a court order for the evacuation of the building. At this stage, the Amsterdam City Council stepped in to pre-empt the violence that was certain to accompany such an action: they bought the villa for f350,000 – giving the owners an easy f73,000 profit. The squatters weren't happy, but agreed to leave the building if it were used for young people's housing. On October 11, 1982, two days before a meeting between the Council and the squatters, twelve policemen from the Special Squad broke into Lucky Luyk through the roof and arrested the five occupants – a surprise attack that enraged squatters across the country and resulted in sympathy actions in many other cities.

In Amsterdam, riots soon started and lasted for three days. Supporters of the Lucky Luyk, who included many non-squatters, built barricades, wrecked cars, destroyed property and set fire to a tram, while police retaliated with tear gas and water cannons. The mayor declared unprecedented emergency measures, permitting police to arrest anyone suspected of disrupting public order.

The squatters had learned a lesson: the authorities had had enough and were learning new and easier methods of eviction – and were prepared to evict at any cost. Squatters needed to develop a new defence tactic. They hit on politics, and found a new case to fight – **Wyers**. This building, a former distribution centre for a textile firm, had been occupied in October 1981 by about a hundred squatters from all over the city. They were soon informed that *Hollandse Beton Maatschapij*, one of the country's largest building companies, had just obtained permission to build luxury apartments and shops on the site. Trouble was postponed, however, when *HBM* decided the time was not right for their financial investment and scrapped their plans. But in the spring of 1982 they reapplied for building rights, this time to put up a hotel on behalf of Holiday Inn. The initial application was turned down, but an amended plan was approved by the Council in June 1983. An eviction order was presented to the Wyers inhabitants, but the squatters found legal loopholes within the eviction order and the clearance was delayed.

The squatters were also busy preparing an alternative plan to present to the Council, which involved using the building as a combined cultural-residential complex with space for small businesses and studios. This constructive alternative won the support of many people, and even the Council considered it a viable idea. Dialogue between the Council and squatters continued, but Wyers was cleared in February 1984, with the usual pictures of water cannons and tear gas spread across Europe's front pages. The eviction itself was relatively peaceful: the squatters had decided not to resist and instead linked arms around the site and waited for the police onslaught. Today the Holiday Inn stands on N. Z. Voorburgwal as a testament to the fact that the squatters failed here: but as banners proclaimed after the eviction, "You can demolish Wyers but will never destroy the ideas behind Wyers".

AMSTERDAM TODAY

Some of those ideas surfaced recently with the building of the **Muziektheater/Stadhuis** on Waterlooplein. Historically the site chosen for the new opera building was sensitive, as it was part of the old Jodenhoek and had been a public space for centuries; politically, the building of a highbrow cultural centre was attacked as elitist; and architecturally, the plans were a clumsy hybrid, different designers being responsible for each section.

The Muziektheater was bound to come in for flak, and got it from the **Stopera** campaign, named after the early label for the building and a convenient contraction of "Stop the Opera". No doubt the fact that Amsterdam was angling for the **1992 Olympics*** was reason for the Council to railroad the plans through, yet, compared to the previous fracas, protest was surprisingly slight. Though the building is today an ugly intruder on the Amstel, it seems to have won over many of its erstwhile opponents – perhaps because Amsterdammers can accommodate any public building more easily than a

private one. On the other hand, it's a sign of the times (and the city's gentrification) that there's been little protest over the new casino that's about to open just off the Leidseplein, or the private residential and shopping development – of massive and unappealing proportions – that is being built alongside it.

Yet some of the ideas (and idealism) of a few years back seem to be bearing fruit on a national level. In the elections of 1989 **Groen Links**, the Green-Left coalition of mainly small left and ecology parties had a strong showing, and, a year previously, The Netherlands became the first European country to officially adopt a **National Environment Plan**, a radical agenda of Green policies: as yet, however, the Plan has still to be implemented. On the downside, the far-right **Centrum Democratische** party, led by Hans Janmaat, also won enough votes to enable him to gain an unprecedented seat in the Lower House of the country's parliament, an event which occasioned multiple demonstrations. There's something naggingly illiberal too in the City Council's decision to set up an employment scheme-cum-"Guardian Angels"-type force, the **Stadswacht**, which will patrol Leidseplein, Rembrandtsplein and other hot spots on the lookout for drug dealers and sundry petty criminals. Whether the presence of the *Stadswacht* will check the upsurge of minor thefts that has occurred in the wake of the rise of the dealing of hard drugs is a debatable point. But, with the city setting up its own vigilante force, the days of "Happenings", helpful gnomes and white bicycles now seems a world away. . .

---

*During the planning stages for these Olympics, when each city was allowed to plead its suitability before a committee, Amsterdam became the only city in history ever to send an official *anti*-Olympics delegation.

DUTCH ART

This is the very briefest of introductions to the subject, designed to serve only as a quick reference on your way round the major galleries. For more in-depth and academic studies, see the recommendations in the Books listings, p.202. And for where to find the paintings themselves, turn to the hit list at the end.

BEGINNINGS

Until the sixteenth century the area now known as the Low Countries was in effect one country, the most artistically productive part of which was Flanders in modern Belgium, and it was there that the solid realist base of later Dutch painting developed. Today the works of these **early Flemish painters** are pretty sparse in Holland, and even in Belgium few collections are as complete as they might be; indeed, many ended up as the property of the ruling Habsburgs and were removed to Spain. Most Dutch galleries do, however, have a few examples.

Jan van Eyck (1385–1441) is generally regarded as the originator of Low Countries painting, and has even been credited with the invention of oil painting itself – though it seems more likely that he simply perfected a new technique by thinning his paint with the recently discovered turpentine, thus making it more flexible. His most famous work still in the Low Countries, the Ghent *altarpiece* (debatably

painted with the help of his lesser-known brother, Hubert), was revolutionary in its realism, for the first time using elements of native landscape in depicting biblical themes.

Firmly in the van Eyck tradition were the **Master of Flemalle** (1387–1444) and **Rogier van der Weyden** (1400–64). The Flemalle master is a shadowy figure: some believe he was the teacher of van der Weyden, others that the two artists were in fact the same person. There are differences between the two, however: the Flemalle master's paintings are close to van Eyck's, whereas van der Weyden shows a more emotional and religious intensity. Van der Weyden influenced such painters as **Dieric Bouts** (1415–75), who was born in Haarlem but active in Louvain, and is recognisable by his stiff, rather elongated figures. **Hugo van der Goes** (d. 1482) was the next Ghent master after van Eyck, most famous for the *Portinari altarpiece* in Florence's *Uffizi*; after a short painting career, he died insane. Few doubt that **Hans Memling** (1440–94) was a pupil of van der Weyden: active in Bruges throughout his life, he is best remembered for the pastoral charm of his landscapes and the quality of his portraiture, much of which survives on the rescued side panels of triptychs. More renowned are **Hieronymus Bosch** (1450–1516), whose frequently reprinted and discussed religious allegories are filled with macabre visions of tortured people and grotesque beasts, and **Pieter Bruegel the Elder** (1525–69), whose gruesome allegories and innovative interpretations of religious subjects are firmly placed in Low Countries settings.

Meanwhile, there were movements to the north of Flanders. **Geertgen tot Sint Jans** ("Little Gerard of the Brotherhood of St. John") (d. 1490), a student of **Albert van Ouwater**, had been working in **Haarlem**, initiating – in a strangely naive style – an artistic tradition in the city that would prevail throughout the seventeenth century. **Jan Mostaert** (1475–1555) took over after Geertgen's death, and continued to develop a style that diverged more and more from that of the southern provinces. **Lucas van Leyden** (1489–1533) was the first painter to effect real changes in northern painting. Born in Leiden, his bright colours and narrative technique were refreshingly new at the time, and he introduced a novel dynamism into what had become a rigidly formal treatment of devotional subjects. There was rivalry, of course. Eager to publicise Haarlem as the artistic capital of the northern Netherlands, Carel van Mander (see below) claimed Haarlem native **Jan van Scorel** (1495–1562) as the better painter, complaining, too, of Lucas's dandyish ways.

Certainly van Scorel's influence should not be underestimated. At this time every painter was expected to travel to Italy to view the works of Renaissance artists. When the Bishop of Utrecht became Pope Hadrian VI, he took van Scorel with him as court painter, giving him the opportunity to introduce Italian styles into what had been a completely independent tradition. Hadrian died soon after, and van Scorel returned north, combining the ideas he had picked up in Italy with Haarlem realism and passing them on to **Maerten van Heemskerck** (1498–1574), who went off to Italy himself in 1532, staying there five years before returning to Haarlem.

THE GOLDEN AGE

The seventeenth century begins with **Carel van Mander**, Haarlem painter and art impressario and one of the few chroniclers of the art of the Low Countries. His *Schilderboek* of 1604 put Flemish and Dutch traditions into context for the first time, and, in addition, specified the rules of fine painting. Examples of his own work are rare, but his followers were many, among them **Cornelius Cornelisz van Haarlem** (1562–1638), who produced elegant renditions of biblical and mythical themes; and **Hendrik Goltzius** (1558–1616), who was a skilled engraver and an integral member of van Mander's Haarlem academy. These painters' enthusiasm for Italian art, combined with the influence of a late revival of Gothicism, resulted in works that combined mannerist and classical elements. An interest in realism was also felt, and for them, the subject became less important than the way in which it was depicted: biblical stories became merely a vehicle whereby artists could apply their skills in painting the human body, landscapes, or copious displays of food – all of which served to break religion's stranglehold on art, and make legitimate a whole range of everyday subjects for the painter.

In Holland (and this was where the north and the south finally diverged) this break with tradition was compounded by the **Reformation**: the austere Calvinism that had replaced the Catholic faith in the northern provinces had no use for images or symbols of devotion in its churches. Instead, painters catered to the public, and no longer visited Italy to learn their craft; the real giants of the seventeenth century – Hals, Rembrandt, Vermeer – stayed in The Netherlands all their lives. Another innovation was that painting split into more distinct categories – genre, portrait, landscape, etc. – and artists tended (with notable exceptions) to confine themselves to one field throughout their careers. So began the greatest age of Dutch art.

HISTORICAL AND RELIGIOUS PAINTING

If Italy continued to hold sway in The Netherlands it was not through the Renaissance painters but rather via the fashionable new realism of Caravaggio. Many artists – Rembrandt for one – continued to portray classic subjects, but in a way that was totally at odds with the Mannerists' stylish flights of imagination. Though a solid Mannerist throughout his career, the Utrecht artist, **Abraham Bloemaert** (1564–1651), encouraged these new ideas, and his students – **Gerard van Honthorst** (1590–1656), **Hendrik Terbrugghen** (1588–1629), and **Dirck van Baburen** (1590–1624) – formed the nucleus of the influential **Utrecht School**, which followed Caravaggio almost to the point of slavishness. Honthorst was perhaps the leading figure, learning his craft from Bloemaert and travelling to Rome, where he was nicknamed "Gerardo delle Notti" for his ingenious handling of light and shade. This was, however, to become in his later paintings more routine technique than inspired invention, and though a supremely competent artist, Honthorst remains somewhat discredited among critics today. Terbrugghen's reputation seems to have aged rather better: he soon forgot Caravaggio and developed a more personal style, his lighter, later work having a great influence on the young Vermeer. After the obligatory jaunt to Rome, Baburen shared a studio with Terbrugghen and produced some fairly original work – work which also had some influence on Vermeer – but today he is the least studied member of the group and few of his paintings survive.

But it's **Rembrandt** who was considered the most original historical artist of the seventeenth century, painting religious scenes throughout his life. In the 1630s, the poet and statesman Constantijn Huygens procured for him his greatest commission – a series of five paintings of the Passion, beautifully composed and uncompromisingly realistic. Later, however, Rembrandt received fewer and fewer commissions, since his treatment of biblical and historical subjects was far less dramatic than that of his contemporaries. It's significant that while the more conventional Jordaens, Honthorst, and van Everdingen were busy decorating the Huis ten Bosch near The Hague for patron Stadholder Frederick Henry, Rembrandt was having his monumental *Conspiracy of Claudius Civilis* (painted for the new Amsterdam town hall) rejected – probably because it was thought too pagan an interpretation of what was an important symbolic event in Dutch history. **Aert van Gelder** (1645–1727), Rembrandt's last pupil and probably the only one to concentrate on historical painting, followed the style of his master closely, producing shimmering biblical scenes well into the eighteenth century.

GENRE PAINTING

Genre refers to scenes from everyday life, a subject that, with the decline of the church as patron, became popular in Holland by the mid-seventeenth century. Many painters devoted themselves solely to such work. Some genre paintings were simply non-idealised portrayals of common scenes, while others, by means of symbols or carefully disguised details, made moral entreaties to the viewer.

Among early-seventeenth-century painters, **Hendrik Terbrugghen** and **Gerard Honthorst** spent much of their time on religious subjects, but also adapted the realism and strong chiaroscuro learned from Caravaggio to a number of tableaux of everyday life. **Frans Hals**, too, is better known as a portraitist, but his early genre paintings no doubt influenced his pupil, **Adriaen Brouwer** (1605–38), whose riotous tavern scenes were well received in their day and collected by, among others, Rubens and Rembrandt. Brouwer spent only a couple of years in Haarlem under Hals before

returning to his native Flanders to influence the younger **David Teniers**. **Adriaen van Ostade** (1610–85), on the other hand, stayed there most of his life, skilfully painting groups of peasants and tavern brawls – though his later acceptance by the establishment led him to water down the realism he had learnt from Brouwer. He was teacher to his brother **Isaak** (1621–49), who produced a large number of open-air peasant scenes, subtle combinations of genre and landscape work.

The English critic E. V. Lucas dubbed Teniers, Brouwer and Ostade "coarse and boorish" compared with **Jan Steen** (1625–79), who, along with Vermeer, is probably the most admired Dutch genre painter. You can see what he had in mind: Steen's paintings offer the same Rabelaisian peasantry in full fling, but they go their debauched ways in broad daylight, and nowhere do you see the filthy rogues in shadowy hovels favoured by Brouwer and Ostade. Steen offers more humour, too, as well as more moralising, identifying with the hedonistic mob and reproaching them at the same time. Indeed, many of his pictures are illustrations of well-known proverbs of the time – popular epithets on the evils of drink or the transience of human existence that were supposed to teach as well as entertain.

Gerrit Dou (1613–75) was Rembrandt's Leiden contemporary and one of his first pupils. It's difficult to detect any trace of the master's influence in his work, however; Dou initiated a style of his own: tiny, minutely realised, and beautifully finished views of a kind of ordinary life that was decidedly more genteel than Brouwer's – or even Steen's for that matter. He was admired, above all, for his painstaking attention to detail: and he would, they say, sit in his studio for hours waiting for the dust to settle before starting work. Among his students, **Frans van Mieris** (1635–81) continued the highly finished portrayals of the Dutch bourgeoisie, as did **Gabriel Metsu** (1629–67) – perhaps Dou's greatest pupil – whose pictures often convey an overtly moral message. Another pupil of Rembrandt's, though a much later one, was **Nicholaes Maes** (1629–93), whose early paintings were almost entirely genre paintings, sensitively executed and again with a moralising message. His later work shows the influence of a more refined style of portrait, which he had picked up in France.

As a native of Zwolle, **Gerard ter Borch** (1619–81) found himself far from all these Leiden/Rembrandt connections; despite trips abroad to most of the artistic capitals of Europe, he remained very much a provincial painter all his life, depicting Holland's merchant class at play and becoming renowned for his curious doll-like figures and his enormous ability to capture the textures of different cloths. His domestic scenes were not unlike those of **Pieter de Hooch** (1629–after 1684), whose simple depictions of everyday life are deliberately unsentimental, and, for the first time, have little or no moral commentary. De Hooch's favourite trick was to paint darkened rooms with an open door leading through to a sunlit courtyard, a practice that, along with his trademark rusty red colour, makes his work easy to identify – and, at its best, exquisite. That said, his later pictures reflect the encroaching decadence of the Dutch republic: the rooms are more richly decorated, the arrangements more contrived and the subjects far less homely.

It was, however, **Jan Vermeer** (1632–75) who brought the most sophisticated methods to painting interiors, depicting the play of natural light on indoor surfaces with superlative skill. And it's for this and the curious peace and intimacy of his pictures that he's best known. Another recorder of the better-heeled Dutch households, and, like de Hooch, without the moral tone, he is regarded (with Hals and Rembrandt) as one of the big three Dutch painters – though he was, it seems, a slow worker, and only about forty small paintings can be attributed to him with any certainty. Living all his life in Delft, Vermeer is perhaps the epitome of the seventeenth-century Dutch painter – rejecting the pomp and ostentation of the High Renaissance to quietly record his contemporaries at home, painting for a public that demanded no more than that.

PORTRAITS

Naturally, the ruling bourgeoisie of Holland's flourishing mercantile society wanted to put their success on record, and it's little wonder that portraiture was the best way for a young painter to make a living. **Michiel Jansz Miereveld** (1567–1641), court painter to Frederick Henry in The Hague, was the first real portraitist of the Dutch Republic, but it wasn't long before his stiff and rather conservative figures were superseded by the more spontaneous renderings of **Frans Hals** (1585–1666). Hals is perhaps best known for his "corporation-pictures" – portraits of the members of the Dutch civil guard regiments that had been formed in most larger towns while the threat of invasion by the Spanish was still imminent. These large group pieces demanded superlative technique, since the painter had to create a collection of individual portraits while retaining a sense of the group and accord prominence based on the importance of the sitter and the size of the payment each had made. Hals was particularly good at this, using innovative lighting effects, arranging his sitters subtly, and putting all the elements together in a fluid and dynamic composition. He also painted many individual portraits, making the ability to capture fleeting and telling expressions his trademark; his pictures of children are particularly sensitive. Later in life, his work became darker and more akin to Rembrandt's.

Jan Cornelisz Verspronck (1597–1662) and **Bartholomeus van der Helst** (1613–70) were the other great Haarlem portraitists after Frans Hals – Verspronck recognisable by the smooth, shiny glow he always gave to his sitters' faces, van der Helst by a competent but unadventurous style. Of the two, van der Helst was the more popular, influencing a number of later painters and leaving Haarlem while still young to begin a solidly successful career as portrait painter to Amsterdam's burghers.

The reputation of **Rembrandt van Rijn** (1606–69) is still relatively recent – nineteenth-century connoisseurs preferred Gerard Dou – but he is now justly regarded as one of the greatest and most versatile painters of all time. Born in Leiden, the son of a miller, he was apprenticed at an early age to **Jacob van Swanenburgh**, a then quite important, though uninventive, local artist. He shared a studio with **Jan Lievens**, a promising painter and something of a rival for a while (now all but forgotten), before going up to Amsterdam to study under the fashionable **Pieter Lastman**. Soon he was painting commissions for the city elite and he also became an accepted member of their circle. The poet and statesman Constantin Huygens acted as his agent, pulling strings to obtain all of Rembrandt's more lucrative jobs, and in 1634 he married Saskia van

Ulenborch, daughter of the burgomeister of Leeuwarden and quite a catch for the still relatively humble artist. His self-portraits at the time show the confident face of security – on top of things and quite sure of where he's going.

Rembrandt would not always be the darling of the Amsterdam smart set, but his fall from grace was still some way off when he painted the *Night Watch* – a group portrait often associated with the artist's decline in popularity. But, although Rembrandt's fluent arrangement of his subjects was totally original, there's no evidence that the military company who commissioned the painting were anything but pleased with the result. More likely culprits are the artist's later pieces, whose obscure lighting and psychological insight took the conservative Amsterdam burghers by surprise. His patrons were certainly not sufficiently enthusiastic about his work to support his taste for art collecting and his expensive house on Jodenbreestraat, and in 1656 possibly the most brilliant artist the city would ever know was declared bankrupt; he died thirteen years later, as his last self-portraits show, a broken and embittered old man. Throughout his career Rembrandt maintained a large studio, and his influence pervaded the next generation of Dutch painters. Some – Dou, Maes – more famous for their genre work, have already been mentioned. Others turned to portraiture.

Govert Flinck (1615–60) was perhaps Rembrandt's most faithful follower, and he was, ironically, given the job of decorating Amsterdam's new town hall after his teacher had been passed over. He died at a tragically young age before he could execute his designs, and Rembrandt was one of several artists commissioned to paint them – though his contribution was removed shortly afterwards. The work of **Ferdinand Bol** (1616–80) was so heavily influenced by Rembrandt that for a long time art historians couldn't tell the two apart. Most of the pitifully slim extant work of **Carel Fabritius** (1622–54) was portraiture, but he too died young, before he could properly realise his promise as perhaps the most gifted of all Rembrandt's students. Generally regarded as the teacher of Vermeer, he forms a link between the , two masters, combining Rembrandt's technique with his own practice

of painting figures against a dark background, prefiguring the lighting and colouring of the Delft painter.

LANDSCAPES

Aside from Bruegel, whose depictions of his native surroundings make him the first true Low Countries' landscape painter, **Gillis van Coninxloo** (1544–1607) stands out as the earliest Dutch landscapist. He imbued the native scenery with elements of fantasy, painting the richly wooded views he had seen on his travels around Europe as backdrops to biblical scenes. In the early seventeenth century, **Hercules Seghers** (1590–1638), apprenticed to Coninxloo, carried on his mentor's style of depicting forested and mountainous landscapes, some real, others not: his work is scarce but is believed to have had considerable influence on the landscape work of Rembrandt. **Esaias van der Velde's** (1591–1632) quaint and unpretentious scenes show the first real affinity with the Dutch countryside but – though his influence, too, was great – he was soon overtaken in stature by his pupil **Jan van Goyen** (1596–1656), a remarkable painter who belongs to the so-called "tonal phase" of Dutch landscape painting. Van Goyen's early pictures were highly coloured and close to those of his teacher, but it didn't take him long to develop a markedly personal touch, using tones of greens, browns and greys to lend everything a characteristic translucent haze. His paintings are, above all, of nature, and if he included figures it was just for the sake of scale. Neglected until a little over a century ago, his fluid and rapid brushwork became more accepted as the Impressionists rose in stature.

Another "tonal" painter and a native of Haarlem, **Salomon van Ruisdael** (1600–70) was also directly affected by van der Velde, and his simple but atmospheric, though not terribly adventurous, landscapes were for a long time consistently confused with those of van Goyen. More esteemed is his nephew, **Jacob van Ruisdael** (1628–82), generally considered the greatest of all Dutch landscapists, whose fastidiously observed views of quiet flatlands dominated by stormy skies were to influence European painters' impressions of nature right up to the nineteenth century. Constable, certainly, acknowledged a debt to him. Ruisdael's foremost pupil was **Meindert Hobbema** (1638–1709), who followed the master faithfully, sometimes even painting the same views (his *Avenue at Middelharnis* may be familiar).

Nicholas Berchem (1620–83) & **Jan Both** (1618–52) were the "Italianisers" of Dutch landscapes. They studied in Rome and were influenced by Claude, taking back to Holland rich, golden views of the world, full of steep gorges and hills, picturesque ruins and wandering shepherds. **Allart van Everdingen** (1621–75) had a similar approach, but his subject matter stemmed from travels in Scandinavia, which, after his return to Holland, he reproduced in all its mountainous glory.

Aelbert Cuyp (1620–91), on the other hand, stayed in Dordrecht all his life, painting what was probably the favourite city skyline of Dutch landscapists. He inherited the warm tones of the Italianisers, and his pictures are always suffused with a deep, golden glow.

Of a number of **specialist seventeenth-century painters** who can be included here, **Paulus Potter** (1625–54) is rated as the best painter of **domestic animals**. He produced a fair amount of work in a short life, most reputed being his lovingly executed pictures of cows and horses. The accurate rendering of **architectural features** also became a specialised field, in which **Pieter Saenredam** (1597–1665), with his finely realised paintings of Dutch church interiors, is the most widely known exponent. **Emanuel de Witte** (1616–92) continued in the same vein, though his churches lack the spartan crispness of Saenredam's. **Gerrit Berckheyde** (1638–98) worked in Haarlem soon after but he limited his views to the outside of buildings, producing variations on the same scenes around town.

In the seventeenth century another thriving category of painting was the **still-life**, in which objects were gathered together to remind the viewer of the transience of human life and the meaninglessness of all worldly pursuits: often a skull would be joined by a book, a pipe or a goblet, and some half-eaten food. Again, two Haarlem painters dominated this field: **Pieter Claesz** (1598–1660) and **Willem Heda** (1594–1680), who confined themselves almost entirely to these carefully arranged groups of objects.

THE 18TH AND 19TH CENTURIES

With the demise of Holland's economic boom, the quality – and originality – of Dutch painting began to decline. The delicacy of some of the classical seventeenth-century painters was replaced by finnicky still-lifes and minute studies of flowers, or finely finished portraiture and religious scenes, as in the work of **Adrian van der Werff** (1659–1722). Of the era's big names, **Gerard de Lairesse** (1640–1711) spent most of his time decorating the splendid civic halls and palaces that were going up all over the place, and, like the buildings he worked on, his style and influences were French. **Jacob de Wit** (1695–1754) continued where Lairesse left off, receiving more commissions in churches as Catholicism was allowed out of the closet. The period's only painter of any true renown was **Cornelis Troost** (1697–1750) who, although he didn't produce anything really new, painted competent portraits and some neat, faintly satirical pieces that have since earned him the title of "The Dutch Hogarth". Cosy interiors also continued to prove popular and the Haarlem painter, **Wybrand Hendriks** (1744–1831), satisfied demand with numerous proficient examples.

Johann Barthold Jongkind (1819–91) was the first great artist to emerge in the nineteenth century, painting landscapes and seascapes that were to influence Monet and the early Impressionists: he spent most of his life in France and his work was exhibited in Paris with the Barbizon painters, though he owed less to them than to the landscapes of van Goyen and the seventeenth-century "tonal" artists.

Jongkind's work was a logical precursor to the art of the **Hague School**, a group of painters based in and around that city between 1870 and 1900 who tried to re-establish a characteristically Dutch national school of painting. They produced atmospheric studies of the dunes and polderlands around The Hague, nature pictures that are characterised by grey, rain-filled skies, windswept seas, and silvery, flat beaches – pictures that, for some, verge on the sentimental. **J. H. Weissenbruch** (1824–1903) was a founding member, a specialist in low, flat beach scenes dotted with stranded boats. The banker-turned-artist **H. W. Mesdag** (1831–1915) did the same but with more skill than imagination, while **Jacob Maris** (1837–99), one of three artist brothers, was perhaps the most typically Hague School painter, with his rural and sea scenes heavily covered by grey chasing skies. His brother, **Matthijs** (1839–1917), was less predictable, ultimately tiring of his colleagues' interest in straight observation and going to London to design windows, while **Willem** (1844–1910), the youngest, is best known for his small, unpretentious studies of nature.

Anton Mauve (1838–88) is more famous, an exponent of soft, pastel landscapes and an early teacher of van Gogh. Profoundly influenced by the French Barbizon painters – Corot, Millet et al. – he went to Hilversum in 1885 to set up his own group, which became known as the "Dutch Barbizon". **Jozef Israëls** (1826–1911) has often been likened to Millet, though it's generally agreed that he had more in common with the Impressionists, and his best pictures are his melancholy portraits and interiors. Lastly, **Johan Bosboom**'s (1817–91) church interiors may be said to sum up the nostalgia of the Hague School: shadowy and populated by figures in seventeenth-century dress, they seem to yearn for Holland's Golden Age.

Vincent van Gogh (1853–90), on the other hand, was one of the least "Dutch" of Dutch artists, and he lived out most of his relatively short painting career in France. After countless studies of peasant life in his native North Brabant – studies which culminated in the sombre *Potato Eaters* – he went to live in Paris with his art-dealer brother Theo. There, under the influence of the Impressionists, he lightened his palette, following the pointillist work of Seurat and "trying to render intense colour and not a grey harmony". Two years later he went south to Arles, the "land of blue tones and gay colours", and, struck by the harsh Mediterranean light, his characteristic style began to develop. A disastrous attempt to live with Gauguin, and the much-publicised episode when he cut off part of his ear and presented it to a woman in a nearby brothel, led eventually to committal to an asylum at St.-Remy, where he produced some of his most famous, and most expressionistic, canvases – strongly coloured and with the paint thickly, almost frantically, applied.

Like van Gogh, **Jan Toorop** (1858–1928) went through multiple artistic changes, though he didn't need to travel the world to do so; he radically adapted his technique from a fairly conventional pointillism through a tired Expressionism to Symbolism with an art nouveau feel. Roughly contemporary, **G. H. Breitner** (1857–1923) was a better painter, and one who refined his style rather than changed it. His snapshot-like impressions of his beloved Amsterdam figure among his best work and offered a promising start to the new century.

THE 20TH CENTURY: THE SEARCH FOR A STYLE

Most of the trends in the visual arts of the early twentieth century found their way to The Netherlands at one time or another: of many minor names, **Jan Sluyters** (1881–1957) was the Dutch pioneer of Cubism. But only one movement was specifically Dutch – **de Stijl** (literally "the Style").

Piet Mondrian (1872–1944) was de Stijl's leading figure, developing the realism he had learned from the Hague School painters – via Cubism, which he criticised for being too cowardly to depart totally from representation – into a complete abstraction of form which he called **neo-plasticism**. He was something of a mystic, and this was to some extent responsible for the direction that de Stijl – and his paintings – took: canvases painted with grids of lines and blocks made up of the three primary colours and white, black and grey. Mondrian believed this freed the work of art from the vagaries of personal perception, and made it possible to obtain what he called "a true vision of reality".

De Stijl took other forms too: there was a magazine of the same name, and the movement introduced new concepts into every aspect of design, from painting to interior design to architecture. But in all these media lines were kept simple, colours bold and clear. **Theo van Doesburg** (1883–1931) was a de Stijl co-founder and major theorist: his work is similar to Mondrian's except for the noticeable absence of thick, black borders and the diagonals that he introduced into his work, calling his paintings "contra-compositions" – which, he said, were both more dynamic and more in touch with twentieth-century life. **Bart van der Leck** (1876–1958) was the third member of the circle, identifiable by white canvases covered by seemingly randomly placed interlocking coloured triangles.

Mondrian split with de Stijl in 1925, going on to attain new artistic extremes of clarity and soberness before moving to New York in the 1940s and producing atypically exuberant works such as *Victory Boogie Woogie* – so named because of the artist's love of jazz.

During and after de Stijl, a number of other movements flourished, though their impact was not so great and their influence largely confined to The Netherlands. The Expressionist **Bergen School** was probably the most localised, its best-known exponent **Charley Toorop** (1891–1955), daughter of Jan, who developed a distinctively glaring but strangely sensitive realism. **De Ploeg** ("The Plough"), centred in Groningen, was headed by **Jan Wiegers** (1893–1959) and influenced by Kirchner and the German Expressionists; the group's artists set out to capture the uninviting landscapes around their native town, and produced violently coloured canvases that hark back to van Gogh. Another group, known as the **Magic Realists**, surfaced in the 1930s, painting quasi-surrealistic scenes that, according to their leading light, **Carel Willinck** (b. 1900), reveal "a world stranger and more dreadful in its haughty impenetrability than the most terrifying nightmare".

Post-war Dutch art began with **CoBrA**: a loose grouping of like-minded painters from Denmark, Belgium and Holland, whose name derives from the initial letters of their respective capital cities. Their first exhibition at Amsterdam's Stedelijk Museum in 1949 provoked a huge uproar, at the centre of which was **Karel Appel** (b. 1921), whose brutal Abstract Expressionist pieces, plastered with paint inches thick, were, he maintained, necessary for the era – indeed, inevitable reflections of it. "I paint like a barbarian in a barbarous age", he claimed. In the graphic arts the most famous twentieth-century figure is **M. C. Escher** (1898–1970).

As for today, there's as vibrant an art scene as there ever was, best exemplified in Amsterdam by the rotating exhibitions of the Stedelijk or the nearby Overholland Museum. Of contemporary Dutch artists, look out for the abstract work of **Edgar Fernhout** and **Ad Dekkers**; the reliefs of **Jan Schoonhoven**; the multi-media productions of **Jan Dibbets**; the glowering realism of **Marlene Dumas**; the imprecisely coloured geometric designs of **Rob van Koningsbruggen**; the smeary expressionism of **Toon Verhoef**; and the exuberant figures of **Rene Daniels** – to name only the most important figures.

DUTCH GALLERIES: A HIT LIST

In **Amsterdam**, the *Rijksmuseum* gives a complete overview of Dutch art up to the end of the nineteenth century, in particular the work of Rembrandt, Hals, and the major artists of the Golden Age; the *Van Gogh Museum* is best for the Impressionists and, of course, van Gogh; and, for twentieth-century and contemporary Dutch art, there's the *Stedelijk*. Within easy reach of the city, the *Frans Hals Museum* in **Haarlem** holds some of the best work of Hals and the Haarlem School; also in Haarlem, the *Teyler's Museum* is strong on eighteenth- and nineteenth-century Dutch works. In **Leiden**, the *Lakenhal* has works by, among others, local artists Dou and Rembrandt, and the *Centraal* in **Utrecht** has paintings by van Scorel and the Utrecht School. Also in Utrecht, the *Catherine Convent Museum* boasts an excellent collection of works by Flemish artists and by Hals and Rembrandt.

Further afield, **The Hague's** *Gemeente Museum* owns the country's largest set of Mondrians, and its *Mauritshuis* collection contains works by Rembrandt, Vermeer and others of the era. The *Boymans van Beuningen Museum* in **Rotterdam** has a weighty stock of Flemish primitives and surrealists, as well as works by Rembrandt and other seventeenth-century artists, and nearby **Dordrecht's** *Municipal Museum* offers an assortment of seventeenth-century paintings that includes work by Albert Cuyp, and later canvases by the Hague School and Breitner.

The *Kroller-Muller Museum*, just outside **Arnhem**, is probably the country's finest modern art collection, and has a superb collection of van Goghs; a little further east, **Enschede's** *Rijksmuseum Twenthe* has quality works from the Golden Age to the twentieth century.

THE CITY IN FICTION

Creator of the Dutch detective van der Valk, NICOLAS FREELING was born in England but has lived all his life in Europe, where most of his novels are set. He actually left Amsterdam over twenty years ago and nowadays rarely returns. But in the van der Valk novels he evokes Amsterdam (and Amsterdammers) as well as any writer ever has, subtly and unsentimentally using the city and its people as a vivid backdrop to his fast-moving action. The following extract is from *A Long Silence*, first published in 1972.

Arlette came out into the open air and saw that spring had come to Amsterdam. The pale, acid sun of late afternoon lay on the inner harbour beyond the Prins Hendrik Kade: the wind off the water was sharp. It gave her a shock. A succession of quick rhythmic taps, as at the start of a violin concerto of Beethoven. That she noticed this means, I think, that from that moment she was sane again. But it is possible that I am mistaken. Even if insane one can have, surely, the same perceptions as other people, and this "click" is a familiar thing. Exactly the same happens when one takes a night train down from Paris to the Coast, and one wakes somewhere between Saint Raphael and Cannes and looks out, and there is the Mediterranean. Or was.

The pungent salt smell, the northern, maritime keynotes of seagull and herring, the pointed brick buildings, tall and narrow like herons, with their mosaic of parti-coloured shutters, eaves, sills, that gives the landscapes their stiff, heraldic look (one is back beyond Brueghel, beyond Van Eyck, to the primitives whose artists we do not know, so that they have names like the Master of the Saint Ursula Legend). The lavish use of paint in flat bright primary colours which typifies these Baltic, Hanseatic quay-sides is startling to the visitor from central Europe. Even the Dutch flags waving everywhere (there are no more determined flag-wavers) upset and worried Arlette: she had not realised how in a short time her eye had accustomed itself to the subtle and faded colourings of France, so that it was as though she had never left home. The sharp flat brightness of Holland! The painters' light which hurts the unaccustomed eye. . . Arlette never wore sunglasses in France, except on the sea, or on the snow, yet here, she remembered suddenly, she had practically gone to bed in them. It was all so familiar. She had lived here, she had to keep reminding herself, for twenty years.

She had no notion of where she wanted to go, but she knew that now she was here, a small pause would bring the spinning, whirling patterns of the kaleidoscope to rest. She crossed the road and down the steps to the little wooden terrace – a drink, and get her breath back! Everything was new – the pale heavy squatness of the Dutch café's cup-and-saucer, left on her table by the last occupant; the delightful rhythmic skyline across the harbour of the Saint Nicolaas church and the corner of the Zeedijk! Tourists were flocking into waterbuses, and now she was a tourist too. An old waiter was wiping the table while holding a tray full of empty bottles, which wavered in front of her eye.

"Mevrouw?"

"Give me a chocomilk, if at least you've got one that's good and cold".

Another click! She was talking Dutch, and as fluently as ever she had! He was back before she had got over it.

"Nou, mevrouwtje – cold as Finnegan's feet". His voice had the real Amsterdam caw to it. "You aren't Dutch though, are you now?"

"Only a tourist", smiling.

"Well now, by-your-leave: proper-sounding Dutch you talk there", chattily, bumping the glass down and pouring in the clawky chocomilk.

"Thank you very much".

"Tot Uw dienst. Ja ja ja, kom er aan" to a fussy man, waving and banging his saucer with a coin.

Neem mij niet kwa-a-lijk; een be-hoor-lijk Nederlands spreekt U daar. Like a flock of rooks. *Yah, yah ya-ah, kom er a-an.* And she was blinded by tears again, hearing her husband's exact intonation – when with her he spoke a Dutch whose accent sometimes unconsciously – ludicrously – copied hers, but when with the real thing, the *rasecht* like himself his accent would begin to caw too as though in self-parody.

Next door to her were sitting two American girls, earnest, quiet, dusty-haired, looking quite clean though their jeans were as darkly greasy as the mud the dredger over there was turning up off the harbour bottom. Scraps of conversation floated across.

"She's a lovely person, ever so quiet but really mature, you know what I mean, yes, from Toledo". Arlette knew that Van der Valk would have guffawed and her eyes cleared.

I see her there, at the start of her absurd and terrifying mission. She has the characteristic feminine memory for detail, the naively earnest certainty that she has to get everything right. Had I asked what those two girls were drinking she would have known for sure, and been delighted at my asking.

I have not seen Amsterdam for four or five years, and it might be as long again before I shall. This is just as well. I do not want my imagination to get in the way of Arlette's senses. Piet, whose imagination worked like mine, saw things in an entirely different way to her. We were sitting once together on that same terrace.

"Look at that dam" building", pointing at the Central Station, a construction I am fond of, built with loving attention to every useless detail by an architect of the last century whose name I have forgotten (a Dutch equivalent of Sir Giles Gilbert Scott). "Isn't it lovely?" Lovely is not the word I would have chosen but it is oddly right.

"The Railway Age", he went on. "Make a wonderful museum — old wooden carriages, tuff-tuff locos with long funnels, Madame Tussaud figures of station-masters with beards, policemen wearing helmets, huge great soup-strainer moustaches, women with bustle and reticules. . ". Yes, indeed, and children in sailor suits. Arlette's mind does not behave like this.

I am changed, thought Arlette, and unchanged. I am the same housewife, familiar with these streets, this people. I am not pricked or tickled by anything here, like a tourist. I see all this with the coolness and objectivity of experience. I am not going to rush into anything stupid or imprudent. This is a town I know, and I am going to find myself perfectly able to cope with the problem. I am not alone or helpless; I have here many friends, and there are many more who were Piet's friends and who will

help me for his sake. But I am no longer the thoughtless and innocent little wife of a little man in a little job, standing on the corner with shopping bag wondering whether to have a cabbage or a cauli. I am a liberated woman, and that is going to make a difference.

A tout was circling around the cluster of tables, sizing up likely suckers. A year or so ago he would have been handing out cards for a restaurant or hotel, hooking for a quickie trip around the sights, with waterbus, Anne Frank and the Rembrandthuis all thrown in for only ten gulden. Now — he had closed in on the two American girls and she could hear his pidgin-German patois that is the international language of the European tout — selling live sex-shows. The two girls glanced up for a second with polite indifference, and went back to their earnest, careful, intense conversation, paying no further attention to him at all. He broke off the patter, circled backwards like a boxer and gave Arlette a careful glance: Frenchwomen, generally fascinated by the immoralities and debaucheries of these English and these Scandinavians — a likely buyer, as long as they have first done their duty with a really good orgy at Marks and Spencer's. Arlette met his eye with such a chill and knowing look that he shuffled back into the ropes and made off sideways: cow has been to the sex-show and has no money left. Amsterdam too has changed and not changed, she thought.

"Raffishness" was always the first cliché-tourists used, the Amsterdammers were always intensely, idiotically proud of their red-light district and since time immemorial a stroll to look at "the ladies behind the windows" was proposed to every eager tourist the very first night.

They have taken now with such relish to the new role of exhibitionist shop-window that it is hard not to laugh — the visitor's first reaction generally is roars of laughter. The Dutch have a belief that sex has made them less provincial somehow — for few attitudes are more provincial than the anxious striving to be modern-and-progressive. Paris doesn't exist any more, and London is slipping, they will tell one with a boastful pathos, and Holland-is-where-it's-at. A bit immature, really, as the two nineteen-year olds from Dubuque were probably at that moment saying. Arlette was a humble woman. She saw herself as snobbish, narrow, rigid,

French provincial bourgeois. Piet, born and bred in Amsterdam, used to describe himself as a peasant. This humility gave them both an unusual breadth, stability, balance. I remember his telling me once how to his mind his career if not his life had been an abject failure.

"But there", drinking brandy reflectively, being indeed a real soak and loving it, "what else could I have done?"

Arlette, walking through the lazy, dirty sunshine of late afternoon in Amsterdam, was thinking too, "What else could I have done?" She had come to lay a ghost. Not that she — hardheaded woman — believed in ghosts, but she had lived long enough to know they were there. Piet was a believer in ghosts. "I have known malign influences outside the bathroom door, " he used to say. He was delighted when I gave him to read the finely-made old thriller of Mr A.E.W. Mason which is called *The Prisoner in the Opal*: he saw the point at once, and when he brought it back he said that he too, with the most sordid, materialistic, bourgeois of enquiries, always made the effort "to pierce the opal crust". Poor old Piet.

Once we were having dinner together in a Japanese restaurant. We had had three pernods, big ones, the ones Piet with his horrible Dutch ideas of wit which he took for *esprit* described as "*Des Grand Pers*". We were watching the cook slicing raw fish into fine transparent slices.

"There is poetry", said Piet suddenly, "in those fingers". I turned around suspiciously, because this is a paraphrase from a good writer, whom Piet had certainly not read. I used the phrase as an epigraph to a book I once wrote about cooks — which Piet had not read either. "Poetry in the fat fingers of cooks" — I looked at Piet suspiciously.

"So", with tactful calm, "is that a quotation?"

"No", innocent, "Just a phrase. Thought it would please you, haw". That crude guffaw; completely Piet. The stinker; to this day I don't know whether he was kidding me. A skilful user of flattery, but damn it, a friend.

The Damrak, the Dam, the Rokin. Squalid remnants of food, flung upon the pavements. The young were unable or unwilling to spend much on food, she thought, and what they got for their money probably deserved to be flung:

one could not blame them too much, just because one felt revolted. But one did blame them: beastly children.

The Utrechtsestraat. The Frederickplein. And once out of the tourist stamping-ground, Arlette knew suddenly where she was going. She was heading unerringly and as though she had never been away straight towards the flat where she had lived for twenty years. It was a longish way to walk, all the way from the Central Station and carrying a suitcase too. Why had she done it? She would have said, "What else could I have done?" crossly, for when she got there she was very tired and slightly footsore, dishevelled, her hair full of dust, smelling of sweat and ready to cry.

"Arlette! My dear girl! What Are you doing? — but come in! I'm so happy to see you — and at the same time, my poor child, I'm so sad! Not that we know Anything — what one reads in the paper nowadays — Pah! And again Pah! come in, my dear girl, come in — you don't mean to say you walked. . . from the station? You Didn't! You couldn't! Sit down child, do. The lavy? But of course you know where it is, that's not something you'll have forgotten. I'll make some coffee. My dear girl, marvellous to see you, and the dear boys? — no no, I must be patient, go and have a pee child, and a wash, do you good". The old biddy who had always had a ground floor flat, and still did. . . She taught the piano. It had been the most familiar background noise to Arlette's life throughout the boys' childhood; her voice carried tremendously.

"One, Two, not so hasty. Pedal there, you're not giving those notes their value, that's a sharp, can't you hear it?" And coming back from shopping an hour later another one was being put through its hoops. "Watch your tempo, not so much espressivo, you're sentimentalising, this is the Ruysdaelskade not the Wiener Wald or something".

"Lumpenpack", she would mutter, coming out on the landing for a breather and finding Arlette emptying the dustbin.

Old Mother Counterpoint, Piet always called her, and sometimes in deference to Jane Austen "Bates" ("Mother hears perfectly well; you only have to shout a little and say it two or at the most three times"). A wonderful person really. A mine of information on the quarter, possessor of efficient intelligence networks in every shop, an endless gabble on the telephone, forever fixing things for someone else. She could find anything for you; a furnished room, a secondhand pram scarcely used, a boy's bike, a shop where they were having a sale of materials ever so cheap – even if she didn't have her finger on it she knew a man who would let you have it wholesale. Warm hearted old girl. Gushing, but wonderfully kind, and gentle, and sometimes even tactful.

"You take yours black, dear, oh yes, I hadn't forgotten – you think I'd forget a thing like that? Not gaga yet, thank God. Good heavens, it must be seven years. But you haven't aged, dear a few lines yes – badges of honour my pet, that's what I call them. Tell me – can you bear to talk about it? Where are you staying? By the look of you you could do with a square meal".

"I don't know, I was wondering . . ."

"But my poor pet of course, how can you ask, you know I'd be more than pleased and I've plenty of room, it's just can you bear all the little fussinesses of a frightened old maid – oh nonsense child, now don't be tiresome. Now I'll tell you what, no don't interrupt, I'm going to the butcher, yes still the same awful fellow, all those terrible people, how they'll be thrilled, just wait till he hears, I'll frighten him, he gave me an escalope last week and tough... my poor girl, since you left he thinks everything is permitted him. I'll get a couple of nice veal cutlets and we'll have dinner, just you wait and I'll get something to drink too, I love the excuse and what's more I'll make pancakes. I never bother by myself, you take your shoes off and put your feet up and read the paper, nonsense you'll do no such thing, I want to and anyway I'll enjoy it: would you perhaps love a bath, my pet?" The voice floated off into the hallway. "Where's my goloshes, oh dear, oh here they are now how did they get that way, oh wait till I tell the wretch the cutlets are for you, he'll jump out of his skin . . ." The front door slammed. Arlette was home.

It was a nice evening. Bates brought Beaujolais – Beaujolais! "I remember you used to buy it, child, I hope you still like it. Cutlets".

"He practically went on his knees when he heard, with the tears in his eyes he swore on his mother's grave you'd be able to cut them

with a fork and I just looked and said "She'd better," that's all".

"Bananas – I've got some rum somewhere, hasn't been touched in five years I'd say, pah, all dusty, do you think it'll still be all right dear, not gone poisonous or anything, one never knows now, they put chemicals in to make things smell better, awful man in the supermarket and I swear he squirts the oranges with an aerosol thing to make them smell like oranges, forlorn hope is all I can say".

The rum was tasted, and pronounced fit for pancakes.

"And how's Amsterdam?" asked Arlette, laughing.

It wasn't what it was; it wasn't what it had been. Arlette had been prepared to be bored with old-maidish gush about how we don't sleep safe in our beds of nights, not like when we had a policeman in the house, which did give someone a sense of security somehow. She ought to have known better really, because old mother Counterpoint had the tough dryness, the voluble energy, the inconsequent loquacity she expected – and indeed remembered, but the warm-hearted kindness was illuminated by a shrewd observation she had never given the old biddy credit for.

"Well, my dear, it would ill become me to complain. I'll have this flat for as long as I live and they can't put my rent up, I have to spread my butter thinner but I'm getting old and I need less of it. I have the sunshine still and the plants and my birds and they'll all last my time. I think it comes much harder on a girl your age, who can remember what things used to be, and who still has to move with the changes and accept them, whereas people expect me to be eccentric and silly. And I'm sorrier still for the young ones. They don't have any patterns to move by: it must give a terrible sense of insecurity and I think that's what makes them so unhappy. Everyone kowtows to them and it must be horrid really. Look at the word young, I mean it used to mean what it said and no more, young cheese or a young woman and that was that – and now they talk about a young chair or a young frock and it's supposed to mean good, and when you keep ascribing virtue to people, and implying all the time that they should be admired and imitated, well dear, it makes their life very difficult and wearisome; I used to know a holy nun and she said sometimes that everybody being convinced one was good made a heavy cross to carry. When the young do wicked things I can't help feeling that it's because they're dreadfully unhappy. Of course there's progress, lots and lots of progress, and it makes me very happy. I don't have many pupils now, but I'm always struck when they come, so tall and healthy and active, so unlike the pale little tots when I was a young woman, and I remember very hard times, my dear, all the men drunk always because their lives were so hard, but they don't seem to me any happier or more contented and they complain more because they expect much more. I can't really see what they mean talking about progress because that seems to me that people are good and get better and the fact is, my pet, as you and I know, people are born bad and tend to get worse and putting good before evil is always a dreadful struggle dear, whatever they say. One is so vain and so selfish".

And Arlette, who had had a good rest, a delicious bath, and a good supper, found herself pouring out her whole tale and most of her heart.

"Well", said Bates at the end with great commonsense, "that has done you a great deal of good my dear, and that's a fact, just like taking off one's stays, girls don't wear stays any more and they don't know what they miss".

Arlette felt inclined to argue that it was a good thing to be no longer obliged to wear stays.

"Of course dear, don't think I don't agree with you, healthy girls with good stomach muscles playing tennis, and no more of that fainting and vapouring. But I maintain that it was a good thing for a girl to know constraint. Sex education and women's lib, all dreadful cant. Girls who married without knowing the meaning of the word sex were sometimes very happy and sometimes very unhappy, and I don't believe they are any happier now. I married a sailor, dear, and learned how to go without".

"It doesn't make me any happier now", said Arlette dryly.

"No dear, and that's just what I felt in 1940 when my ship got torpedoed. So now let's be very sensible. You've come here very confused and embittered, and you don't want anything to do with the police, and you're probably quite right because really poor dears they've simply no notion, but at the present you've no notion either. You'd never of thought about asking my advice because I'm a silly old bag but I'll give it you, and it is that you probably can find out who killed your husband, because it's surprising what you can do when you try, but it's as well to have friends you can count on, and you can count on me for a start, and with that my dear we'll go to bed, your eyes are dropping out".

"Did you join the resistance, in 1940 I mean?" asked Arlette.

"Yes I did, and what's more once I threw a bomb at a bad man in the Euterpestraat, and that was a dreadful place, the Gestapo headquarters here in Amsterdam and it was very hard because I was horribly frightened of the bomb, and even more frightened of the bad man who had soldiers with him and most of all because I knew they would take hostages and execute them, but it had to be done, you see".

"I do see", said Arlette seriously, "it wasn't the moment to take off one's stays and feel comfortable".

"Right, my pet, right", said old mother Counterpoint.

SIMON CARMIGGELT is a Dutch literary institution. For nigh on forty years he contributed a regular column to *Het Parool*, originally a war-time anti-German newssheet. He wrote under the pen-name "Kronkel" (twist or kink), short pieces that are concise comments on everyday life, mixing wry anecdote with razor-sharp observation. As the author himself said: "I write about people, what makes them tick, what they do, what they say". It's a much-imitated form, and annual collections of the pieces are perpetual best-sellers. Carmiggelt produced something like 9000 of his "Kronkels" in all and three are reprinted below from a book called *I'm Just Kidding*, translated by Elizabeth Willems-Treeman and first published in English in 1972. He died in 1989.

CORNER

In a café in the Albert Cuypstraat, where the open-air market pulses with sounds and colour, I ran into my friend Ben.

"Did you know Joop Groenteman?" he asked.

"You mean the one who sold fruit?" I replied.

"Yes. You heard about his death?"

I nodded. A fishmonger had told me. "It's a shame", said Ben. "A real loss for the market. He had a nice stall – always polished his fruit. And he had that typical Amsterdam sense of humour that seems to be disappearing. He'd say "Hi" to big people and "lo" to little ones. If somebody wanted to buy two apples, he'd ask where the party was. No one was allowed to pick and choose his fruit. Joop handed it out from behind the plank. Somebody asked him once if he had a plastic bag, and he said, "I got false teeth. Ain't that bad enough?" He never lost his touch, not even in the hospital".

"Did you go see him there?" I enquired.

"Yes, several times", Ben said. "Once his bed was empty. On the pillow lay a note: "Back in two hours. Put whatever you brought on the bed." He had to go on a diet because he was too fat. They weighed him every day. One morning he tied a portable radio around his waist with a rope, put his bathrobe over it, and got on the scale. To the nurse's alarm he'd suddenly gained eight pounds. That was his idea of fun in the hospital. During one visit I asked him when he'd get out. He said, "Oh, someday soon, either through the front door or the back.'"

Ben smiled sadly.

"He died rather unexpectedly", he resumed. "There was an enormous crowd at his funeral. I was touched by the sight of all his friends from the market standing round the grave with their hats on and each one of them shovelling three spadesful of earth on to his coffin. Oh well, he at least attained the goal of his life".

"What goal?" I asked.

"The same one every open air merchant has", Ben answered, "a place on a corner. If you're on a corner, you sell more. But it's awfully hard to get a corner place".

"Joop managed it, though?"

"Yes – but not in the Albert Cuyp", said Ben. "That corner place was a sort of obsession to him. He knew his chance was practically nil. So then he decided that if he couldn't get one while he was alive, he'd make sure of it when he died. Every time the collector for the burial insurance came along, he'd say "Remember, I want a corner grave." But when he did die, there wasn't a single corner to be had. Well, that's not quite right. It just happened that there was one corner with a stone to the memory of someone who had died in the furnaces of a concentration camp. Nobody was really buried there. And the cemetery people gave permission to have the stone placed somewhere else and to let Joop have that plot. So he finally got what he wanted. A place on the corner".

SMELLS

When I entered the pub with the morning papers, I found only the proprietor – a sombre toper who was voraciously swilling down beer as if trying to put out a fire. I limited myself to a cup of coffee – a rarity in this establishment – which he went grudgingly to fetch from the kitchen. As he pushed open the door marked "Private", a pleasant aroma emerged to mingle with the stale smell of yesterday's drinking session.

A small grey man came in from outside and sniffed the air thoughtfully.

"Pancakes?" he asked when the publican returned with my coffee.

"Yes, my wife's frying them for my grand-son; he's coming this afternoon" was the reply.

"What'll you have?"

"Coffee", said the man.

The publican opened the kitchen door again, and the smell became stronger.

"You know", the man said to me, "there was a time when I cried because of a pancake".

"When you were a child, no doubt", I suggested.

"No, I was a grown-up", he answered. "It was 1943 – during the German occupation. My wife and I and four other Jews were hiding in the house of a very devout couple. Baptists, that's what they were. Religious fanatics. One day the man said to me, "Do you realise that, by the power of prayer, I can move the tree in front of the house?" I said, "Don't do it. That tree looks just fine where it is." Strange people, those two. The six of us stayed with them for a year and a half, and every day they fed us sugar-beet mush until we choked on it. One evening a visitor came. A friend. We were all sitting in the living room. The woman got up and walked into the kitchen and began to fry pancakes. Oh, the smell! The wonderful smell! It almost made me faint. When the pancakes were ready, the man whose faith could move trees said, "All hiders to bed." We didn't get a single pancake. Off we went meekly, shooed away. Then I lay in my bed and cried. Not because of the pancakes, but out of sheer rage – because of our terrible helplessness".

The pubkeeper put a cup of coffee down in front of the man and tapped himself another large glass of beer.

"We're supposed to forget all that", the man went on, "but how can we forget? If I smell pancakes, I can't help thinking about that night I lay in bed sobbing with rage".

He pointed at the glass from which our host was taking a huge swig.

"Beer", said the man. "I don't like beer. But one time in my life I said "God bless beer." You know why?"

He smiled rather bitterly.

"It was in 1942", he said. "My wife and I were hiding at another address then. In a little attic room full of junk. One night we heard a car stop outside. German police – the Grüne. We heard them come into the house. We heard them bellowing. My wife and I thought: this is the end. We stood crushed against the wall of that tiny room, beside the door. The door could

only open a crack because a heavy piece of furniture was shoved close behind it. As we were standing there stock-still, we heard footsteps coming up the stair towards the attic room. The handle turned and the door opened – as far as it could. A normal person would have been able to get through. But the Grüne was from Bavaria, I think, for he had an enormous beer-belly. Two or three times he tried to worm his belly inside. But he couldn't. So he closed the door, without having seen us. "God bless beer," I whispered then".

He looked at me.

"Forget?" he said. "If I smell or see beer, that moment comes back to me. And it always will".

And to the publican, "Come on, have another beer, on me. It's a life saver".

FAREWELL

My mother died as she had always hoped she would: gentle death called for her at night while she slept in her own bed in her own house. She had lived there thirty-nine years, first with her family, and after the war alone. All our attempts to persuade her to move to a rest-home were frustrated by the steadfast refusal.

"I'm not going to live with all those old women", she said to me. She was then over eighty. We could observe the marks of this age upon her when we entered the room on the first floor where she spent her last years, but after talking a quarter of an hour her face became young, probably because she laughed so much. Her humour could not be destroyed, although life did its best.

I remember how merrily she told us, not long ago, about an arrangement she had made with a friend who lived next door – a widow in her late seventies. The friend had said, "You're all alone all day. Give me a key and I'll drop in every morning to see how you are".

"Very well", my mother had replied, "but you're also alone everyday, so you give me your key, or I won't give you mine".

The exchange was made. When Mother heard her neighbour opening the door in the morning she always called down from upstairs, "No, I'm not dead yet".

But on that Friday morning she could no longer give this reassurance. She had gone to sleep for ever – without becoming senile, without suffering, and without ever having had to be dependent on anyone. The evening before she had enjoyed herself immensely watching a play on television. And on her calendar for Friday she'd written, "Go to hairdresser", for we were coming to visit her on Saturday, and she wanted to look her best for us.

I have happy memories of our visits to her because they were always so much fun. She'd tell us everything that had happened to her recently, and that was a great deal, for her life was busy and her schedule full through to her very last day. Good weather or bad, she travelled about The Hague by bus or tram. She refused to take a taxi, no matter how much I pleaded with her.

"If I listened to you", she'd say, "I'd end up in the poor house".

As a matter of principle she never telephoned me.

"If you're interested in me", she decreed, "it's up to you to call". When I did so and enquired how she was, she always answered "I'm fine", although she had all sorts of infirmities. But she refused to whimper about them.

A couple of years ago she had to go to a hospital to have her gall-bladder removed. I heard of it quite by chance from an acquaintance, because my mother had told me nothing. When I entered her hospital room that evening, she said in astonishment, "Have you found me already?"

She had not expected it. That was the fundamental principle by which she lived: she wished to expect nothing from others and to build upon her own strength alone. Swift death had allowed her to stick to it till her last breath. There was but one little blemish: she died on my wife's birthday, so that the party for our grandchildren, with cakes and decoration, had to be cancelled at the last moment. Mother would have blamed herself harshly, for her love for little children was inexhaustible.

Day after day my wife and I have said to each other, "She could not have longed for a more perfect death". And that is true. But the memories of her courageous life still well up unavoidably.

When my granddaughter – five years old and every inch a woman – heard that her great-grandmother had died, she flew straight to the essence by asking piteously, "Oh are all her things by themselves now? All her pans and her dishes – are they all alone?"

"Yes", I said.

BOOKS

HISTORY

Dedalo Carasso *A Short History of Amsterdam* (Amsterdam Historical Museum f17,50]. Brief, socialist-slanted account, well illustrated with artefacts from the Historical Museum.

Geoffrey Cotterell *Amsterdam* (Saxon House o/p). Popularised, offbeat history giving a highly readable account of the city up to the late 1960s.

Pieter Geyl, *The Revolt of The Netherlands 1555–1609; The Netherlands in the Seventeenth Century 1609–1648* (Cassell £8.95 each). Geyl's History of the Dutch-Speaking Peoples is the definitive account of Holland's history during its formative years, chronicling the uprising against the Spanish and the formation of the United Provinces. Quite the best thing you can read on the period.

Mark Girouard *Cities and People: A Social and Architectural History* (Yale University Press £16.95). Has an informed and well-illustrated chapter on the city's social history.

Christopher Hibbert *Cities and Civilisation* (Weidenfeld and Nicolson £15). Includes a chapter on Amsterdam in the age of Rembrandt. Some interesting facts about seventeenth-century daily life.

J. H. Huizinga *Dutch Civilisation in the 17th Century* [Collins o/p). Analysis of life and culture in the Dutch Republic by the country's most widely respected historian.

J. L. Price *Culture and Society in the Dutch Republic in the 17th Century* (Batsford o/p). An accurate, intelligent account of the Golden Age.

Simon Schama *The Embarrassment of Riches: An Interpretation of Dutch Culture in the Golden Age* (Collins £12.95). The most recent – and one of the most accessible – works on the Golden Age, drawing on a wide variety of archive sources.

Jan Stoutenbeek et al. *A Guide to Jewish Amsterdam* (De Haan £9.50). Fascinating, if perhaps over-detailed, guide to just about every Jewish monument in the city. You can purchase a copy before you leave from the *Netherlands Board of Tourism*, or in better Amsterdam bookshops.

Sir William Temple *Observations upon the United Provinces of The Netherlands* (OUP £20). Written by a seventeenth-century English diplomat, and a good, evocative account of the country at the time.

ART AND ARCHITECTURE

Kenneth Clark *Civilisation* (Penguin £3.95). This includes a warm and scholarly rundown on the Golden Age, with illuminating insights on the way in which the art reflected the period.

Eugene Fromentin *The Masters of Past Time: Dutch and Flemish Painting from Van Eyck to Rembrandt* (Phaidon £6.50). Entertaining essays on the major Dutch and Flemish painters.

R. H. Fuchs *Dutch Painting* (Thames & Hudson £4.95). As complete an introduction to the subject – from Flemish origins to the present day – as you could wish for in a couple of hundred pages.

Jacob Rosenberg et al. *Dutch Art and Architecture 1600–1800* (Penguin £17). Full and erudite anthology of essays on the art and buildings of the Golden Age and after. Strictly for dedicated Dutch art fans.

Christopher White *Rembrandt* (Thames & Hudson £4.95). The most widely available – and wide-ranging – study of the painter and his work.

Pierre Cabanne *Van Gogh* (Thames & Hudson £4.95). Standard mix of art criticism and biography, drawing heavily on the artist's letters themselves, published by Flamingo at £3.50.

Irving Stone *Lust for Life* (Methuen £2.95). Everything you ever wanted to know about Vincent van Gogh in a pop genius-is-pain biography.

Guus Kemme (ed.) *Amsterdam Architecture: A Guide* (Thoth f29,50]. Illustrated guide to the architecture of Amsterdam, with potted accounts of the major buildings.

Christian Rheinwald *Amsterdam Art Guide* [Art Guide Pubs. £5.95]. Comprehensive guide to the city's galleries, shops and contact points for both artists and those wanting to tour the art scene.

LITERATURE

Simon Carmiggelt *Kronkels* (De Arbeiderspers o/p). Second collection of Carmiggelt's 'slight adventures', three of which are reprinted here, beginning on p.199.

Anne Frank *The Diary of a Young Girl* (Pan £1.95). Lucid and moving, the most revealing thing you can read on the plight of Amsterdam's Jews during the war years.

Nicolas Freeling *A City Solitary, Love in Amsterdam, Cold Iron, Strike Out Where Not Applicable* (all published by Penguin at £2.25-2.50). Freeling writes detective novels, and his most famous creation is the rebel cop, van der Valk, around whom a successful British TV series was made. Light, carefully crafted tales, with just the right amount of twists to make them classic cops 'n' robbers reading – and with some good Amsterdam (and Dutch) locations. See also the extract from *A Long Silence* on p.194.

Etty Hillesum *Etty: An Interrupted Life* (Granada £2.50). Diary of an Amsterdam Jewish young woman uprooted from her life in the city and taken to Auschwitz, where she died. As with Anne Frank's more famous jour-nal, penetratingly written – though on the whole much less readable.

Harry Mulisch *The Assault* (Penguin £2.50). Set part in Haarlem, part in Amsterdam, this traces the story of a young boy who loses his family in a reprisal-raid by the Nazis. A powerful tale, made into an excellent and effective film.

Multatuli *Max Havelaar: or the Coffee Auctions of the Dutch Trading Company* (Penguin £4.50). Classic nineteenth-century Dutch satire of colonial life in the East Indies. Eloquent and, at times, amusing.

Cees Noteboom *Rituals* [Penguin £2.95]. An existentialist novel of the 1980's, mapping the empty existence of a rich Amsterdammer who dabbles in antiques. Bleak, but absorbing.

Jona Oberski *Childhood* (Hodder & Stoughton £5.95). First published in 1978, this is a Jewish child's eye-witness account of the war years, the camps and executions. Written with feeling and precision.

Janwillem van de Wetering *Hard Rain* (Gollancz £9.95). An offbeat detective tale set in Amsterdam and provincial Holland. Like van de Wetering's other stories, sadly only available in the US, it's a humane, quirky and humourous story, worth reading for characters and locations as much as for inventive narrative.

Jan Wolkers *Turkish Delight* (Marion Boyars £3.95). Wolkers is one of The Netherlands' best-known artists and writers, and this is one of his early novels, examining closely a relationship between a bitter, working-class sculptor and his young, middle-class wife. A compelling, though at times misogynistic, even offensive, work, by a writer who above all seeks reaction.

LANGUAGE

It's unlikely you'll need to speak anything other than English in Amsterdam: the Dutch have a seemingly natural talent for languages, and your attempts at speaking theirs may be met with amusement. Outside Amsterdam people aren't quite as cosmopolitan, but even so the following words and phrases of Dutch should be the most you'll need to get by; supplement these with our detailed Food Glossary on p.114.

Of the available phrase books/dictionaries, *Dutch at your Fingertips* [RKP £3.95] is the most up-to-date and useful companion. To continue your studies, take a look at *Colloquial Dutch* (RKP £3.95).

PRONUNCIATION

Dutch is pronounced much the same as English, but with a few differences:

v is like the English f in **f**ar

w like the v in **v**at

j like the initial sound of **y**ellow

ch and g are like the Scottish lo**ch**

ng is as in bri**ng**

nj as in o**ni**on

Otherwise double consonants keep their separate sounds – kn, for example, is never like the English "knight".

Doubling the letter lengthens the vowel sound:

a is like the English c**a**t

aa like c**a**rt

e like l**e**t

ee like l**a**te

o as in p**o**p

oo in p**o**pe

u is like w**oo**d

uu the French t**u**

au and ou like h**ow**

ei and ij as in f**i**ne

oe as in s**oo**n

eu is like the dipthong in the French l**eu**r

DUTCH WORDS AND PHRASES

Basics and Greetings

yes	*ja*	do you speak English?	*spreekt u Engels?*
no	*nee*	I don't understand	*Ik begrijp het niet*
please	*alstublieft*	women/men	*vrouwen/mannen*
(no) thank you	*[nee] dank u* or *bedankt*	children	*kinderen*
hello	*hallo* or *dag*	when?	*wanneer?*
good morning	*goedemeorgen*	I want	*ik wil*
good afternoon	*goedemiddag*	I don't want	*Ik wil niet. . .(+verb)*
good evening	*goedenavond*		*ik wil geen. . .(+noun)*
goodbye	*tot ziens*	how much is. . .?	*wat kost. . .?*
see you later	*tot straks*		

Finding the way

how do I get to. . .?	*hoe kom ik in. . .?*	left/right	*inks/rechts*
where is. . .?	*waar is. . .?*	straight ahead	*echtuit gaan*
how far is it to. . .?	*hoe ver is her naar. . .?*	platform	*spoor* or *perron*
far/near	*ver/dichtbij*		

Money

post office	*postkantoor*	cashier	*kassa*
stamp(s)	*postzegel(en)*	ticket office	*loket*
money exchange	*wisselkantoor*		

Useful Words

good/bad	*goed/slecht*	cheap/expensive	*goedkoop/duur*
big/small	*groot/klein*	hot/cold	*heet/koud*
open/shut	*open/gesloten*	with/without	*met/zonder*
push/pull	*duwen/trekken*	here/there	*hier/daar*
new/old	*nieuw/oud*	men's/women's toilets	*heren/damen*

Days and Times

Sunday	*Sondag*	tomorrow	*morgen*
Monday	*Maandag*	tomorrow morning	*morgenochtend*
Tuesday	*Dinsdag*	minute	*minuut*
Wednesday	*Woensdag*	hour	*uur*
Thursday	*Donderdag*	day	*dag*
Friday	*Vrijdag*	week	*week*
Saturday	*Zaterdag*	month	*maand*
yesterday	*gisteren*	year	*jaar*
today	*vandaag*		

Numbers

When saying a number, the Dutch generally transpose the last two digits: e.g., *drie guilden vijf en twintig* is f3.25.

0	*nul*	9	*negen*	18	*achttien*	80	*tachtig*
1	*een*	10	*ien*	19	*negentien*	90	*negentig*
2	*twee*	11	*elf*	20	*wintig*	100	*honderd*
3	*drie*	12	*waalf*	21	*een en twintig*	101	*honderd een*
4	*vier*	13	*dertien*	30	*dertig*	200	*twee honderd*
5	*vijf*	14	*veertien*	40	*veertig*	201	*twee honderd een*
6	*zes*	15	*vijftien*	50	*vijftig*	500	*vijf honderd*
7	*zeven*	16	*zestien*	60	*zestig*	1000	*duizend*
8	*acht*	17	*zeventien*	70	*zeventig*		

A GLOSSARY OF DUTCH AND ARCHITECTURAL TERMS

AMBULATORY Covered passage around the outer edge of the choir of a church.

AMSTERDAMMERTJE Phallic-shaped objects placed alongside Amsterdam streets to keep drivers off the pavements and out of the canals.

APSE Semi-circular protrusion at (usually) the east end of a church.

BAROQUE High-Renaissance period of art and architecture, distinguished by extreme ornateness.

BEGIJNHOF Similar to a *hofje* but occupied by Catholic women (*Begijns*) who led semi-religious lives without taking full vows.

BURGHER Member of the upper or mercantile classes of a town, usually with certain civic powers.

CABINET-PIECE Small, finely detailed painting of a domestic scene.

CARILLON A set of tuned church bells, either operated by an automatic mechanism or played by a keyboard.

FIETSPAD Bicycle path.

GASTHUIS Hospice for the sick or infirm.

GEMEENTE Municipal; e.g. *Gemeentehuis* – town hall.

GESLOTEN Closed.

GEVEL Gable. The only decoration practical on the narrow-fronted canal house was on its gables. Initially fairly simple, they developed into an ostentatious riot of individualism in the late seventeenth century before turning to a more restrained classicism in the eighteenth and nineteenth centuries.

GRACHT Canal.

HIJSTBALK Pulley beam, often decorated, affixed to the top of a gable to lift goods, furniture etc. Essential in canal houses whose staircases were narrow and steep, *hijstbalken* are still very much in use today.

HOF Courtyard.

HOFJE Almshouse, usually for elderly women who could look after themselves but needed small charities such as food and fuel; usually a number of buildings centred around a small, peaceful courtyard. (See pp.56 and 158).

HUIS House.

KERK Church.

KONINKLIJK Royal.

MARKT Central town square and the heart of most Dutch communities, normally still the site of weekly markets.

MISERICORD Ledge on choir stall on which occupant can be supported while standing; often carved.

MOKUM A Yiddish word meaning "city", originally used by the Jewish community to indicate Amsterdam. Now in general usage.

NEOCLASSICAL Architectural style derived from Greek and Roman elements – pillars, domes, colonnades, etc. – popular in The Netherlands during French rule in the early nineteenth century.

POLDER An area of land reclaimed from the sea.

POSTBUS Post office box.

PLEIN A square or open space.

RAADHUIS Town hall.

RIJKS State.

SPIONNETJE Small mirror on canal house enabling occupant to see who is at the door without descending stairs.

STADHUIS Most commonly used word for a town hall.

STICHTING An institute or foundation.

STEDELIJK Civic, municipal.

WAAG Old public weighing-house, a common feature of most towns – usually found on the *Markt*.

HELP US UPDATE

We've gone to a lot of effort to make sure this edition of the Rough Guide to Amsterdam is completely up-to-date and accurate. However things do change -- openings times vary, restaurants close, prices increase -- and any suggestions, recommendations or corrections would be much appreciated. We'll credit all contributions and send a copy of the new edition (or any other Rough Guide, if you prefer) for the best letters. Send them along to: The Rough Guides, 149 Kennington Lane, London SE11 4EZ.

INDEX